David Wilson is Emeritus Pr[...] [...] founding Director of the Centre for Applied Criminology at Birmingham City University. Prior to taking up an academic appointment in 1997, David was a prison governor working at a variety of establishments in a number of different roles.

Professor Wilson appears in the print and broadcast media as a commentator and presenter. His publishing includes *Hunting Evil, A History of British Serial Killing, Signs of Murder, A Plot to Kill* and his professional memoir, *My Life with Murderers,* which was shortlisted for the Saltire Prize for Non-Fiction.

MURDER AT HOME

How Our Safest Space is Where We're Most in Danger

DAVID WILSON

SPHERE

SPHERE

First published in Great Britain in 2023 by Sphere
This paperback edition published in Great Britain in 2024 by Sphere

1 3 5 7 9 10 8 6 4 2

A CIP catalogue record for this book is available from the British Library.

ISBN 978-0-7515-8497-4

Typeset in Warnock by M Rules
Printed and bound in Great Britain by Clays Ltd, Elcograf S.p.A.

Papers used by Sphere are from well-managed forests
and other responsible sources.

Sphere
An imprint of
Little, Brown Book Group
Carmelite House
50 Victoria Embankment
London EC4Y 0DZ

An Hachette UK Company
www.hachette.co.uk

www.littlebrown.co.uk

For Fleur

Evil is unspectacular and always human,
Shares our bed and eats at our own table.

W. H. Auden, 'Herman Melville'

Introduction

'There's no place like Home'

Dorothy in *The Wizard of Oz* (1939)

I n *A Lust for Window Sills*, Harry Mount's brilliant and idiosyncratic celebration of British architecture, he sets out to encourage his readers to develop and then share his own excitement about buildings of all shapes and sizes, historic and modern. As an architectural historian Mount has a few tricks up his sleeve to help him achieve this objective. First, he asks his readers to look up rather than stare into the middle distance, so that they can see and appreciate weathervanes, crockets and spires because, as he explains, 'we take in the function of buildings, but not much else'. Thereafter, as we approach each new building, we need to 'push open the door and step inside, not knowing what beauties, great and small, quirky and mainstream lie inside'.

I also want you to step inside a series of buildings, but with a different purpose in mind. Not so much to look up as to look

1

differently, because, just occasionally, the answers to some pressing social problems are staring us in the face. As a criminologist rather than an architectural historian, I want you to consider something which is rarely discussed: that the home is the primary site for murder in this country. Whether male or female, the victims of murder are more likely to have been killed in or around a house, or what the Office for National Statistics (ONS) rather primly describes as 'a residential dwelling', than in a public space – be that outdoors, such as in a street, or an indoor public space like a pub or night club.

The figures underlying this truism are doggedly consistent, although there are gender differences. In the three years between 2017 and 2019, in England and Wales, on average 75 per cent of women and 39 per cent of men were murdered in a house, or residential dwelling. There was a slight change in 2020 when 78 per cent of women and 38 per cent of men were murdered in a residential dwelling but, for the very first time, there was one more murder of a man in a 'street, path or alleyway'. Often, but not in every case, there was a prior or ongoing relationship between the victim and the perpetrator. Leaving 2020 and England and Wales to one side, this pattern is even more marked in the separate and independent criminal justice system of Scotland, where between 2010 and 2020, 83 per cent of all female murder victims and 55 per cent of male victims were killed in a residential dwelling. Whether in England, Scotland or Wales, a much higher percentage of women than men are murdered indoors, but overall the space where a murder is most likely to occur in Britain will be in the home.

This reality about the banal site of British murder has long been ignored or under-appreciated, even as we try to find solutions to reduce the amount of murder while at the same time continuing to consume murder as a form of entertainment in our homes, in the books and newspaper articles that we read, on the television programmes that we watch, or in the social media that we subscribe to. That consumption often blinds us to reality both now and in the past. In his famous but mistaken essay, 'Decline of the English Murder', George Orwell conjures up a Sunday afternoon before the Second World War: .

The wife is already asleep in the armchair, and the children have been sent out for a nice long walk. You put your feet up on the sofa, settle your spectacles on your nose, and open the *News of the World*. Roast beef and Yorkshire, or roast pork and apple sauce, followed up by suet pudding and driven home, as it were, by a cup of mahogany-brown tea, have put you in just the right mood. Your pipe is drawing sweetly, the sofa cushions are soft underneath you, the fire is well alight, the air is warm and stagnant. In these blissful circumstances, what is it that you want to read about?

Naturally, about a murder.

Orwell goes on to compare 'our great period in murder' – which he sees as between about 1850 and 1925 – with the murders that had occurred during the war. In the 'great period' he cites nine murderers 'whose reputation has stood the test of time'. These are: 'Dr Palmer of Rugeley, Jack the Ripper, Neill Cream, Mrs Maybrick, Dr Crippen, Seddon, Joseph Smith, Armstrong, and Bywaters and Thompson'. Most of their murders, but certainly not all of them (the crimes of

Jack the Ripper most obviously), involved poisoning, and that seems to be Orwell's point about decline: how murder was committed changed during the war, and something about it now reeked of the 'atmosphere of dance-halls, movie-palaces, cheap perfume, false names and stolen cars'. Murder had become Americanised and 'meaningless', compared with 'the old domestic poisoning dramas' that had been a product of an earlier time.

Orwell, while acknowledging the domesticity that characterised his 'great period' of English murder, does not really question, or even explore, why most of the murders that he cites took place within a domestic setting – ironically very much like the one he evokes at the start of his essay. And, in emphasising a change that he saw as having been created by war, he does not seem to appreciate that that domestic setting still dominated, and continues to dominate, murder, no matter what period in our history we are describing. Though Orwell was not to know it when he wrote his essay in 1946, the serial killers Reginald Christie and John George Haigh had already murdered several people – and to be fair to Orwell, it would be three years after his death before the first of them (Christie) was brought to justice, but the settings for their murders were also domestic and just as 'English'. In fact, those committed by Christie even involved poisoning, and his squalid home at 10 Rillington Place in Notting Hill, London, was the gothic backdrop to his crimes.

So far I have used the terms 'house', 'home' and 'residential dwelling' interchangeably. However, as the social historian Judith Flanders reminds us, there is a difference between these terms and how, and where, they are used. A house is simply a pile of bricks, a physical shape that can be 'safe as houses', whereas a home implies something different altogether – it is a dwelling place; the place where you live and where the business of domesticity takes place. Home is 'where the heart is', 'home sweet home', and 'there's no place like it'. In other words, it is a personal, interior space cut off from the glare of the outside real world; it is a private sanctuary that should not routinely be made visible and public. Homes are, Flanders argues, intimate and private and, as the centuries wore on, the sphere that was to become 'a woman's place' – although later this phrase would be applied more specifically to the kitchen.

So a house – the pile of bricks – has been designed and built by someone else and thereafter becomes merely a commodity to be bought and sold, whereas a home is something that you create; a home is personal, it is an extension of you. The home reflects who you are – your hopes, aspirations, tastes, desires, fears, dreams and disappointments. And there's the rub. What if those dreams and aspirations are unfulfilled and it is disappointment and fear, rather than hopes, that come to dominate your home? When that happens it can all too easily become a prison, an altogether darker space that traps you. You might sit on the same sofa to read the newspaper or eat at the same table in the kitchen as you have always done, but these familiar spaces, routines and even furnishings begin to take on a more menacing hue. Sometimes violence begins to seep out of the very essence of that space, the routines which take place there, and even the bits and pieces that you bought to make your house a home.

When I use the term home, I am employing that word to capture something about a space that is private and intimate, although, for purely stylistic reasons, I will also refer to houses, flats and other residential dwellings where a murder has taken place. Ironically, it is murder that will make these intimate and private spaces become public, and so offer to us a glimpse of what had been going on behind the front door and after the curtains have been drawn. Murder, in my experience, is so much more authentic about the reality of these private spaces than the photos of interiors that get posted on Instagram or Facebook, or appear in glossy magazines.

Let's get back to Orwell.

Of Orwell's nine chosen murders, those committed by the serial killers Neill Cream and Jack the Ripper, and by Frederick Bywaters are different from the rest of his list in that they took place outside, or in public settings. The other cases Orwell mentions took place indoors, and often in a private house. But we can be even more specific. Those committed by Joseph Smith all happened in the bathroom – his crimes are sometimes known as the 'brides in the bath murders', as he drowned several of his new wives as they took a bath shortly after they had been married. He wanted their life assurance. We might want to quibble that two of Smith's murders took place in guesthouses, but there can be no such objections about the site of Hawley Crippen's murder of his wife Cora, after a party they had held at their house, 38 Hilldrop Crescent, Holloway, on 31 January 1910. Cora's body was eventually found in the basement – buried in the coal cellar – by which time Crippen and his lover had left London and fled across the Atlantic to Canada on the SS *Montrose*.

After Crippen had been hanged at HMP Pentonville in November 1910, his house was bought for £500 by a

Glaswegian comedian called Sandy McNab, who turned it into a 'dark tourist' destination. As part of his sales pitch, McNab described in almost breathless detail his exploration of his new purchase:

> I made my way all over the premises, and at last I came to the fateful cellar. I will not attempt to hide the fact that as my foot stepped upon the concrete floor, hardly yet dried, I felt a queer sensation at the pit of my stomach and a choking sensation in my throat ... Then I imagined the officers of the law examining the dark, damp, dungeon-like cellar, while the culprit stood calmly behind them.

McNab's use of the house is to make public what had once been private – it allows us to peek behind the curtains which had been drawn on Cora and Crippen's domestic life; it makes that life and their personal arrangements visible. But there is more going on here too. Inevitably, the press of the time labelled 38 Hilldrop Crescent a 'house of horrors'. This is a newspaper trope that we can trace back to, at the very least, the Ratcliffe Highway Murders of December 1811, when there were attacks in London on two different families in just twelve days, leaving seven people dead. Understandably, this caused a panic in the capital, and a media sensation. McNab is very consciously playing on this idea, with phrases such as 'queer sensation' and 'dark, damp, dungeon-like cellar'. It's actually no more than a teasing come-on to satisfy our morbid curiosity and at the same time play on our repulsion at what had taken place.

The 'house of horrors' phrase still crops up frequently – especially in relation to the houses or flats occupied by serial killers such as Dennis Nilsen or Fred and Rose West, and not just in this country. I remember it being applied to the house in Amstetten in Austria where Josef Fritzl held one of his daughters, Elisabeth, captive for more than twenty years in a specially designed concealed basement, where he would repeatedly rape and abuse her. Standing on the steps to their front door in 2008, after the story came to light, I was amazed most of all by the house's closeness to a baker's shop just next door, and a tattoo parlour across the road. I filled up my car at a petrol station less than two hundred yards away. Had no one noticed what had been going on? This 'house of horror' had been the perfect embodiment of Austrian decency and respectability, and was still standing defiantly against any arguments to the contrary.

In the USA, the phrase has been applied most recently to the Florida case of Russell Tillis, who kept a number of women imprisoned as 'sex slaves', and who then killed two of these women, and to the Cleveland home of Ariel Castro, who for over a decade kept three women – Michelle Knight, Amanda Berry and Gina DeJesus – locked up in his house undetected, just three miles away from the block where they had all gone missing between 2002 and 2004. One of the many books about that case – *Captive* – is subtitled *One House, Three Women, Ten Years in Hell*. Much further back in American history we might cite the case of Herman Webster Mudgett. He is perhaps better known as H. H. Holmes, a serial killer who murdered at least twenty-seven people, having lured them to his hotel in Chicago between 1891 and 1894. The hotel became known as the 'Murder Castle', with soundproofed rooms, a maze of hallways, and chutes that would drop a victim from his or her room into the basement, and a vat of acid.

I want to discuss 'houses of horror' (even if many of them were in actuality flats) and also interrogate this generic description further. For example, there is a difference between Fritzl's home, where there was a hellish 'below stairs' cut off from the rest of the house, and 25 Cromwell Street in Gloucester, where Fred and Rose West would torture, kill and bury the bodies of many of their victims. Almost every room of that house had been adapted to facilitate the range of sexual behaviours that were of interest to the couple, and their cellar and back garden converted to accommodate the bodies of their victims. What happens to these houses of horror after the perpetrators have been brought to justice also varies. Some, such as the house in Amstetten, are left standing while others, including 25 Cromwell Street, are destroyed, almost as if by doing so we can exorcise the evil they contained and banish it from our community. Yet the flats occupied by Dennis Nilsen – whom we should remember was unmasked as a killer because he had blocked the drains with human remains – regularly come up for sale on the open market and they have always found a buyer. How are we to make sense of these differences? Are they a reflection of the 'body count' that is associated with the house, the nature of the murders themselves, or are other cultural and social factors at play?

In the same way that Harry Mount wanted his readers to 'push open the door and step inside' the buildings he described, so too will I take you into specific rooms within these and other houses of horror. I want to discuss attics and cellars; bedrooms and kitchens; living rooms; and the self-effacing back garden. What roles do these specific places – these guilty and tainted spaces – play in the commission or aftermath of a murder? It might be obvious that cellars, attics and back gardens are good places to dispose of bodies, but why should the bedroom produce more extreme and unusual murders than any other room? What unique role does the kitchen play in the history of British murder? I even want to consider the role of the stairs and the humble doorstep – the latter as a liminal space that connects our private world to the public life we lead outside the house and, as I have discovered in my academic research, is the preferred site for contract killers to complete their hits.

The tension between the public and the private that we encounter on the doorstep is only one of a number of similar stresses that exist within our homes, after we have crossed the threshold and closed the front door. Our home is where we feel intimate and private, but it is also a site where we socialise. Some rooms are kept scrupulously clean, while others are left to collect mess and dirt. We display what we think is socially acceptable, perhaps even desirable, but that very visibility often serves to hide and mask who we really are and what our true interests might actually be. As many social commentators and academics have argued, the house and what is bought and displayed within it is an extension of the self. However, I am going to argue it is no more an extension of the self than those aspects of our identity we know we cannot make public. How we present ourselves to other people might appear rational, coherent and stable, but that does not mean that we are necessarily all of those things all of the time. So as an extension of the self, we consciously use some rooms and what those rooms contain to perform a public role, but ensure that others are much more guarded and private, and execute a 'backstage' function. In doing so they permit, and sometimes provoke, different actions and behaviour from those which are regarded as socially acceptable.

As I see it, the house is a complex site where the true self can be revealed not only through what we buy, appropriate, consume and display, but also through what we hide, conceal, dispose of and bury. In some circumstances each room might allow us to act and behave in different ways – including being violent, and sometimes committing murder. This interaction between the physical and the criminological is at the very heart of my study of these spaces.

So far I have mentioned, among other things, drains, baths, gardens, doorsteps and specific spaces in houses where murders have taken place, or where bodies have been buried. I have characterised all of this as banal – the ordinary and everyday. To use an old-fashioned description, the backdrop to murder is 'homely'. Let's think about that word. Just over a hundred years ago, Freud wrote a paper on 'The Uncanny' about his belief that what is frightening, distressing and even repulsive is rooted in our everyday experiences. In Freud's native German, 'uncanny' is *unheimlich*, the opposite of *heimlich*, which is the German word for 'homely'. *Unheimlich* is literarily to be 'un-homely'. At the root of Freud's thinking is the belief that the uncanny and terrifying are located in the strangeness of the ordinary – not the fear of some alien other, but a fear we supress about those things which surround us, and that over time we have come to take for granted as being safe and harmless. It was this psychoanalytical idea that first started to make me think about the issues at the heart of the book.

Let me tell you the story of a murder by way of explanation.

Angelika Kluk was murdered in September 2006 at St Patrick's Church in Anderston in Glasgow, and suspicion soon fell on the church's handyman, Pat McLaughlin. Angelika's body was found buried under the floor of the church near the confessional; she had been repeatedly bludgeoned and stabbed sixteen times in the adjacent garage that belonged to the priest, and then dragged into the church. She might still have been alive when she was being pushed under the floorboards. McLaughlin fled to London after the murder, where he was arrested, and the police soon realised that he was in fact a notorious sex offender by the name of Peter Tobin, who had been released from prison a few years earlier. The way that Angelika had been murdered and how her body had been concealed made the police suspect that Tobin might have been responsible for several other crimes. They quickly began to piece together what was known about his movements and identified the specific places where he had once lived. They knew that in the early 1990s he had lived at Bathgate in West Lothian, but that he had arranged for a swap to a council house in Margate, Kent in 1991 – a three-bedroom mid-terrace property at 50 Irvine Drive, where Tobin was to stay until 1993. The police also knew that two young women had disappeared about this time: fifteen-year-old Vicky Hamilton, who had gone missing in Bathgate in February 1991 – just a few weeks before Tobin had moved to England – and eighteen-year-old Dinah McNicol, who was last seen alive in August 1991, after attending a music festival in Hampshire.

In the wake of Angelika's murder, the police started to excavate the back garden of the house in Margate. David Martin, one of the neighbours, remembered that Tobin had once started to dig a rather elaborate sandpit for his son, a pit which had never actually materialised. Tobin had explained to his neighbour that 'health and safety issues' raised by the council had put paid to the sandpit, but in November 2007 the police discovered a grave in the garden, located under a shed that stood on top of a concrete base where David remembered that Tobin had been digging all those years ago. There they found Dinah's body, tightly bound and gagged, and wrapped in sixteen heavy-duty refuse sacks. A few metres away was Vicky's body, also wrapped in bin bags – Tobin must have brought her body with him from Scotland during his house swap.

With the discovery of the bodies of the two young women, the tenants of 50 Irvine Drive were immediately re-housed by the council and, through various contacts which I cannot reveal, I was allowed to visit the property for myself. Clearly there had been a number of cosmetic changes to the house since Tobin had moved out in 1993, but the structural layout remained intact. I was particularly drawn to the kitchen, which had a breakfast bar with a view out onto his small back garden just a few metres away. This wasn't a private space, but one that was overlooked by scores of neighbours. I sat down on a chair and looked out of the window – as Tobin must have done, drinking his tea, eating toast, getting his supper ready, or doing the washing-up. I realised that as he did so he would be looking out onto the bodies of his two young victims. Every day as he prepared a meal, or switched on the kettle, he would be aware of who he had buried in his garden; it was his secret – a secret that gave him private pleasure, and was no doubt made all the more intense because he had done all of it in a very public manner. After all, his neighbour had noticed the digging. But there was more. He had also kept the bodies of his victims close to him, and that meant that he could always relive the moment when he had taken their lives; he was still in control even after their deaths. They had not been returned to their families, who could bury them in a proper grave; it was Tobin who was still powerful – you might even say omnipotent and God-like.

I attended Tobin's trial for Dinah's murder at Chelmsford Crown Court in December 2009. He pleaded not guilty, although it took the jury just thirteen minutes to convict him. He'd already been convicted of Vicky's murder earlier in the year. After the trial had ended Ian McNicol, Dinah's father, told the press that he wanted 50 Irvine Drive to be 'bulldozed and a memorial garden put in its place'. However, Thanet Council explained that there was a shortage of houses and, as 50 Irvine Drive was mid-terrace, adjacent properties would have had to be destroyed too. In any event, the house soon had a new tenant.

Abigail Dengate had been living in a cramped flat around the corner in Palmer Court with her father and two children who, at the time of the trial, were eleven and six years old. She was desperate for space and, having waited for a new home for four years, she put in a bid to move to 50 Irvine Drive. She admitted that the decision at the time did raise eyebrows but, what with everyone having to share bedrooms where they were currently living, she saw the move as a positive one. Abigail has lived there ever since and, in an interview that she gave to *KentOnline*, she called it a family home and said that 'even though people might have thought it strange that we wanted to live here, to us we didn't care about what had happened in the past – it's a house. I don't mean that we don't care what happened to the girls, that was horrible, but I mean it didn't bother us living here.' The newspaper noted that the front garden was tidy (front gardens usually are), and discusses the normality of the house:

> Inside, the cosy living room is filled with toys, and the garden has been transformed with a colourful fence running down the middle and a children's play zone with a slide, play house and trampoline. [...] The previously grim spot in the back left-hand corner of the garden is now sectioned off with a new fence and is covered in decking, with a pergola and colourful plant pots hanging from the fence. Bird feeders and a decorative mobile hang down, and a bench with a bright pink cushion provides a place to sit. It has been turned into a spot to enjoy, with all trace of death and misery erased.

The temptation here is to see what I have been describing and then how Abigail discusses her family home as being in some form of opposition given the house's history. On the one hand, we have my thoughts about a serial killer and how he had used his back garden as a burial site, where he could savour the moment when he had taken the lives of two young women. A serial killer who had justified his digging to his neighbour by explaining that he was creating a sandpit for his son, so trying to create the impression that he was just behaving like a good father. On the other hand, the reporter notes that Abigail has made her living room 'cosy', and the garden now has a child's play area – it has been 'transformed' with a trampoline, a pergola and bird feeders. Abigail thinks of 50 Irvine Drive simply as 'a house', and the journalist agrees that 'the house appears like any other'. It is familiar and safe – like the houses in any street and in which you and I might live, and call our home.

But this is my point.

The homes where murders occur do not need to look any different from ours, or that of our family, neighbours or our friends. They can all have the same cosy sitting rooms, children's play areas, bird feeders in the garden. It is the uncanny of the familiar that is being described by us both. It is the things we are accustomed to and which are ordinary that really begin to raise the hairs on the back of my neck – like taking a shower after watching *Psycho* – rather than those that are strange, bizarre or astonishing. *Heimlich* and *unheimlich* – homely and unhomely at the same time; safe and dangerous; a place to live, but also to die. Of course Freud was interested in what was hidden and repressed in us as individuals, buried deep in our unconscious, but here I am using his idea of the uncanny in a more elaborate and a broader way. Specifically, what is it that is submerged in the history of the spaces where we live, that we come to call home, and how, and when, might they surface in a way that leads to death? So I'm not interested in the disorientating, alien, shape-shifting spaces so beloved by film-makers, but by the all-too-real spaces where we actually live our lives.

Sadly in my work I have had to visit many houses, flats and

lodgings where a murder has taken place. Sometimes these murders took place in the distant past, and I have visited the houses where they were committed as part of my research for an academic article or a book, or when I was filming a documentary. I have, for example, visited the Victorian serial killer Mary Ann Cotton's terraced house in Front Street, West Auckland and the house in Abertillery in Wales, where in 1921 Harold Jones hid the body of eleven-year-old Florence Little in his father's attic. I climbed into the cramped loft myself. More recently, I have been to the flat in Bradford where the serial killer Stephen Griffiths – the self-styled 'Crossbow Cannibal' – murdered three women between 2009 and 2010, and the home of Peter Farquhar in Maids Moreton in Buckinghamshire, where he was murdered by Ben Field in October 2015. I have even been inside the priest's garage beside St Patrick's Church in Anderston, where Peter Tobin first attacked Angelika Kluk before moving her body into the church and leaving it under the floor, near to the confessional. Was that choice of deposition site significant, or merely chosen for practical reasons? I think that it was profoundly significant, and that Angelika's burial in the church was carefully staged to tell a story – Tobin's. Above all, I remember having to explain why there was blood on the ceiling of the garage, where he had started his attack: each time Tobin raised the weapon that he used to strike another blow, blood from Angelika's head, which was now also on the weapon, would fly off and upwards into the air. Some of that blood got stuck on the ceiling.

I will use these and other experiences as part of the case-study approach to the book, but I have also had to draw on secondary research for one obvious reason: sometimes the house, flat or 'residential dwelling' where a murder took place no longer exists. 10 Rillington Place is no more, nor is 38 Hilldrop Crescent, and, as mentioned, 25 Cromwell Street was destroyed after the crimes committed by the Wests came to light. The house was compulsory-purchased by Gloucester City Council in 1996 and razed to the ground. The contents and the remains of the building were then pulverised so as to prevent them becoming ghoulish souvenirs – 'murderabilia', as it is now called. The disappearance of the physical sites of murder have sometimes been decisions quite consciously taken, as in the case of the Wests, but on other occasions has been the consequence of urban development, especially after the Second World War. It is relatively unusual to have a house such as the one lived in by Mary Ann Cotton still in existence. I have therefore had to rely on other people's accounts of some of the homes where a murder took place, as opposed to being able to describe them from first-hand experience. I have also interviewed a number of the murderers that you are going to meet or, for very different reasons, have spoken with the families or friends of some of their victims.

My choice of cases is a mix of those murders which often get called, or are thought of, as 'ordinary' murders – sometimes also rather dismissively termed as 'domestics' – and those which have been committed in more unusual circumstances, such as when the offender is unknown to the victim, or is a serial killer. This combination of the extreme and the ordinary not only allows me to consider a range of cases but also to determine what common patterns, or dissimilarities, exist. However, is any murder ever really ordinary: average, normal, commonplace? Thankfully murder, no matter what we might think, remains a relatively unusual crime, and so it is hard to see how there can be such a thing as an ordinary murder, and it will certainly not be ordinary to the family of the victim. What is perhaps more interesting is how these murders allow us to build up a picture of people who rarely trouble history, to the extent that if the victim had not been killed, we would probably never have gained any understanding of how they had once lived. All murders create a public record, not just police and court reports, but also print and broadcast accounts. These records offer a different way to think about our culture – in this case, where and how we live – and to tell us stories about Britain and the British from a very different perspective. Even so, I remain acutely aware from my applied work that murder is always a tragedy and continues to create ripples – sometimes many years afterwards – in the lives of those who survive, and in the community where the murder took place. This awareness means that I also have had to be mindful about how I use, or choose not to use, some of the details about these cases, and I only provide as much infor- mation as is necessary to shape and illustrate my argument.

As outlined, I will use these case studies to guide you through a number of rooms in different flats and houses, so as to discuss the specific room or space that is the focus of the chapter. I describe the roles played by living rooms, kitchens and bedrooms in the commission of murder, as well as stairs, attics and cellars. However, perhaps reflecting changes in architectural design and the rapid expansion of home ownership between the wars, or the demands of rented accommodation, I have never actually visited a house in the

UK where the killer used a cellar to commit a murder or hide his victim's body. As a result, I only briefly discuss cellars, and the example that I use is a recent and well-known case. So too bathrooms and front gardens make only a brief appearance, especially in comparison to the role of back gardens – which are obviously more private. 'Digging the garden' is a perfectly banal excuse to hide more malevolent intentions. After all, who doesn't like that British obsession, gardening? My question hints at a perennial practical problem for a killer: what to do with the body of his victim after they have died. Decomposing bodies smell, as trapped gases in the intestinal tract begin to build up, and then release a pungent odour not unlike rotting fruit. That too has to be managed if you want to escape detection. Dennis Nilsen, when he had access to a garden, buried or burned his victims there, but when he moved to a top-floor flat he had to flush their body parts down the toilet or stuff their bodies under the floorboards, along with copious air fresheners. Other murderers I am going to describe found even more ingenious ways of hiding human remains in their homes, or destroying what was left of their victims.

So come with me. Let's park the car, walk down the street map in hand (remember those?), find the right house, open the gate and walk up the garden path to knock on the front door. Stand on the doorstep for a moment or two, as you might do when you are looking for the keys to your own home, and look around. What do you see? Something different from what you expected, or strangely familiar? Deep breaths; stay calm – get a grip of yourself! Was that a curtain I just saw twitching and a light being switched on? As we step inside, please don't think that you are visiting somewhere exotic and unusual, but marvel instead at how everything reminds you of where you live.

There really is no place like home.

CHAPTER ONE

The Door and the Doorstep

'Knock, knock, knock! Who's there, i'th' name of
Beelzebub?'

The Porter in *Macbeth*, Act 2, Scene 3

I don't imagine that you've ever given much thought to your
front door. And certainly not as much of your time and
attention as you've spent thinking about the new sofa that you
want to buy, or the bed that you sleep on every night. After
all, it's just a front door. You close it in the morning, perhaps
jiggling the key and then trying the handle just to make sure it
really is locked, before setting out for work and the day ahead
with your game face on. Several hours later that routine gets
reversed. You park the car, or walk from the train station or
bus stop, silently cursing that you didn't remember to put out
the bins, and then navigate the garden path (if there is one),
all the while fishing in your bag or pockets for the front-door
key. Perhaps you are just catching your breath, having climbed
the stairs to your flat. In any event, you're still mulling over

what happened at work as you do this, or wondering what you'll make for supper and if there's post lying on the floor beneath the letterbox. At last you find the key, thrust it into the lock, turn it quickly, push the handle and then you step inside; you take off your coat, throw your bag to one side and consider changing into some comfier clothes. Your guard is down now, and your game face safely stored away until tomorrow morning.

As I say, you don't really think too much about your front door.

I do, for as a criminologist I've learned that front doors – and the front doorstep – are very important. They are a threshold between the private and intimate world of domesticity and the external, public world of work, business and socialising. They form a boundary between the public and the private self; a neutral border that can act as both the beginning and the end of a journey. That this boundary has also become the preferred site of professional hitmen is something I will come on to, but we can already glimpse a little of the criminological that I am describing in why our police, and sometimes tabloid journalists, 'doorstep' to deliver bad news with a 'death knock'. Death is an obvious ending as far as murder is concerned, but it also starts the process of trying to uncover how these public and private worlds might have converged to produce such a traumatic conclusion. Does that coming together need to be further investigated, or should our attention be drawn more to the private or the public self as an explanation for the murder?

I only started to think about front doors and doorsteps in this way by knocking on a very different front door from my own.

I first crossed the threshold of 10 Downing Street in April 2006, as a guest of the Howard League for Penal Reform. The league is the oldest penal reform charity in the world, named in honour of John Howard, who had championed better prison conditions as a reforming high sheriff of Bedfordshire in the eighteenth century. Cherie Blair, QC hosted the event, held in honour of the Howard League's 150th anniversary, and as part of our visit she very graciously gave us a tour of the prime ministerial quarters.

I was struck by two things. The front door that I had walked through looked just like any you might encounter on a Georgian terrace. The front door might suggest a democratic ordinariness of being just like anywhere else, but inside it is quite obvious that appearances can be deceptive: 10 Downing Street is a rather grand mansion (created by knocking two houses into one for the country's first prime minister, Sir Robert Walpole). That front door was not only a means of entering the building, but also a portal into a different world, where decisions are taken that have an impact on how we all live our lives. That famous threshold led to an inside private reality about government that I had always understood existed but had never previously experienced. Now I could see, feel and touch that reality.

The academic term that I want to use here is borrowed from social anthropology: 'liminality'. Coined by Arnold van Gennep in the early twentieth century, liminality is about the rituals and rites of passage in our own and other cultures. According to van Gennep, these have three stages: first, when the individual is separated from his old status, identity, place or time; next, the liminal stage when that individual no longer holds his pre-ritual status, but has not yet begun to transition to the status that he will hold after the ritual has been completed; and then, finally, when he is reintegrated into society with a new identity or status. So liminality is the middle stage, where people are on the threshold of changing their identity. We can think about this in some of our societal structures, such as a university graduation ceremony, or when we exchange rings with a partner to become married.

Liminality is a fluid moment in time that might be exciting, or perhaps filled with uncertainty and doubt. Over the years, this concept of the liminal has been applied to various other events and settings. We can now think about temporal liminality, such as when the sun begins to set – when time is neither day nor night, but in between; liminal spaces like beaches, which are neither the sea nor the land; or perhaps even the demilitarised zone that often exists between two warring or hostile neighbours, but which does not belong to either country.

After my visit to 10 Downing Street, I began to think of the doors of houses, and even the modest doorstep, as being liminal – an in-between space both public and private, and the threshold that connects one aspect of our lives to another. Or, to put this in more poetic language, a fluid space where everything is but is not; a site of the before and the after. Because of that fluidity, there can sometimes be seepage between the private and the public within this space. Perhaps that's why our front gardens, which are always on public display, are often neater and tidier than our back gardens, which are more scruffy and personal.

As strange as it might seem, these ideas had quite an impact on my thinking about hitmen – those almost exclusively male killers who accept a contract to murder on behalf of a third party. What was it about this liminal space that seemed to facilitate murder, and was the answer to be found in the public or the private world of those who are killed? Clearly there is one obvious instrumental reason that needs to be acknowledged: the hitman knows where he can find you if you are at home. Not only that, your guard is down and you're not expecting death to come calling. However, I soon realised that when trying to understand a hit you have to assess if the victim has been murdered because of issues, tensions or disputes in their domestic and private life, or because of work and the problems that might have arisen when they engaged with people outside their home. The case studies I have chosen throw some light onto how we should answer this question, and why it is that a surprising number of people get killed at their front door.

*

Gulistan Subasi was murdered in Hackney, London on 22 March 2010, as she opened the front door of her mother's flat. Her killer was a fifteen-year-old called Santre Sanchez Gayle, who went by the street name Riot. As his age suggests, he was more of a 'hitboy' than a hitman. We know a great deal about this hit: the specific location; how it was performed; that Gayle was quiet in the taxi that he used to travel from his home in Kensal Green to Hackney; that he wore a white forensic suit with the hood covering his head, a mask over his mouth and gloves on his hands. We even know the exact time that it happened – twenty past eight in the evening. Gayle was carrying a plastic bag, which he must have used to hide his sawn-off shotgun.

We know most of this information because the hit was captured on CCTV – almost unbelievably, at the time of writing it is still available to view on YouTube. We also know that Gayle seemed just 'ordinary' in the taxi home after the hit, as the police tracked down and interviewed the driver. The grainy footage captures Gayle, first with an older accomplice called Izak Billy and then by himself, resting his sawn-off shotgun on the front gate to the building. As the door to the flat is opened Gayle immediately pulls the trigger from the gate, seemingly without bothering to check whether he was firing at Gulistan or her mother, or anyone else who might have been inside. The flash of the shot momentarily lights up the screen. Gulistan collapses into her mother's arms as Gayle calmly jogs away to catch his taxi back to Kensal Green, still clutching the sawn-off shotgun.

The hit was so well executed that Gayle was only caught because he bragged about it to other people, and that local intelligence eventually got back to the police. I interviewed DCI Jackie Sabire, who was the senior investigating officer on the case, and she said: 'When we saw the CCTV we all thought that it was a professional hitman. There was no hesitation and he shows no nerves. It did not look like a fifteen-year-old boy.' Jackie learned that Gayle was paid just £200, with which he bought a fake Gucci hat. Gulistan's estranged partner, Serdar Ozbek, was arrested and tried with contracting Gayle, although he was later cleared in court. As a result we still do not know who commissioned the hit. However, Gulistan had just returned from Turkey, where she had established a new relationship, so the temptation is to see this hit as emanating from her changing domestic circumstances – from what was happening inside her home, rather than the world beyond her mother's front door.

Let's think about Gayle's motivation. Two hundred pounds seems like a vanishingly small amount to induce someone to take another person's life and, even if Gayle had been promised more, was there actually a different incentive? In the course of the investigation it became clear that he was undergoing a deadly rite of passage, and that the hit on Gulistan was his initiation. Successfully completing the hit was the passport that would allow him to rise up the hierarchy of the Kensal Green Boys (KGB) – the gang that he belonged to in northwest London, which had in effect become his family. Gayle, described in court as a low-level cannabis dealer, had been excluded from school the previous year, already had convictions for attempted robbery and was living by himself. Gayle's two half-brothers were each serving life sentences for murder. In other words, he had been nurtured within an environment that prioritised offending over everything else, and he realised that if he wanted to progress and be successful in that world he needed to behave just like the older men who surrounded him. Like many other fifteen-year-olds he might have been interested in girls, football and Xbox, but those other boys would progress by staying at school and eventually finding jobs. Gayle's path was already different, and he needed to show everyone that he could use violence and, when the need arose, that he would be prepared to kill.

On that night in March 2010, Santre Sanchez Gayle was on the threshold of transforming his identity; of transitioning from his old status as a low-level drug dealer to someone with more standing; and of the promise of new respect and prestige in the KGB. As he stood with his sawn-off shotgun perched on the gate he occupied a liminal space – an in-between space that served to measure his value in a world with very different priorities to our own. That liminal space in Hackney marked for him a before and an after.

The CCTV footage seems to suggest that Gayle didn't doubt his abilities: he did not hesitate; when the occasion demanded it, he pulled the trigger. In other words, he was successful, at least on those twisted terms. He was calm and cool as he stood on the brink of this new status, and then professional and skilled when Gulistan opened the door. With Gulistan's murder he had crossed the threshold and completed his rite of passage. Just like his half-brothers, he could take another person's life, but what let Gayle down was that he did not have the maturity to realise that he shouldn't brag about what had happened; he was too eager to let everyone know that he had graduated. More mature and seasoned hitmen I have studied never made this sort of schoolboy error. Gayle had become a hitman, but he was still a fifteen-year-old boy. He is now serving twenty years in prison.

*

Let's keep thinking about the door and the doorstep. I've used the story of the murder committed by Sanchez Gayle to describe a typical ritual that is not so different from the classic rite-of-passage narratives found in social anthropology. The liminality I've outlined concerns his transition from an old to a new identity, and his subsequent standing in his social group – in Gayle's case the KGB. However, I now want to use the idea of liminality not to discuss rites of passage but to focus on the door and the doorstep themselves. In other words, the door and the doorstep as thresholds between the public and the private; the boundary between the civic and communal and the intimate, interior life that exists within the home. Thinking in this way about doorstep hits allow us to better understand why they might have been contracted, and by whom. This thinking, I am going to suggest, puts the victim rather than the hitman at the heart of the narrative, and can be an aid to detection. By the time Shakespeare's drunken porter hears knocking on the castle door, King Duncan had already been murdered by Macbeth, although in my case studies the door and the doorstep work in a very different way because it really is the *knock, knock, knock* – metaphorical, and in one case almost literally – that facilitates murder. The door and the doorstep become an almost perfect example of when the homely can become uncanny and frightening – *heimlich* and *unheimlich* – and how violence can seep without notice into the most ordinary of routines, objects and spaces. Opening the front door can be the beginning of the rest of your life, or its end.

Knock, knock, knock.

*

There are three murders that I will use to illustrate my point: the murder of Jill Dando on the doorstep of her home in 29 Gowan Avenue, Fulham, London on 26 April 1999; the hit on Frank McPhie outside the front door of his ground-floor flat at 6 Guthrie Street, Maryhill in Glasgow on 10 May 2000; and finally the murder of Alistair Wilson at the door of the home that he shared with his wife, father-in-law and two sons at 10 Crescent Road, Nairn, an ancient fishing port and market town in the north-east of Scotland, on 28 November

2004. As a general background to these case studies, and a fact that links all three, it's worth remembering that none of these murders has been solved. However, I am suggesting that thinking about doorstep hits in the way that I have outlined helps us to determine more generally who might have been responsible for these crimes and can help the police to focus their investigation.

When the police say that they are 'following multiple lines of enquiries', they are essentially looking at one of three possibilities. First, that the explanation for the hit stems from the domestic circumstances of the victim. Husbands contract a hit on their wife or their former partner, and sometimes wives commission a third party to kill their husband or lover. They've had an affair, want to move on but can't, or don't want to deal with the huge legal bill they will be landed with if they break up. Second, that the motive for the hit stems from the professional background of the victim, and tensions or difficulties that may have developed within that aspect of the victim's life. These are usually, but not exclusively, financial. Finally, there are always other unique elements to each particular case that might prove to be a fruitful line of enquiry. I suggest that we can better understand which of these three possibilities best explains why the hit had been commissioned by thinking about the space where the murder took place. Some background to each case is therefore important.

Jill Dando had worked for the BBC since 1979, at first in regional news and then from 1988 onwards as a national newsreader. Such was her popularity, she also presented a range of other programmes including *Songs of Praise*, *Crimewatch* and *Holiday*. In 1997 she was the BBC's

Personality of the Year, and at the time of her murder she was on the front cover of that week's *Radio Times*. She was sometimes described as the corporation's golden girl and, given her high public profile, 'the face of the BBC'. Her house in Gowan Avenue, Fulham was up for sale, and from early 1999 Jill had been living in Chiswick with Alan Farthing, her new fiancé. She drove alone from Chiswick to Fulham on an April morning in 1999 and at around half past eleven she parked her car on the street and opened the garden gate onto the short path that led up to her house. As she was about to put the keys in the lock to open the front door she was grabbed from behind. Her assailant held her with his right hand and forced her to the ground, so that her face was almost touching the tiled step of the front porch. Then, with his other hand, he fired a single shot that hit her just above the left ear, parallel to the ground; the bullet went through her head, coming out on the right side. The weapon used was a 9mm semi-automatic pistol, and the gun was pressed close to her head. The bullet, but not the gun, was recovered near by. Jill died instantly, her keys still in her hand.

A local resident called Helen Doble discovered her body about fifteen minutes later and called the police. Jill was taken to Charing Cross Hospital where she was declared dead on arrival. Later, her next-door neighbour, a man called Richard Hughes, remembered that he had heard Jill make a surprised cry as if she were greeting a friend, but he hadn't heard a gun being fired. Nonetheless, Richard had looked out of his front window and seen a man – undoubtedly the killer – whom he described as being white, six foot tall and aged around forty, walking away from Jill's house. This man walked down Gowan

Avenue, perhaps to where he had an accomplice waiting in a car, and has never been identified.

This was a high-profile murder of a much-loved public figure, and the Metropolitan Police would go on to take tens of thousands of statements and interview hundreds of people as part of their investigation. It was codenamed Operation Oxborough and, despite its scale, as I have mentioned above, their lines of enquiry concentrated on ruling out someone close to Jill, events in her professional life – it should be remembered that she presented a very popular BBC programme which aimed to bring offenders to justice – and finding out if there were any unique elements to the case beyond Jill's status and celebrity. Operation Oxborough hired the services of Dr Adrian West, a forensic psychologist who often acted as a profiler for the police, who produced three separate profiles of the type of person who might have been involved in the crime.

Jill had been in a long-term relationship with a BBC executive called Bob Wheaton between 1989 and 1996, and then had a brief affair with Simon Basil. However, the biggest change in her domestic circumstances related to her engagement to Alan Farthing at the end of January 1999, and the date of their wedding had been set for September that year. She was living at Farthing's house at the time of her murder, and their relationship was blossoming. All of this implies there was very little to indicate that the motive for her murder was linked to her personal life.

Dr Adrian West suggested that, despite the seemingly professional execution of the hit, it might have been undertaken by an 'obsessed loner' – perhaps a fan of Dando's – who had simply got lucky. This line of enquiry would eventually lead to the arrest and conviction of a rather odd local man called Barry George, who lived about half a mile from Jill's house. He had previously stalked a number of women, and had a history of anti-social and attention-seeking behaviour. George was eventually convicted of Jill's murder at the Old Bailey in July 2001 and sentenced to life imprisonment. His conviction, largely based on forensic evidence (a tiny particle of explosives residue was found in the lining of his coat, although this would later be discredited), was eventually overturned, and George was acquitted in August 2008.

At George's trial his defence barrister, Michael Mansfield, QC, put forward the hypothesis that Jill had been executed by a professional hitman, working on behalf of the Serbian government. Mansfield argued the killer was not a local man at all, and a number of pieces of evidence were cited to support this claim. The ballistics evidence revealed that Jill had been shot in a professional way – even down to the fact that her next-door neighbour had not heard a shot being fired. This could be explained by the gases escaping from the gun as it was being discharged being released inside Jill's head, rather than into the air and thus creating a noise. This sophisticated MO had other advantages for the killer, as he – I'm making the assumption here, as murder typically has a male perpetrator – would not have been covered in blood and other human matter, making it easier for him to have escaped without being detected. The fact that only one shot was fired again suggested competence and experience, and of course the hit was over in seconds – that meant that the killer did not need to linger on the doorstep of 29 Gowan Avenue. Nor were there any rifling marks found on the bullet, which implied that it had been custom made and that the gun itself was a smooth-bore, short-range weapon.

A Serbian hitman was suggested because on 6 April Jill had presented a high-profile BBC appeal on behalf of Kosovan Albanian refugees (no friends of the Serbs), which raised over a million pounds in the first twenty-four hours. Mansfield theorised that the hit had been ordered by the Serbian warlord Arkan on behalf of Slobodan Milošević, Serbia's hard-line leader, who would eventually be charged with war crimes by the International Criminal Tribunal for the former Yugoslavia. He died in March 2006 in a prison cell in The Hague. Just three days before Jill was murdered, NATO had bombed the Belgrade headquarters of Radio Television of Serbia, which had been established in 1992, was part-owned by the Milošević family and which was used to spread nationalist propaganda. Sixteen staff died in the raid. This was NATO's first offensive action against a sovereign country in its fifty-year history and, as Mansfield put it:

> The television station was owned and run by the Milošević family and was deliberately targeted by NATO, using a cruise missile, because it was seen as the main purveyor of Serbian state propaganda. Jill Dando by this stage had become one of the, if not the, face[s] of the BBC. In short, she was the personification and embodiment of the BBC.

In other words, Jill was targeted in retaliation for the NATO attack at a time when Britain was in effect at war with Serbia. This might all seem rather far-fetched and rooted in conspiracy theory, but there was in fact a history of Serbian hitmen working within Britain, although this was not much commented upon at the time. Another doorstep hit, from Scotland in the previous decade, can throw some light onto what might have happened to Jill.

On the morning of 20 October 1988, Nikola Štedul, a Croatian separatist leader living with his Scottish-born wife and their two daughters in Kirkcaldy, Fife, was returning to his house in Glen Lyon Road. He had been walking his dog Pasha. He was just yards from his front door when he noticed a black Mini Metro car slow down, as if the driver was lost and wanted directions. The car was actually being driven by Vinko Sindičić, a notorious Yugoslavian hitman who had entered the country on a false passport alleging that he wanted to attend the Scotland vs Yugoslavia World Cup qualifying match. Sindičić fired at least five shots at Nikola; the first two smashed his teeth and another hit him in the chest. Miraculously Nikola survived, in no small part saved because Pasha started to bark and the commotion attracted the attention of Nikola's neighbours. One neighbour noted down the number of the Mini Metro as it sped away, and Sindičić was arrested later that day as he tried to board a plane at Heathrow. A few days later two guns used in the hit were discovered on a grass verge by workmen employed by Fife Regional Council.

After his ordeal, Nikola said that 'the bullets in the mouth were a sign to shut up', as he had become a vocal advocate in exile for Croatian independence, at a time when it was still part of Yugoslavia. Support for this suggestion comes from government papers released in 2021. In a briefing note to Mrs Thatcher from 1988, Charles Powell, the prime minister's foreign policy adviser, wrote that 'we suspect that the Yugoslav security services were responsible for the shooting of the Croatian émigré in Scotland', although he did not have independent evidence to back this up. In May 1989 Sindičić was sentenced to fifteen years in prison, which he served at HMP Perth. According to my sources, while Sindičić was in prison he was regularly interviewed by Interpol as he was linked to a number of other assassinations and assassination attempts throughout Europe. It is of note that Milošević became president of Serbia in 1989 and, perhaps learning from the somewhat botched job that had been done on Nikola Štedul, set up the Jedinicia za Specijalne Operacije (JSO) within the country's security services. The JSO was known informally as 'the assassination department'.

With this background, it doesn't seem so far-fetched to link Jill's death to a Serbian hitman, given that one had been active on British soil in the decade before she had been murdered; that the victim had been targeted as he was seen to be undermining Serbia in some way; and that the doorstep was the site of the hit, which was undertaken just as the victim was returning home. This pattern would also be repeated over a decade later in Glasgow.

*

Frank McPhie was a father of five, enjoyed dog-fighting, and lived a life patterned by violent crime and spells in prison. He was one of Glasgow's major underworld figures, and had been involved in organised crime since the 1970s; he was a close associate of the legendary crime boss Arthur Thompson. One police officer who knew him described McPhie as 'savage, brutal and utterly callous', and added for good measure that 'he had a killer's eyes'. In fact, McPhie had been *cleared* of two murder charges: the death of a fellow prisoner called William Toye in 1996, and later the murder of Christopher McGrory in 1997. However, he had served time for armed robbery in 1978 and again in 1986, and in 1992 received an eight-year sentence for being in possession of £200,000 worth of drugs. It was on McPhie's release from that sentence that he was accused of having murdered McGrory, in what was perceived at the time to have been a drug deal gone wrong. In short, Frank McPhie's life was a world away from that inhabited by Jill Dando, even if they were both killed on their doorstep.

McPhie was murdered just before 9 p.m. on 10 May 2000 – shot in the head outside the door of his ground-floor flat in a sandstone tenement block at 6 Guthrie Street. The flat was less than half a mile away from Maryhill Police Station. The hitman had positioned himself on the eighth-floor drying area at the top of an adjacent tower block on Carrbridge Drive, which gave him a perfect view of McPhie's front door. The killer only needed one shot, and left behind his Czech-made ACZ Brno rifle; it yielded no useful forensic evidence. There were no witnesses who saw the hit taking place or the hitman exiting the scene of the crime. As the police said at the time, quoted in the *Glasgow Herald*, 'there was no sign of a man running off, or cars being driven away at high speed'. Indeed, several years later, when I questioned local people about the hit, they described the culprit as a 'ghost', or as a 'ghoster', by which they meant someone who had come into the area for the hit and then left again shortly afterwards. There was local suspicion that the killer had been contracted in and came from Ireland.

Given his background, there must have been many people who would have liked to have seen Frank McPhie dead. He lived in a world that operated outside the law; a world where tensions, slights and disagreements had serious and often life-threatening consequences. To that end, the police were also aware that McPhie had been involved in a recent road-rage incident with a member of the Daniel gang – a rival criminal family – and eventually John McCabe, a key member of that gang, was arrested for McPhie's murder, although charges were eventually dropped for lack of evidence.

As with the arrest and eventual conviction of Barry George, the idea that the killer was a local did not advance the police's investigation or solve the crime. The motive for the hit has always been presumed to have emanated from the external world in which McPhie operated, rather than his domestic circumstances. In that respect, we also have a clue as to what was happening in the weeks leading up to the murder, as the police had delivered an Osman Warning to McPhie. These official warnings are issued by the police when they have credible intelligence about a death threat against a potential victim's life. Detective Sergeant Gerry Gallagher had gone to 6 Guthrie Street to deliver the Osman Warning, although it has never been made public what that intelligence contained. DS Gallagher remembered that McPhie was unconcerned about the threat to his life, and made it clear that the police officer was not welcome in his home, as he later recalled in the *Daily Record*:

> During our short meeting he bristled with aggression ... I told him that I was there to give him a warning that his life

was in danger and he should take precautions regarding his movements. But he wasn't interested in hearing this. He said, 'You've given it, now goodbye.'

Six weeks later McPhie was murdered.

*

In these first two case studies we have seen how the door, or doorstep, was the site for the hit, although there are subtle differences. In Jill Dando's murder the killer completes his hit in only a few minutes and does not dwell for any length of time at her doorstep. However, Frank McPhie's killer did not go to the doorstep of the flat at all, but used a rifle from some distance away to carry out the hit as his victim was at the door of the block of flats – a communal space rather than the entry point of a private dwelling. Standing in these liminal spaces would have been dangerous for the hitman, as it increased the chances of his being detected, or might even have prevented him from accomplishing the hit, and so he wanted to mini-mise or eradicate completely the time he might spend there. This was not the case in our final murder.

Alistair Wilson was shot on the doorstep of his imposing three-storey, double-fronted Victorian house at 10 Crescent Road in Nairn at about 7 p.m. on 28 November 2004. In her excellent podcast about the case, called *The Doorstep Murder*, the BBC broadcast journalist Fiona Walker evokes a picture of Nairn as a coastal town; a place of 'sea gulls and sandcastles', but also a town that has a hint of grandeur, with an annual agricultural show and a Highland games. It was not the sort of place that was associated with violent crime, and before 2004 the last time there had been a murder in Nairn was in

1986. The Wilson house stands in the middle of a quiet street, tucked behind the main road and opposite a pub called the Havelock House Hotel, although most of the eleven thousand inhabitants of Nairn call it the Havelock. Number 10 dominates Crescent Road, and at one time the Wilsons had run it as a hotel, although that venture had failed. There are six steep steps leading up to the house, and the front door is visible from the street. The night of the murder was a Sunday, and that evening Alistair was upstairs in a bedroom reading his two sons, aged four and two, a bedtime story after they had had their bath when the doorbell rang. Also in the house were Veronica, his wife of six years, and her father.

It was Veronica who answered the door, and later she would remember that the man standing outside had asked for her husband by name; that he was white, clean-shaven, aged between thirty and forty, with a stocky build and between 5' 6" and 5' 10" tall. He was wearing a baseball cap and a dark blouson-style jacket. No e-fit of the man who rang their doorbell has ever been produced. Veronica went upstairs to get her husband, and presumed that the man must have had something to do with Alistair's work – he was the leader of a business banking team at HBOS, responsible for securing loans for small to medium-sized businesses in the north of Scotland, from the Orkneys to Oban. Alistair had recently resigned from the bank, and had only two weeks of his notice period left before starting a new job at BRE Highlands, an environmental consultancy. He was thirty years old, ambitious, and had studied accountancy and business law at Stirling University, from where he graduated in 1996.

Alistair went to see who was at the door, and shortly

afterwards went back upstairs to speak with Veronica, who was now with their two boys. He had with him an envelope – the type that usually comes with a birthday card, made of good-quality paper. Written on the front was the name Paul, but the envelope itself was empty. Veronica remembered that Alistair was confused about whether the man at the door was really looking for him, despite asking for him by name. Perhaps, she thought, it was a case of mistaken identity. When he went back into the house, Alistair had closed the door, leaving their caller on the doorstep. Veronica later recalled in an anniversary appeal about the case that:

Alistair was just a bit bewildered as to what the gentleman had said, because the envelope wasn't addressed to him. He was puzzled by the name; that it was not addressed to himself and there was nothing in the envelope. I said, 'No, he definitely asked for you by name.' It wasn't threatening, it was just very unusual. But there was no fear, otherwise I wouldn't have let him go back downstairs. He didn't need to; he was in the house now.

Veronica believed that, inside their house, Alistair was safe from whatever it was that had caused the man to ring their doorbell. Alistair went back downstairs and opened the door again; he was, for whatever reason, being pulled back to the external. The man was still standing on the doorstep. Veronica heard 'muffled' conversation downstairs, and then what she described as the sound of wooden pallets dropping to the floor. She now went back downstairs and saw that Alistair had been shot at close range, twice in the head and once in the body. The gun used to fire these shots was later found down a drain on a nearby street, giving us some clue as to where the hitman travelled after killing Alistair. The gun was a Haenel Schmeisser semi-automatic, sometimes called a 'pocket pistol', manufactured in Germany before the Second World War. Alistair was still breathing when Veronica reached him, but had lost a great deal of blood. Their four-year-old son Andrew saw his father lying in a pool of blood, and Veronica had to shout for her father to come and look after the children. She dialled 999 at 7.11 p.m., and then ran across the road to the Havelock, asking for help. When she didn't recognise anyone in the bar she returned to Alistair, although she would return to the Havelock again, desperately seeking assistance. The ambulance arrived at 7.19 p.m. and Alistair was taken to Raigmore Hospital in Inverness, where he died.

Even after nearly two decades there are many questions still needing answers about Alistair's brutal death. The search for the truth is not helped by the fact that the original police investigation, conducted by the old Northern Constabulary (one of the eight regional police forces that were merged when Police Scotland was created in April 2013), was a shambles from the outset. The crime scene at the doorstep was not preserved as it should have been, perhaps because the two police officers who originally answered the 999 call had little or no experience of murders. One witness, who later spoke with the former Metropolitan Police detective and author Peter Bleksley, remembered that he had put Alistair's watch, which had fallen off, back onto the dying man's wrist. Bleksley was also told that Alistair's body slipped from the stretcher as he was being carried to the ambulance, such was the steepness of the steps at the front of the house. Bleksley would go on to write an extraordinary book about the case, and he and I have discussed Alistair's murder on many occasions – conversations initiated by us both being contacted by the same man, who went by the pseudonym Nate.

Anniversaries of high-profile but unsolved murders often generate a great deal of media attention. On the thirteenth anniversary of Alistair's death, and soon after I had spoken about my hitmen research to the Scottish media, a package with a Glasgow postmark dropped into my pigeon hole at my university address. The package contained eight typed pages, and was entitled 'Alistair Wilson: A Cold Case Thesis'. No author was identified, although it was signed Nate. It is not unusual for me to receive packages, letters or emails of this kind, either asking for help or offering new lines of enquiry in relation to a cold case, and I have to admit that I have sometimes benefited from what has been suggested. Nate's views were trenchant, and at times had the whiff of conspiracy theory about them, as he stated that the police hadn't actually wanted to solve the case at all, partly because powerful regional business interests were at the root of Alistair's murder.

However, as I started to read his thesis I became aware that Nate was drawing my attention to two pieces of information that were at that stage unknown to me. I had always known that Veronica opened the door to her husband's killer, and that he had handed over an envelope, although the police had not at that time disclosed its contents. What I was unaware of was that the name Paul was written on the envelope, which Nate revealed in his document. Nate also referred to an independent witness called Tommy Hogg, who claimed that he had seen the killer and could describe him. In addition, he made a number of comments about Alistair Wilson's work at the bank, which, as I have mentioned, he was to leave in the coming weeks, and suggested that he was not as 'squeaky clean' in his personal life as he had been portrayed in the media.

This information was news to me, and I wondered if what Nate had written was already in the public domain.

I called one or two people who knew about the case, but they were equally surprised by Nate's claims. I appeared on BBC Scotland talking about the murder and, leaving aside the accusations about Alistair's personal life, suggested that there were consequently two particular lines of enquiry that could be pursued based on what Nate had written – if it was accurate. First, that we could attempt to identify his killer by having Tommy Hogg produce an e-fit, as Veronica had also seen her husband's killer; and, second, that a forensic accountant could look more closely at Alistair's dealings at the bank and identify any potentially suspicious transactions. I ended the interview saying that: 'I always thought that this case was unsolvable, but if what Nate says is true now I'm increasingly of the view that I'm surprised it hasn't been solved already. It is eminently solvable.'

My confidence was based on my knowledge of hits, who conducts them and how professional hits were usually undertaken on the doorstep of the victim. Pointing this out resulted in a small volcanic eruption both in the reporting of the case and in how Police Scotland reacted.

Local and regional journalists, and Police Scotland

themselves, appeared to know all about what Nate had described, and, as if to distance themselves from what he had said, suggested that everything that he had written was already well known. Of course, if it was already well known it could be discounted. The deputy senior investigating officer sent an email to my university address, and we subsequently had a very pleasant conversation during which he suggested that no e-fit had been produced as perhaps Tommy hadn't got a good look at the man. That comment only made me more curious, especially when Tommy Hogg then went on a radio show a day later, and assured the host that he had been able to get a very good look at the man he had seen walk in the direction of the Wilsons' house, wearing clothing that appeared to him to be remarkably like the clothes worn by the killer, as had been described by Veronica.

I called Mr Hogg (he was in the local Nairn telephone directory), and he told me all about his statements to the police and, specifically, that he was shown an e-fit that had already been produced when he went to the police station. 'It was the spitting image' of the person he had seen. Who had provided the description for the e-fit? Perhaps Veronica, who had opened the door to the killer? If this e-fit was already in existence, why had it never been circulated to the public? Police Scotland then issued another statement saying that the person whom Mr Hogg had identified had been traced and eliminated from their enquiries. If that was true, Mr Hogg didn't seem to know about it, and how had the police been able to track down this person without appealing for help from the public? Did they themselves know who was being described in the e-fit? Was he well known locally?

Perhaps he might even have been a policeman, or an ex-policeman? It might even have been Nate.

If all of these details were already in the public domain why didn't the police, or indeed any number of Scottish crime correspondents, seem to be connecting the dots between any business deals completed by Alistair in the course of his work at the bank, which would establish a motive for him to have been murdered, and the likely contractor of the hit? Indeed Peter Bleksley, in his book about the case, *To Catch a Killer*, noted that Alistair was universally known in the town as 'the Banker', and suggested that the key to unlocking this case was the financial affairs of Livingston Football Club, which had serious money problems in 2004, and was on the verge of going into liquidation before a deal was eventually arranged.

In short, this hit increasingly bears the hallmarks of white-collar crime, as opposed to the blue-collar crimes of drug dealers, crime families and Serbian hitmen. This is not about the internal domestic circumstances of the Wilsons – Alistair really was safe at home – but about his world beyond 10 Crescent Road, and beyond Nairn; a world that he was about to leave behind. My hypothesis is that the contractor of the hit was likely to have been a regional – perhaps even national – businessman, who had it in his interests to kill Alistair after he had outlived his usefulness. What's important here is to allow the necessary forensic accounting that would need to be done to test this hypothesis, and Police Scotland have suggested that this is an 'active line of the investigation'. Really? Has it actually taken all these years to identify the one aspect of Alistair's life that transcended the local and the tranquil, and which took him into a world where fortunes could be made or lost?

It is imperative that Alistair's murder continues to be seen as a tragedy; finding his killer is not a parlour game. A man was murdered, and so his wife has been left without a husband, his children without a father. Someone out there, more than likely living and doing business in the area, had a man killed and, if a similar situation arises again, what's to prevent them from commissioning another doorstep hit in the future?

*

What should we conclude about these three unsolved doorstep murders?

All of them seem to have been related to the external and not the internal domestic worlds of the victims. This is perhaps most obvious in the cases of Jill Dando and Frank McPhie, but if my hypothesis is correct the solution to Alistair Wilson's murder lies in his work at HBOS and his decision to leave the bank. In fact, all three murders seem to have been precipitated by an event that took place in the professional lives of the victims in the weeks leading up to their murder. Jill had presented the BBC appeal on behalf of Kosovan Albanian refugees, which was seen in Serbia as being harmful to Serbs; Alistair had resigned from the bank and was going to be employed elsewhere; and Frank was involved in a road-rage incident with a member of another notorious crime family and, whether related to that or not, he had received an Osman Warning from the police. Their murders were a form of retaliation and revenge, and we can even detect some of that motivation in how the hits were executed.

Jill, who was shot in the head, was also a presenter who was seen to be the 'face of the BBC' – a state broadcaster, just like Radio Television of Serbia – and so attacking her head made her murder both personal and symbolic. Frank was murdered in sight of Maryhill Police Station, which seems to suggest that his killer cared little about the authority of the police – he was 'above the law' – and of course no one has ever been convicted of this murder. And what about Alistair? It is perhaps here we need to think about the envelope that he was handed on his doorstep. Perhaps the name Paul is a red herring – although I have heard it suggested that Paul was an acronym for 'Pay And U Live' – but more generally envelopes really are expected to be filled and, above all, they deliver messages from the world outside; they remind you that people 'out there' are still connected to you, and involved with your life even after you close the front door.

Weapons were recovered in two cases but neither yielded any useful forensic evidence, and there are descriptions of the killer in two of the hits: on Jill and on Alistair. In both instances there was direct contact between the victim and the perpetrator, and, in the case of Alistair, also between the killer and Veronica. Only Frank McPhie did not interact with his killer – perhaps because he was known for being able to look after himself during a confrontation, and so his assailant didn't want to take any chances that he might be overpowered. Without doubt the least 'professional' of these hits was that perpetrated on Alistair. For example, three shots were necessary to kill him, rather than one, and his killer was on the doorstep for the longest period of time. As I have suggested, the hitman wants to minimise or eradicate the time he spends in this liminal space. For Peter Bleksley, this implies that the hitman had not necessarily come to kill but to negotiate, and it was only when it became clear that this negotiation was going nowhere that Alistair was murdered. There's a lot to be said for that analysis. Indeed, we can sense something of the confusion of that negotiation being played out with first Veronica at the door, and then Alistair coming and going with the envelope in his hand. He'd received the message but didn't know what it meant, or perhaps was confused about how to react. Could he have just been playing for time, thinking that it would all be sorted out? The deadly *pas de deux* on the doorstep brought Alistair back into a world that he thought he was leaving behind when he resigned from the bank; it wasn't going to be that easy. He was in his domestic, internal world on a Sunday night, surrounded by his family, and yet trying to make sense of a set of circumstances that I believe came from beyond 10 Crescent Road.

That is also different about the hit on Alistair. He was at home, rather than coming home, as was the case with Jill and Frank. As Veronica put it, what was happening was 'unusual' but not 'threatening', for 'he was in the house now'. Neither Jill nor Frank had got that far. The house was a place where Alistair and Veronica could safely leave the world outside and concentrate on raising their family. He was within the world of baths and bedtime stories for his boys; the familiar rhythms of family life that make us all feel human; above all, the rituals of domesticity that create an atmosphere of safety and protection. The homely and the unhomely; bedtime for the children disturbed by callers carrying empty envelopes that are nonetheless filled with meaning. *Knock, knock, knock, who's there?* Whether in Nairn, London or Glasgow, we would be wrong to think of the doorstep as a safe and comfortable space, despite its familiarity, for it is one which is liminal, and so fluid and unpredictable. It can, if the occasion demands it, lead to death.

Let's now cross that threshold ourselves and walk inside.

CHAPTER TWO

The Living Room

'His living room is a box in the theatre of the
world ... the interior is not just the universe but
also the etui of the private individual. To dwell
means to leave traces. In the interior these are
accentuated. Coverlets and antimacassars, cases
and containers are devised in abundance; in these
the traces of the most ordinary objects of use are
imprinted. In just the same way, the traces of the
inhabitant are imprinted in the interior. Enter the
detective story, which pursues these traces.'

Walter Benjamin, *Paris, the Capital of the
Nineteenth Century*

What do you call the room in your home where you do
most, if not all, of your socialising with your family
and friends? The room where you watch television – sometimes with a meal on your lap – but also the place where you
try to catch up with that day's headlines, or finish the book

you've been reading for the last few weeks? If you had the space, would you try to put the television somewhere else, or make sure that meals were always eaten in the kitchen or even a dining room? Is this room that I am describing your drawing room (after you have 'withdrawn' from the dining room), sitting room or living room? Perhaps you call it a lounge, though maybe you reserve that description for the disinfected and impersonal spaces where people sit in airports.

How you answer this question, and even whether you might have couches, settees or sofas in this room to sit on, is redolent of that most British of obsessions: class. As the social anthropologist Kate Fox pointed out in *Watching the English*, the everyday terminology that we use for these intimate spaces can tell other people whether we are working class, lower-middle, middle-middle, upper-middle class, or upper class.

However, I am not trying to pick up the class, or perhaps even the generational, clues that your answer to this question might reveal, and have called this chapter 'The Living Room' because, given what I am going to describe, it feels darkly ironic. For what it's worth, we call this space the fire room in my own home, for this is what my children called it when they were very young, as it's the room that has a wood burner. All that I am trying to do is to get you to think about that space in your home which is not a bedroom, kitchen, dining room (if you have one) or bathroom and, like the hall of a medieval house, is the place where leisure time is spent. It is the room where you sit, as opposed to sleep, and which over time has become the place that you have decorated to reveal something of your personal tastes, wealth and social standing, because it is also a space where you receive and entertain guests and so want to show yourself at your best. It is the room that has become the ornamental case, or etui, as the German cultural critic Walter Benjamin put it, of the hidden and private individual.

Benjamin was also describing much more than this in his pre-war essay quoted at the start of the chapter, for, like a crime scene itself, he also pointed out that traces of the supposedly private person are 'imprinted in the interior'. This was all part of his critique of capitalism, modernisation and consumerism, and how the changes that had occurred as a result of these broad social, economic and cultural shifts affected the way people lived their lives. He argued that the living room might be a private 'box in the theatre of the world', but it was also a space that exposed something of the person who lived there through the 'ordinary objects' that were bought and displayed. It might have become a private space (another British obsession), but if you were invited to enter, or had to do so for other reasons, it offered clues about the person, or people, who occupied that place. The private, in other words, could just as easily become public.

Benjamin's final suggestion, that all of this permitted the development of the detective story, is an allusion to Edgar Allan Poe's 'The Murders in the Rue Morgue'. Published in 1841 in *Graham's Magazine*, this is generally considered to be the first ever piece of detective fiction. This short story came hard on the heels of an essay called 'The Philosophy of Furniture', in which Poe described the importance of curtains, lampshades, mirrors, dinner plates, sofas and so forth. He suggested, with only a slight hint of sarcasm, that a 'judge at common law may be an ordinary man; a good judge of a carpet must be a genius'. This theme is taken up in 'The Murders in the Rue Morgue', in which his amateur detective, Auguste Dupin, unravels the mystery of the horrific murders of Madame L'Espanaye and her daughter. Inevitably, as would become the norm with detective fiction, this was a case the police found baffling.

Poe, who employs a friend of Dupin to act as the narrator, puts a great deal of emphasis on the state of the room where the murders had taken place. Dupin notes, for example, that the room, where the inhabitants both lived and slept, was 'in the wildest disorder', and 'a spectacle presented itself which struck everyone present not less with horror than with astonishment'. Chairs and tables had been broken and:

There was only one bedstead; and from this the bed had been removed, and thrown into the middle of the floor. On a chair lay a razor, besmeared with blood. On the hearth were two or three long and thick tresses of grey human hair, also dabbled in blood, and seeming to have been pulled out by the roots. Upon the floor were found four Napoleons, an ear-ring of topaz, three large silver spoons, three smaller of *métal d'Alger*, and two bags, containing nearly four thousand francs in gold. The drawers of a *bureau*, which stood in one corner was open, and had been, apparently, rifled, although many articles still remained in them. A small iron safe was discovered under the *bed* (not under the bedstead). It was open, with the key still in the door. It had no contents beyond a few old letters, and other papers of little consequence.

I will not spoil the somewhat preposterous ending of the story, but suffice to say Dupin solves the mystery, and his understanding of the murder and the murderer is grounded on how the room had been left by the killer. Poe might have prioritised the name of the street in this story, but he could equally have called it 'The Murders in a Living Room situated on the Rue Morgue'.

I now want us to consider three other living rooms, although this trio are real rather than fictional and, as before, I will use case studies of murders that have taken place in these spaces. These are: the murders of forty-five-year-old Janice Sheridan and her seventy-nine-year-old mother Connie in 1999, in the isolated cottage that they shared near the village of Upwell in Norfolk; the murder of seventeen-year-old Edward Evans by Ian Brady in October 1965, at 16 Wardle Brook Avenue in Hattersley, Cheshire; and, finally, the murder of forty-two-year-old Julia Rawson in May 2019, in a flat located on Mission Drive, Tipton, in the West Midlands, by Nathan Maynard-Ellis and his partner David Leesley. These murders make public what had been private and, in the case of Brady, also offer an insight into his development as a serial killer. Of course there is an immediate variance that should be acknowledged: both killer couples – Brady and Hindley, and Maynard-Ellis and Leesley – committed the murder of other people, who they had invited into these spaces, whereas Janice and her mother were slain in their own living room, which their killer illegally entered. This does create a difference that we need to think about when we consider this case, but my general point about how using this space within the commission of a murder is part of a process of showing the private self to the outside world still holds true. I also want to start with these two murders in Norfolk because, rather uncannily, they echo what happened to Madame L'Espayane and her daughter.

*

Connie Sheridan and her daughter Janice were pedigree-dog breeders who lived together in a cottage in the fens of Norfolk, situated about a mile and half down a dead-end track from the village of Upwell. After their murders their relatives explained that they had chosen the house precisely because its isolation meant that there wouldn't be neighbours to object to their whippets barking, and there was also plenty of space just outside the front door to take the dogs for a walk. At the time of their deaths twenty-four whippets were living in a ground-floor annexe, which could be easily accessed by a door in the living room. Connie, who was nearly eighty, rarely left the house. However Janice was regularly seen out and about in the local community and, in 1994, had taken a part-time job helping out at Country Kennels. It was her failure to turn up for work on Sunday 10 January 1999 that alerted people to the fact that something was seriously wrong.

The police who entered the house found Connie in the living room. She had been stabbed ten times: eight wounds in her chest; one on her stomach; and another on her forearm – likely to have been caused as she raised her arm to protect herself. After her death her arms had been folded across her chest, and the sofa on which she lay had been pushed against the door to the annexe. Janice was also dead. She had been stabbed a total of eleven times, including in the middle of her back – perhaps sustained as she tried to flee from her attacker. She also had stab wounds on her neck, although the bulk of her injuries were to her chest, which, it would later become clear, had been inflicted after her killer had removed her blouse. Janice was lying on her back on the floor with her head pointing towards the fireplace; her legs – bound at the ankles with duct tape – were raised and resting on a chair. Forensic tests would reveal that her wrists had also at one stage been bound in a similar way. Her breasts were exposed, and Janice's trousers and underwear had been removed by the killer. Neither of the women had been raped.

There was no sign of any great struggle, and both Connie's and Janice's bodies had obviously been posed – 'staged' – after they died. Staging, which is often divided into primary and secondary staging, is a criminological term for the conscious choice made by an offender at the crime scene to either thwart the criminal investigation (primary staging) or engage in behaviours that give the offender perverted pleasure (secondary staging). This latter type of staging is sometimes meant to tell a story – a story that might also shock the post-mortem investigators. It was estimated that Connie and Janice were killed on 7 January, and so had lain undiscovered for three days. The dogs were extremely distressed when the police entered the property, although none had been harmed by the killer. As might be imagined, the room was covered in blood and, given the interaction between the killer and the two women (especially with Janice), a great deal of forensic evidence could be gathered. Detective Inspector Paul Chapman, who led the investigation, stated that he'd never seen a scene like it, and in a later ITV documentary about the case he said 'we still don't know what the motive was', although this perhaps reveals how unusual this type of offence and the crime scene associated with it must have been in his experience.

However, there are actually a number of things we can infer from the crime scene about the murders, and about the motive of the offender in relation to how the living room had been staged. At an instrumental level it is difficult to control two victims at the same time, even if one of those victims is elderly, and so the killer had to have planned how he was going to manage the two women once he had gained entry to the house. He has thought about all of this very carefully, and how he is going to use these murders to tell us something about himself. The isolation of the cottage also meant that if either Connie or Janice had screamed they would not have been heard, and nor would the dogs barking have raised the alarm – that gave the killer an advantage. We obviously do not know what he said to his victims, or what they might have said in return, but he was undoubtedly unmoved by any appeals not to cause them harm.

It is also clear from the crime scene that he was methodical, rather than frenzied and chaotic, and so we can infer that he offended in phases: he needed to subdue Connie (and prevent the dogs from entering the living room) so that he could concentrate his attentions on Janice; he incapacitated Janice and tied her wrists prior to removing her clothes; he then laid her on her back, bound her legs and elevated her feet before stabbing her. All this means that he spent a considerable amount of time with his victims; it was not a blitz attack during which the killer was out of control, but one in which each element was constructed so as to be enjoyed and savoured. Finally, it doesn't seem particularly insightful to suggest that from what had happened to Connie, and especially to Janice, the killer's motive was sexual, despite the fact that neither of the women was raped, although the use of a knife to stab the breasts can be viewed as a form of penetrative sexual assault. Janice was stabbed in the chest after her killer had removed her blouse; looking and then being looked at was part of his enjoyment.

These attacks took place in the living room, rather than in the bedroom, which would have afforded a degree of privacy. But that was not what the killer sought. For him this was a stage as much as it was a crime scene – he wanted what he had done to be viewed, perhaps even admired, by those who entered the crime scene after he had left. In much the same way as we might praise a new sofa that a friend had just purchased, or a picture they had chosen to hang on a wall, the murders of Connie and Janice were indicators of his tastes and sexual fantasies, and he wanted compliments too; he wanted to dazzle us. He was also making his fantasies become a reality, which is perhaps best revealed by the binding of Janice's ankles and the raising of her legs. This would have meant that he would have been able to view her vagina, and so by putting her in this position he wanted us to view her vagina too. The binding is also significant, and hints at the sadism inherent in the attack. So too the stabbing, which is a form of piquerism – a paraphilia associated with sadism in which there is an interest in penetrating the skin of another person with a sharp object. The areas most commonly targeted by the piquer are the breasts, groin and buttocks. No semen was found at the crime scene, which implies that either he did not ejaculate – which seems doubtful – or, more likely, the killer wore a condom when committing these attacks (and took it with him when he left), which is again an indication of some planning and shrewdness.

The killer's calculation took him only so far. A great deal of forensic evidence was found in the living room – including a boot mark, and a thumb print on the fireplace belonging to the killer – and subsequent forensic tests would also reveal his DNA on the tape that he had used to bind Janice's legs, and also on her breasts. However, there was no match on the National DNA Database, and so it would be more traditional methods that unmasked thirty-three-year-old Kevin Cotterell, a travelling salesman who worked for a Swindon-based company called Kleeneze (which used the slogan 'The Friendly Face of Home Shopping'), as Janice and Connie's killer. A local from the village who lived close to the Sheridans had observed a green car parked outside their house and noted down the number plate, G567PVF, which was a close match to Cotterell's car, and it would later become clear that he had visited the Sheridans the previous year to sell them double glazing. He knew the property, and that the women lived alone. He had moved from double glazing to double murder, although not in one jump. Cotterell had a previous conviction for two burglaries, and an indecent act which he had committed in 1983, when he was seventeen, and he had also broken into a girl's bedroom and masturbated on her underwear – an offence for which he received twelve months' probation. However, given the age when he had committed these offences, his details were not kept on file. As for the murders of the Sheridans, materials, including a bloody holdall, found in Cotterell's house, which he shared with his father in Pentney in Norfolk, also connected him to their deaths. Pentney is about twenty-five miles away from Upwell.

Cotterell initially pleaded not guilty to the charges, but he then changed his plea on the day of the trial at Norwich Crown Court, and thus didn't have to explain his behaviour to the court. This guilty plea was not entered out of sympathy for Connie and Janice's surviving family, or as a belated form of remorse, but was probably a way of keeping control of what might be learned about the murders; it was another form of calculation – Cotterell was again being methodical. He was given two life sentences.

*

By the time that seventeen-year-old Edward Evans was murdered on the evening of 6 October 1965, Ian Brady and his partner Myra Hindley were already serial killers. They had killed four children in the preceding two years, and Edward was to be their last victim; he was also the oldest. Their first three victims had been, in various ways, lured to their deaths, killed in the open air and then buried on Saddleworth Moor. The murder of the fourth, Lesley Ann Downey, was different in that she was killed inside 16 Wardle Brook Avenue – the council house that was shared by Brady, Hindley and Hindley's grandmother, as well as two dogs and a budgerigar – upstairs in one of the two tiny bedrooms. After her death, she was also buried on Saddleworth Moor. There is clear evidence of escalation from their previous crimes in the murderous behaviour of Brady and Hindley, and what they did to Lesley Ann: not only was she murdered indoors, but she was also photographed and recorded pleading for her life. There is also escalation in how they dealt with Edward, who too was killed indoors, but in the living room rather than a bedroom, and they involved a third party – Myra's brother-in-law David

Smith, who lived close by. It was this final escalation that brought Brady and Hindley's killing cycle to an end.

We have two good sources about what happened to Edward, offering us an intimate picture of the house and the living room where he was killed. First, we have Dr Alan Keightley's book about the murders, *Ian Brady: The Untold Story of the Moors Murders*, published after Brady's death in May 2017, which can be regarded almost as an authorised biography. Keightley, a former religious studies teacher, describes himself as a confidant of Brady. He started to write to him in 1992 and then visited him every three weeks from March 1994 onwards, after Brady had been moved to the high security Ashworth Hospital on Merseyside. A measure of their twenty-five-year relationship can be gleaned from the fact that in 1997 Keightley opened up an account for Brady at the local branch of the bookmaker William Hill. The second source is David Smith himself, and his compelling autobiography *Witness: The Story of David Smith, Chief Prosecution Witness in the Moors Murders Case.* We also have court reports, police testimony and newspaper accounts, of course, but I have tended to prioritise what Smith describes.

Brady and Hindley had moved to Wardle Brook Avenue in September 1964. Number 16 was the end of a terrace of four houses and overlooked the road between Hyde and Mottram; it had a front and a back garden, and was surrounded by a white picket fence. Three doors down, 10 Wardle Brook Avenue, was on the same level as the road, but number 16 was some ten feet above it, and you either had to use the path that ran along the front of the terrace of houses to reach the front door or scramble up a grass slope. On the horizon, and clearly visible from the house, were the moors which were situated some ten miles away. The house would eventually be pulled down in 1987.

Inside number 16 was a living room with a window at each end, a serving hatch that opened into the kitchen, and a fireplace. Upstairs were two bedrooms and a bathroom. The living room was painted pink, with wallpaper that looked like brickwork surrounding the fireplace. There was a red carpet on the floor and, according to Keightley, 'a red moquette settee that converted into a bed and green armchair. A cigarette machine was installed in the house, refilled every Sunday morning and emptied of half-crown coins.' Moquette is a tough woollen fabric often used for the upholstery on public transport. There was a TV in the living room, a record player and some records; David Smith also remembers a Formica coffee table that displayed 'the usual still life: empty bottles, overflowing ashtrays and an abandoned chessboard'. A decade younger than Brady, he would later describe 16 Wardle Brook Avenue as a 'dreary little house at the end of a dreary little terrace', and 'Godless'. It was for him just a place 'to get stoned on booze and talk about nothing'. Smith suspects that Brady had been grooming him to become a participant in his criminal activities, and he remembered that there was always a great deal of discussion about bank robberies, violent crime and murder – especially after they had been drinking. Keightley also notes that Brady had added 'his own touch to the living room decor' and quotes him directly: 'I put an SS dagger on the wall. I bought it from an antique shop. It had a metal scabbard decorated with rune stone signs and an eagle holding a swastika.' This seemed to be a perfect symbol for

Brady's nihilism, which he first cultivated and then justified by his reading – and often his misunderstanding – of the works of a number of existential philosophers and authors, including Friedrich Nietzsche and the Marquis de Sade.

Edward was an apprentice engineer who had arranged to meet with his friend Michael Mahone to go and see Manchester United play Helsinki at Old Trafford. However, Michael never appeared, and that meant that Edward was left drinking in the city centre by himself. Brady eventually picked him up at the railway station, having been driven there by Hindley (he told Edward that she was his sister), and they brought him back to 16 Wardle Brook Avenue.

There has always been a version of events that has suggested that Edward was gay – partly because of the evidence that Brady gave at court, where he claimed that he recognised him from a gay bar in the city, although the two had never previously spoken. Brady said that Edward knew that he was being invited back to the house for sex, and Keightley argues that 'the truth is that Brady did take part in sexual acts with Edward Evans. These included oral sex.' This 'truth' must have come from Brady, and so it cannot be taken as proof. What can be stated more definitively is that when the police found Edward's body he wasn't wearing his shoes and his flies were undone; and that later forensic tests found dog hairs from the house on his legs and anus after his jeans had been removed. Brady said that his intention in picking up Edward had been to 'roll a queer' – in other words, steal his money in the belief that the theft wouldn't be reported as being gay was still illegal. Above all, it would appear to have been a way to test David Smith's willingness to carry out crimes at Brady's bidding.

Leaving Edward and Brady alone on their return to 16 Wardle Brook Avenue (which may have given them the opportunity to have sex), Hindley took a short walk to fetch David. When they returned, Brady answered the door and said, in a voice loud enough for Edward to hear, 'Do you want those miniature wine bottles? They are in the kitchen.' In his police statement David then said that Brady led him into the kitchen. The door to the living room was closed, but after he had handed over the wine bottles Brady went back into the living room while David stayed in the kitchen. He waited for a minute or two and then heard the screams, and Hindley shouting 'Dave, help him!' In his memoir he describes what happened:

Fucking cunt, dirty bastard ... In a nice, normal overspill living room Ian is killing a lad with an axe, repeating those same words over and over again. The lad is lying with his head and shoulders on the settee, his legs sprawled on the floor, facing upwards. Ian stands over him, legs on either side of the screaming lad. The television is the only light in the room.

The lad falls onto the floor, onto his stomach, still screaming. Ian keeps hitting him; even when the lad falls beneath the table, Ian goes after him, drags him out and hits him again. He swings the axe and it grazes the top of Myra's head. There is blood everywhere. Then he stops and shouts: *get the fucking dogs away from the blood, get the fucking things out of it ...*

The lad is lying on his face, feet near the door. Ian kneels down and strangles him, pulling something tight around his throat. The lad's head is destroyed already; he rattles and gurgles, a thick, wet sound, a low sound. Then lower: more effort from Ian, and lower, and lower, then nothing but silence, everlasting silence.

I have used this very graphic account offered by David as it's already in the public domain, and it offers us an insight into what happens at the moment when a living room becomes the site of a murder – and therefore the atmosphere, actions and behaviour that take place before it becomes a crime scene. Here we should note how the room is lit by the light from the television; how poor Edward falls to the ground and appears to try to hide under the table; pets become anxious or involved and have to be removed from the room; and there are shouts and screams – which are eventually replaced by deadening silence. There is now also a body in the living room, along with blood and other forensic evidence.

David helped put Edward's body in a blanket and some polythene, and carried him upstairs with Brady to the second bedroom – the room where Hindley and Brady had killed Lesley Ann Downey – and then they began to try to clean up the living room as best as they could. David noted that Hindley, who had tried to reassure her grandmother that the screams she heard were only because she had dropped something on her foot, organised all the cloths, disinfectant and bowls of water that were necessary to get the blood off the carpet and the walls. David described how there was 'a wicked smell of blood, brains and defecation, more in common with a battlefield than a suburban living room' and, above all, he was anxious that he might be about to become Brady and Hindley's next victim. They worked for several hours smoking, scrubbing and cleaning, and then the living room was 'back to normal'. Brady then started to worry that they would need to move Edward's body out of the house, and this provided David with his excuse to get out of 16 Wardle Brook Avenue and go home. He suggested that they could use his baby's pram to move the body in the morning – an offer of help that was accepted. In fact, David used the opportunity to call the police.

*

More than fifty years later, and almost exactly two years to the day after Brady died, another living room would become the central backdrop to murder, with Brady himself looking on from the bookshelves.

Julia Rawson, a talented artist who had studied at Stafford Art College, and who ran a local market stall to sell her work, decided to meet up with an old girlfriend on 11 May 2019. They drank for a few hours and then decided to go home, but Julia caught the wrong bus and, one thing after another, she ended up in the Bottle & Cork pub in New Mill Street in Dudley. Julia was friendly and outgoing, and it was there that she met and got talking to thirty-year-old Nathan Maynard-Ellis, who was out on the town without his younger partner, David Leesley. It is unlikely that Julia knew that Maynard-Ellis was gay, or that he had in the past seen a psychiatrist because of his violent sexual fantasies. Later newspaper accounts would reveal that Julia was a lesbian, but also claim that she could often be flirtatious with men, especially when she was drunk. Maynard-Ellis, who was sober, although he had been drinking, suggested at around 2 a.m. that they take a taxi back to his flat in Tipton, and Julia accepted the offer.

We do not know how long Julia had been in the tiny flat on Mission Drive before she was killed by Maynard-Ellis and Leesley, but she is unlikely to have been in their company for very long. Maynard-Ellis would later claim that as they sat together on the sofa in the living room, she had made sexually provocative moves towards him and this had triggered memories of early traumas in his life. He said that he had panicked and hit her over the head four times with a rolling pin – a weapon that just happened to be close by. Julia had fallen to the floor and so, Maynard-Ellis stated, he had taken her into the bathroom to wash her wounds. He said that it was only when they were in the bathroom that he realised she was dead. Undoubtedly Julia had died on the sofa. Maynard-Ellis and Leesley then dismembered Julia's body in the bathroom, cutting it into twelve pieces with a hacksaw. Her hands were cut off at the wrists; her feet cut off at the ankles; her legs were removed below the hips and her arms below the shoulders; her spine was cut through at waist level; and she was decapitated. For good measure, her right kidney was removed; later investigation would suggest that this was taken as a trophy. This scale of dismemberment was beyond what would be necessary to dispose of Julia's remains, and so was clearly related to some sexual fantasy either shared by both men or simply favoured by Maynard-Ellis.

Maynard-Ellis and Leesley then put the body parts into black plastic bin bags and, a few days later, discarded them near a local canal. They also disposed of the bloodstained sofa and carpet at a refuse tip on Shidas Lane in Oldbury, and bought a new carpet that same day from Carpetright – insisting that it had to be laid immediately but, the manager later remembered, saying that they only needed one square metre of underlay (presumably this was where the blood had soaked through). Meanwhile the police had started to search for Julia and, tipped off by a member of the public who had observed her with Maynard-Ellis and was suspicious about what had happened, they began to focus their attentions on him and Leesley. There was a great deal of CCTV evidence that connected Maynard-Ellis to Julia captured on the cameras in the Bottle & Cork, and also CCTV of both Maynard-Ellis and Leesley disposing of bin bags around their flat, as well as at the tip. The police searched the site where the rubbish from Shidas Lane was removed to and recovered the sofa, which was then subjected to forensic tests, and it was this that gave them the evidence they needed to bring charges. Until that time, and despite clearly resembling the person in the CCTV footage, Maynard-Ellis had maintained his innocence and denied that he was the man on the film.

After the tip-off by the member of the public, the police searched Maynard-Ellis and Leesley's flat, and it gave them a number of reasons to be concerned. The flat was filled from top to bottom with knives, saws, axes and other bladed instruments; there were Chucky dolls holding knives, other dolls' heads and plastic severed hands; there were home-made horror-movie masks and balaclavas; a collection of films depicting decapitation and necrophilia, such as *Nekromantic 1* and *Nekromantic 2*; scattered around were a great many newspaper cuttings, books and films about serial killers; and there were odd stuffed creatures dotted here and there. More importantly, the police also found bloodstains.

Maynard-Ellis explained that he had studied film and TV,

and that his rather bizarre collecting habits related to his studies; he also claimed to have studied criminology, which was why he had so many books about serial killers. After the pair had been charged, the police took photographs of what was found in the flat and then, following their conviction, released these photographs to the media. On one of the groaning bookshelves that was photographed I noticed that, sandwiched between *The World's Top Twenty Worst Crimes* and *World-Famous Serial Killers*, was my own *A History of British Serial Killing*. I took some comfort from the fact that they obviously hadn't read the book, or if they had they can't have appreciated the central argument that I had made in it, given that it was a history of the victims of serial killers rather than about the serial killers themselves. Further along the shelf were works by Gordon Burn, Michael Bilton and Brian Masters, and a copy of John Lisners's *House of Horrors*, a book about Dennis Nilsen. Inevitably, there were also books about Jack the Ripper, and *Face to Face with Evil* by Chris Cowley, which has a picture of Ian Brady on the front cover, staring blankly at the viewer.

The presence of these books, and the pair's serial-killer fascination, perhaps offers us a different understanding of why they had removed Julia's kidney: Maynard-Ellis and Leesley would seem to have been inspired to do this by the activities of Jack the Ripper. The left kidney of Catherine Eddowes had been removed by her killer; and the kidneys of Mary Jane Kelly, as well as her other internal organs, were removed and placed around her body in 13 Miller's Court, where she was killed. We might debate the significance of taking the kidneys – believed by some faiths to be the site of temperament, prudence and wisdom – although, more generally, the removal of the organs of a victim as a trophy is a psychopathological behaviour that does seem to have special meaning for the killer, as well as allowing him (or them) to maintain post-mortem control.

After a month-long trial at Coventry Crown Court, the pair were convicted in November 2020. A month later, Maynard-Ellis was sentenced to life in prison and the judge ruled that he would have to serve a minimum of thirty years inside before being eligible for parole. He was also convicted of a series of sexual offences against another woman. Leesley was also sentenced to life in prison but, reflecting the different roles that they played within the commission of the murder, his minimum term was set at nineteen years. Just as well that another of the books that they seemed to have read was *Banged Up* by Ronnie Thompson.

*

With three case studies that cover a period from the 1960s until 2019, it is perhaps inevitable that we should encounter significant social, cultural and criminological developments within that sixty-year time frame. Chief amongst these is the fact that when Brady wanted to 'roll a queer', homosexuality was still against the law and would not become legal (for those over the age of twenty-one) until 1967, with the passage of the Sexual Offences Act. Successive Acts of Parliament would strengthen this process so that by 2013 the Marriage (Same Sex Couples) Act allowed civil partners to convert their civil partnership into marriage, and also allowed people to change their legal gender without necessarily having to end their existing marriage. All of this is a noteworthy cultural backdrop as sexuality, as much as sex, features in at least two of these case studies.

Three other developments are also striking, and provide a wider context for what these case studies reveal. First is the growth of closed-circuit television to the extent that it is now a dominant, if rarely discussed or commented on, feature of our civic life – a phenomenon that could not have been envisaged when Brady and Hindley set out on their criminal careers. It is estimated that there is now one CCTV camera for every fourteen people in the UK. Indeed, technology more generally has had a major impact on how crime is detected, and also the types of skills that our police are expected to possess. Today it is blithely accepted that detectives will harvest the mobile phone records and the various forms of social media connected to a victim or an alleged perpetrator, and so Facebook, Twitter, Instagram and email are just as much on the frontline of detection as fingerprints and fibres were when Hindley and Brady were arrested.

What's interesting is how we might see Brady and Hindley as 'early adopters' of technology. They photographed their victims, especially where they had been buried, and in the case of Lesley Ann Downey recorded her on tape. These technologies were a central part of their offending for a number of reasons. Photographing each other near, or standing on, the graves of their victims allowed them to relive the moment when they had taken a life; it was proof of what they had done together and therefore also a way of cementing their commitment to each other. In displaying these photographs (some of which were on the mantelpiece at 16 Wardle Brook Avenue) it became a secret that, paradoxically, they sought to make public. In this way we might see these photographs in the living room as a physical form of what Freud called parapraxes – slips of the tongue. Such slips, Freud suggested, were the result of an irresolvable conflict between the urge to express something and yet an anxiety to which that urge gives rise, and were a window onto the unconscious. In other words, despite knowing that what they had done was to have committed murder, Brady and Hindley nonetheless wanted these murders to be viewed, to be seen and, as they might have regarded it, admired – so why not put them on display in the living room, in much the same way others might hang photographs of graduating children and new grandchildren?

Brady was not by any stretch of the imagination a criminal mastermind, but can we really be certain that he didn't want his diabolical tape of Lesley Ann to be heard? It seems to me that he needed their secrets to be broadcast, despite all the condemnation this would bring down on their heads. In the 1960s all of this was regarded as shocking and unprecedented – yet another example of how evil their crimes were – but it was a trend that would become more prevalent in violent offending as time progressed. Brady's early adoption of electronic technology simply gave him more ways of being surrounded in his living room, his box in the theatre of the world, by the sights and sounds of murder.

Ironically, if CCTV had been as prevalent in the 1960s as it is today, Brady and Hindley would have been apprehended much more quickly, and what might have been captured on camera could have filled in some of the gaps in our knowledge that remain about various aspects of the case. We would certainly have had CCTV footage of Brady picking up Edward at the railway station, just as nearly sixty years later we can actually view the initial encounter between Maynard-Ellis and Julia in the Cork & Bottle. We even have images of Maynard-Ellis and Leesley disposing of her dismembered body, casually walking by a canal as if they are simply out for a stroll. We watch as the sofa on which Julia was murdered was discarded at the local refuse site. The killers chose that sofa and the carpet, and we can perhaps infer something about the state of their minds in that they were now having to dispose of them in the hope of not getting caught.

That's the second development. Forensic science, which is now a broad and diverse discipline, has advanced from a time when blood grouping, fibres and fingerprints were the basis of criminal investigations, to the situation today where forensic officers investigate both the physical and the digital worlds of the alleged perpetrator and victim. In relation to the former, the first murderer to be caught as a result of the development of DNA fingerprinting – a technique developed by the geneticist Sir Alec Jeffreys at the University of Leicester – was Colin Pitchfork in 1987, who murdered Lynda Mann in 1983 and Dawn Ashworth in 1986. Since then DNA has been at the forefront of criminal investigations, and it has been estimated that more than fifty million people have had their DNA tested as a result of a crime being committed. The UK National DNA Database, the oldest and largest in the world, was established in 1995 and as of 2020 it had 6.6 million profiles, although this has been subject to several legal challenges, resulting in the database's indefinite retention policy being abolished. Between 2001 and 2014 the National DNA Database produced just under half a million matches to crimes that had been committed, and it has been estimated that when a DNA profile found at a crime scene is searched against the database there is a 61.9 per cent chance of a match. DNA would feature in the trials of both Nathan Maynard-Ellis and David Leesley, but Kevin Cotterill's first offence was more than a decade before the establishment of the database; a seventeen-year-old convicted of a similar crime today would have his DNA sample stored.

The final development is our growing understanding of the phenomenon of serial murder more generally, specific serial killers and the typical groups that they will target: women, especially older women and sex workers, and gay men. This is in part related to the growth in popularity of criminology and forensic psychology courses at universities since the 1990s – Maynard-Ellis even claimed to have been a criminology student. However, we should remember that while Brady and Hindley were serial killers by the standard definition – that they killed three or more victims in a period of greater than thirty days – Maynard-Ellis and Leesley were wannabes. They read and collected books about serial murder and even bought memorabilia, but they were not themselves serial murderers. They were obsessive fans who might have wanted to emulate their idols, but they were not the real thing, despite their murder of Julia. Perhaps this is the strangest development of all: serial murder has become a commodity to be packaged and then sold, like trainers or mobile phones, rather than something which is simply shocking and abhorrent. Since the conviction of Brady and Hindley, consumer culture has found it relatively easy to accommodate murder, even serial murder.

*

How do these developments help us to make sense on these three living-room crime scenes? What do these three ornamental cases – 'boxes in the theatre of the world' – tell us about these murders, and the personal tastes of the killers? I was struck by David Smith's observation that the living room at 16 Wardle Brook Avenue was characterised by 'the usual still life: empty bottles, overflowing ashtrays and an abandoned chessboard', and that he went there to get 'stoned' on alcohol and talk about 'nothing'. What was being consumed was tobacco – to the extent that a cigarette machine had been installed in the house – and copious quantities of whisky and wine. Picking up miniature wine bottles was even the excuse that was used to get Smith to come to the house on the night that Edward was murdered. The use of alcohol and tobacco might have been widespread at the time, but the patterns of consumption described by Smith seem to be excessive, to the extent that Hindley and Brady's use can be viewed as unrestrained and self-indulgent – they were bingeing. The link between cigarette smoking and cancer had been established in 1962, the year before Brady and Hindley started to kill, in a seminal document published by the Royal College of Physicians, and resulted in the government restricting tobacco advertising, imposing higher taxation and disseminating information about tar and nicotine content. All of this meant that cigarette sales fell for the first time in a decade, although clearly this was not the case at 16 Wardle Brook Avenue.

We also know that Brady added his own 'touch' to the living room, by putting an SS dagger on the wall. This seems to be a counterpoint to the 'abandoned chessboard', in that chess can be seen as an allusion to the more esoteric interests of the people who live in the house, and the former to a nihilism and existential emptiness. We shouldn't be surprised that government recommendations in relation to the consumption of tobacco would have fallen on deaf ears, or that a huge amount of alcohol was used to dull the senses, and to make the people who inhabited that living room reckless and disinhibited. Brady thought of himself as a 'new kind of killer' – a type that would become more common as time progressed, accordingly to Alan Keightley. Thanks to some of the developments I have outlined above, this hasn't actually been the case, and we could debate whether or not Brady and Hindley were merely following a pattern that we can trace back to at least Jack the Ripper and 1888, rather than developing a whole new genre of murderer.

Whether Brady and Hindley were or were not a new type of killer, the commodification of serial murder more generally is now so prevalent that it can be binged on too. The living room of Maynard-Ellis and Leesley is a testimony not just to their personal tastes and interests but to a wider Western cultural obsession. It seems legitimate to question where this obsession has come from, and what it might tell us more broadly about ourselves. The most persuasive answer comes from Mark Seltzer, Professor of Literature at UCLA, who argues that our contemporary culture now collects around the sites of violence both as a form of spectacle and as a place 'where private desire and public fantasy cross'. Central to this is Seltzer's view that we live in a 'wound culture', where the public has become fascinated with torn and opened bodies, and where as a result we can now find common ground 'around shock, trauma and the wound'. In other words, consumption of harm, violence and the pathological has become one of the few things that brings people together in late capitalist society – a society which values instant gratification and selfish individualism, and where success is predicated on the demise of others. The wound culture is about the lack – of the absence and emptiness – that lies at the heart of consumer capitalism.

True crime and the serial killer are central to this wound culture, to the extent that Seltzer argues that serial murder is no longer just something that serial killers do, but has become in itself aspirational, and that this phenomenon has been prompted by the popularity of true crime. It has emerged as 'one of the popular genres of the pathological public sphere', and is the basis for our consumption of the violence directed against bodies, especially the bodies of women.

We see this 'public fantasy' in the living room of Maynard-Ellis and Leesley, not only in their fetishised collecting of newspaper articles, films and books about serial killers but also in the way that Julia was murdered. We can only imagine what she must have made of all of this when she first entered the flat. After she had died, Julia's body was literally torn and opened up for Maynard-Ellis and Leesley to view. This was not the mutilation that one would expect to see if a killer was simply trying to dispose of a victim's remains but was clearly a 'private desire' – a longing and a hunger that needed to be satisfied. As Julia's body was slowly reduced to a sum of parts, Maynard-Ellis and Leesley could binge on the spectacle of the wounds that they were inflicting and the trauma that they had caused. It also seems fair to conclude that these post-mortem behaviours were sexual, but it is important to remember that while Brady used an axe – another form of mutilation – before finally strangling Edward, Maynard-Ellis and Leesley only started to stab, cut and saw after Julia had been killed with a rolling pin. How Julia died was not sexual; that was reserved for how her body was handled after her murder.

While more unusual in relation to what I have described, sexual motivation is also apparent in what happened to Connie and Janice. However, it is important to remember that the killer entered their living room, and the context for the crime scene was therefore created by Cotterell. However, like Brady and Hindley he needed his secret to become public to make him feel really powerful. Being looked at was an integral part of his 'private desire'; he wasn't shy about what he had done being observed, and wanted those who encountered the crime scene to bear witness. After all, what the serial killer is really seeking is fame. And while this is not something I can prove definitively, I wonder to what extent he had Connie view what he was doing to Janice. Of course he also wanted to see inside the bodies of these women, especially inside that of Janice; her legs were propped on the chair so that he could get a better view. This was not accidental, but the conclusion of his methodical and controlled criminal 'signature' – the unusual and distinctive themes and behaviours within a crime that an offender commits to satisfy an underlying psychological and emotional need – and, in this case, related more broadly to misogyny and sadism.

Ironically, it was only Maynard-Ellis and Leesley who were observed. Being seen wasn't part of what motivated them to kill and was, on the contrary, something that they knew they would have to manage after they had murdered Julia. In fact,

Maynard-Ellis repeatedly denied to the police that he was the person captured by the CCTV cameras.

My mention of sadism and misogyny is the cultural context in which to understand these crimes and crime scenes. This is about male fantasy and male prejudice, and the desire to hurt others – mainly women. We know that Brady read, and liked to quote, the Marquis de Sade from books that were found in 16 Wardle Brook Avenue. Indeed, Brady's library would feature at his trial, although all of this is somewhat dismissed by Alan Keightley, who argues that Brady had developed his own nihilistic worldview long before he read de Sade. However, Brady really was a voracious reader, to the extent that we might see him bingeing on books as well as alcohol and tobacco. In his own *The Gates of Janus: Serial Killing and its Analysis*, Brady uses the writings of both Nietzsche and de Sade to frame his analysis of serial murder and, like a Sadean hero who believes that life is meaningless, he persistently prioritises his own sexual satisfaction and desires over all other considerations. What he was seeking was 'power and the will to power', and the freedom to express himself as he so wished in all aspects his life – especially in his sex life. He described to Keightley, for example, how as a young man he had discovered the joy of 'kissing violently' until his mouth bled, and later assured Hindley that 'we were both still individuals, free to indulge as we wished. We laughed together as we exchanged details of our excursions into irregular sex.' He does not expressly outline what this 'irregular sex' actually consisted of, but we can perhaps safely assume that it involved sadism. This is the other change we can observe in these crime scenes, and another broad cultural development: the mainstreaming of sadism, to the extent that *Fifty Shades of Grey*, the 2011 erotic romance that features explicit BDSM scenes, topped bestseller lists around the world, was translated into fifty-two languages and was the UK's fastest selling paperback in history. In short, we have all seemingly become Sadean libertines fond of irregular sex and use moral relativism to justify our own peccadillos.

Finally, these crimes did not baffle the police, and nor were they solved by crime fiction's ever-widening cast of gifted amateurs. They were unravelled by old-fashioned detective work and up-to-date forensic techniques. What's also of interest is how all of these cases initially relied on members of the public coming forward to offer information to the police: David Smith in the case of Brady and Hindley; a local in the village where the Sheridans lived noted down the registration plate of a car he saw parked outside their house; and, finally, an unnamed member of the public who believed that Maynard-Ellis was responsible for Julia's murder. This is a continuity within the time frame of these three case studies, rather than a development or a change. No matter what, policing still relies on the support of the public in bringing offenders to justice.

One other continuity springs to mind. Brady would chain-smoke his way through several packets of Gauloises every day up until his death in May 2017 from chronic obstructive pulmonary disease (COPD). This is characterised by breathing problems and shortness of breath; the most common cause of COPD is tobacco smoking.

These three living-room crime scenes really did tell us something about the private individuals who lived there, and also what might have motivated the killer, or killers, to take a life. The interior offered a way of understanding and then framing a broader context to explain why a murder had taken place there, and as boxes in the theatre of the world they also reflected, and were sometimes even at the cutting edge of, wider developments in society as a whole. Above all, the private could become public and, as Walter Benjamin had indicated, to dwell in these spaces was to leave traces which could then be used to illuminate some monstrous crimes. These interiors were filled with the everyday items we take for granted: carpets, underlay, a rolling pin, photographs, sofas, cigarettes and ashtrays, miniature wine bottles, chess boards, a record player, a tape recorder and books, as well as bin liners, disinfectant, an axe, a hacksaw and knives, and all play a part in telling a story of when the homely became unhomely, and when the safe, innocent, familiar things that surround us could be used to explain a murder. These explanations don't just emerge in detective stories, but are all too evident in real life too.

It's time to leave the living room and find out what's happening in the kitchen.

CHAPTER THREE

The Kitchen

'Meal machine, experimental laboratory, status symbol, domestic prison, or the creative and spiritual heart of the home? Over the course of the past century no other room has been the focus of such intense aesthetic and technological innovation, or as loaded with cultural significance.'

Museum of Modern Art, Design + The Modern Kitchen, Exhibition Guide, 15 September 2010–2 May 2011, New York

In our kitchen, standing proudly on the wooden mantelpiece, is a clock that was given to me by my mother before I went off to university more than forty years ago. Forty years! I wind that clock religiously and send it off for repairs whenever it breaks down – which now seems to be every few months. A couple of weeks later it gets sent back to me, along with an increasingly large bill, and I then return it to its central place in the kitchen. It stands watch like a silent witness to all the activity that takes place in the kitchen: no longer just food preparation and consumption, but noisy games of Monopoly; plans being made around the kitchen table about where to go on holiday; and too many glasses of wine with our friends Sue and Neil on a Friday night, when we sit around and share the stories of our week. It would all be worth the effort (and cost) if the clock kept better time, but it doesn't, and I know that I can't trust it at all. It seems to slow down, or paradoxically to speed up, as if it has a mind of its own. That said, I can't bear the thought of being without it, or of not making the effort to get it repaired when it will yet again break down. It has become something sociologists call an 'evocative object', which connects me to my youth and my long-dead parents, and to moments in time when they were still alive.

I imagine that there are very few kitchens in the country that don't have similar evocative objects, even if these might simply be fridge magnets brought back from a foreign holiday, or a child's painting Blu-tacked to a cupboard door, rather than an unreliable old clock. Perhaps there are still lines on one of the kitchen's walls that marked the height of that child as they grew taller each year and were ceremoniously measured on their birthdays. Many of us will use cutlery or crockery that has been inherited, or perhaps given to us as wedding or anniversary presents, and we will be careful to make certain that these items are on display if the present-giver ever comes to visit. The kitchen unites us with a range of family and friends, and to the different times of our existence, like no other room in the house; it is a central place where memories are collected, and where we feel comfortable to live our lives.

However, the kitchen has not always been the heart of the house in the way that I have described. For a surprisingly long period of our history it was generally shunted away from the main rooms of the home because of the noise and smells associated with food production. At that time, at least until the invention of the cooking range, one of those smells would have been from an open fire, which also meant that there was the constant threat of the fire getting out of control and destroying the rest of the property. As a result, the kitchen was often physically separated from other rooms, including where food was eaten. The kitchen performed a backstage function, a role that mirrored the physical space it occupied. The other rooms were the respectable spaces of the home, and so they were the main stage: the rooms reserved for family, and for friends who might come calling. This also meant that the people who worked in the kitchen – usually women, and the kitchen itself has historically been viewed as a woman's place – were also seen as performing backstage functions, rather than being central to what happened in the house.

As the quotation at the start of this chapter conveys, the kitchen has over time performed many different functions, functions which have been hand in glove with other broad social and cultural changes: the make-up and size of families; the economy; the shifting nature of labour practices, especially the decline of domestic service; and the ever-changing role and status of women. This is why the kitchen is often seen as a contested space, as the career aspirations and paid employment of women served to separate them from the kitchen, which in turn became a significant and symbolic site of women's oppression by domesticity, and which needed to be reconceived to suit their changing needs both within and after they had left that space. Kitchens became more streamlined into triangles in the 1930s, with the layout focused around the fridge, the sink and the cooker so as to cut down on the time that was being spent in the kitchen, therefore allowing for more time away from that space. Women didn't want to stay in this domestic prison, and sought to do more with their lives than simply dreaming about owning a new luxurious fitted kitchen. So, to sum up, the kitchen – for both men and women – has become a place to socialise; a place where the routines that are central to the home take place and domesticity gets performed; a place where we entertain our family and friends.

Before looking at some murders that took place in the kitchen it's important to acknowledge an instrumental function that kitchens still perform: it is where we keep knives. Knives are as important in the history of murder in this country as guns are in the United States; they are the British equivalent of the assault rifle and the AK47. Some statistics help to illustrate this point.

There were 46,265 offences involving knives in the twelve months ending March 2020, almost a 100 per cent increase from March 2014, when there were 23,945 such offences recorded. These figures might be an underestimate of the actual numbers of stabbings and slashings. Not everyone feels able to report such a crime to the police – especially if you are in a relationship with the person who has assaulted you – and it is significant that hospital admissions for assaults involving a 'sharp instrument' (which does not necessarily have to be a knife) over this same period increased at a slightly higher rate than these recorded figures. Most of these knife-crime offences were related to assaults and robberies, but in 2018 there were 285 killings where a knife was the murder weapon – the highest figure recorded since 1946. Some of these murders involved young men fighting other young men in the streets but, of relevance to this chapter, there was also a persistent number of homicides in domestic settings – usually kitchens – involving knives. In London, the Metropolitan Police recorded sixteen homicides involving a knife in a domestic setting in 2019, and twenty-two such killings the following year.

More generally, by 2019 the number of women killed as a result of domestic violence was at its highest level for five years, and just a few examples provide a depressing insight into all of these statistics, and the central role played by knives. Charlotte Huggins was fatally stabbed in Camberwell, London by Michael Rolle just after she had broken up with him; Mary Annie Sowerby was stabbed to death by her son 'with the largest kitchen knife possible' (as was reported in the local newspaper) at her home in Dearham, Cumbria; Alison Hunt was stabbed twenty-two times in the head, chest and neck by her ex-boyfriend Vernon Holmes at her home in Salford, in what was described as 'a grotesque attempt to assert control over her'; and Elize Stevens was stabbed to death in Hendon by her partner Ian Levy 'in a fit of rage'. When the police arrived at their flat they found Elize prone on the floor, having been stabbed eighty-six times with a large kitchen knife, which lay on the floor beside her. One wound on her abdomen was so deep that her intestines were visible. As is clear from these brief snatches of reports about recent murders, knives and kitchens are central to the killing of women in this country.

I will use three case studies to illustrate these themes and to help us to discuss the contested space of kitchens as a site of murder: the murders of Rita Nelson, Kathleen Maloney and Hectorina MacLennan by the serial killer Reg Christie between January and March 1953 in Notting Hill, London; the murder of Hollie Kerrell in April 2018 by her husband Christopher, in the close-knit village of Knucklas in Powys; and, finally, the murder of seventeen-year-old Ellie Gould by her former boyfriend Thomas Griffiths at the home she shared with her parents Matthew and Carole in Calne, Wiltshire the following year.

*

The murder of at least six, and probably eight, women by Reg Christie between 1943 and 1953 at 10 Rillington Place continues to maintain a hold on the public's imagination, especially due to screen adaptations of the story in 1971 and 2016. The first of these adaptations was based on the book written about the case by the Scottish broadcaster and journalist Ludovic Kennedy. Kennedy's primary motivation was to draw attention to a gross miscarriage of justice that saw the father of the family who occupied the top-floor flat at 10 Rillington Place, Timothy Evans, hanged in March 1950 for the murders of his wife Beryl and daughter Jeraldine (there are different spellings of her name). Christie had been the chief prosecution witness. Evans's trial and its outcome is another reason that the case continues to find an audience: was Christie also guilty of the murders of Beryl and Jeraldine, and did an innocent man get sent to the gallows?

It is difficult to answer this question definitively as Christie and Evans – both of whom admitted to the murders, only to later retract their confessions – were incorrigible liars. It was well known that Evans and Beryl often argued, but I would suggest that it is difficult to accept that two different murderers were living under the same roof at exactly the same time, and that it is more than likely that Christie was the killer. However, questions remain not just about Christie's role in these murders but also others that he might have committed. The latter suggestion is given added credence as a tobacco tin found during a search of 10 Rillington Place contained the pubic hair of a number of unidentified women, women who had clearly at some stage found their way into Christie's home. The police sergeant who found the tin, Len Trevallion, had once worked on the local vice squad and believed that Christie and his wife Ethel were actually 'back-street abortionists', although this has never been proven, and was specifically denied by Christie. At a time when the public were being fed stories about the exploits of the ever-dependable *Dixon of Dock Green*, here were the police in real life seemingly to endlessly get things wrong. Whatever your views about the guilt or innocence of Evans, in a search of Christie's garden police officers failed to notice a human femur being used to prop up a trellis. *Heimlich* and *unheimlich* – a theme that resonates throughout Christie's offending.

This is, of course, the final reason that the case continues to fascinate. Christie was a serial killer, and one who employed a rather elaborate modus operandi, with various sexual peccadilloes that served as his offending signature. He was also an apparently respectable member of the community, especially when compared to the other residents of Rillington Place. One former neighbour is quoted in the publicity that surrounded the broadcast of the 2016 television drama about the case, saying that she remembered Christie as 'the poshest man in the street; the smartest. He was someone to be respected.' In reality Christie was often unemployed, had a long history of offending dating back to 1921 and had spent time in prison, although this did not prevent him becoming an assistant Scout master and a constable in the War Reserve Police, with two commendations for good service. He constantly complained of illness and had 'a nervous disposition'. However, when he was out of the house he always wore neatly pressed trousers, a jacket, collar, tie and hat, which, coupled with his round spectacles, must have given him an air of respectability. He particularly revelled in wearing a uniform, and rather liked the structure and hierarchy of the police. This role also gave him the freedom to go where he pleased, and to tell people what they had to do – something that had earned him the local nickname 'the Himmler of Rillington Place'.

Christie's life and offending is riven with this sense of public propriety but private indecency. He was sexually inadequate and found it difficult to gain or sustain an erection, especially with a woman who was conscious. This was something that he had lived with since his teenage years, when he was known to his peers as 'Can't-Make-It Christie'. Though he married Ethel Simpson in 1920, inevitably their marriage was not very successful and the two were separated between 1925 and 1935, although Ethel later returned to her husband and moved into Rillington Place in 1938. They had no children. Christie professed to dislike pubs, masturbation and prostitutes, although in 1929 he set up home with a sex worker by the name of Maud Cole. That relationship came to an end when he hit her over the head with a cricket bat – a crime for which he received six months' hard labour. He would later describe this attack as 'a practice shot'. When he was arrested his shoes were found to be soaked in semen, which suggested that his professed dislike of masturbation must have been easily and regularly overcome. So, like many serial killers, Christie was a house divided, both filthy and fussy at the same time, and this aspect of his personality would become even more apparent in the murders he committed.

We know that it was when he was acting as a War Reserve constable that he killed his first victim, a sex worker called Ruth Fuerst who died in August 1943, and in October the following year he murdered Muriel Eady. He buried the bodies of both women in the back garden at 10 Rillington Place. We then have an interlude of more than five years before he kills Beryl and Jeraldine Evans, and three years after their deaths he murdered his wife on 14 December 1952. Christie extravagantly claimed that this was a 'mercy killing' as Ethel had been ill, although in reality we have no definitive answer as to why he took his wife's life – perhaps simply because he could. Of relevance to this chapter, he buried Ethel's body under the floorboards of the front parlour, and he would later explain his decision to do so to a psychiatrist who interviewed him at HMP Brixton as: 'I think in my mind I did not want to lose her.' This was rather dismissed at the time but surely contains an element of a truth that we have come to see with other serial killers: he liked to keep his victims close, as a way of maintaining power and control over them even when they were dead. Their bodies would also have reminded him of the moment when he had taken their lives, and so they are in that sense evocative objects, just as much as my mother's clock is to me in my own kitchen.

Here it is worth describing 10 Rillington Place, and we have two excellent sources: Len Trevallion's autobiography *Policeman, Pilot and a Guardian Angel*, published in 2008, when he was in his nineties; and Molly Lefebure's *Murder with a Difference: The Cases of Haigh and Christie*, which appeared in 1958. Lefebure was secretary to Dr Keith Simpson, the celebrated Home Office pathologist, during the war. In researching her book she visited 10 Rillington Place, as did Trevallion in his role as a policeman, and Lefebure also consulted the numerous police photographs that were taken within the house at the time of Christie's arrest – some of which are usefully reproduced in her book. It is worth remembering that in the 1940s and 1950s Notting Hill was not the affluent area that it has become today, but a rather down-at-heel district filled with slums and multi-occupancy houses that were rented out cheaply.

At the time that Christie was killing, Rillington Place was a cul-de-sac that terminated at a steep factory wall, and number 10 was the end house on the left-hand side, squashed up against that wall. Lefebure describes it as 'a mean little London house of Victorian ancestry and of average squalor, discomfort and neglect'. The Christies lived in the ground-floor flat, which had a bay-windowed front room; a back room that they used as a bedroom; and, finally, a small kitchen – also characterised as 'squalid' by Lefebure – which contained a gas stove, a kitchen range and a small, recessed cupboard, which would later be used by Christie to store the bodies of his final three victims. The stove ran on 'town gas' – which was produced by burning coal and had a very high carbon monoxide content – and would prove to be central to Christie's MO. A narrow set of stairs in the hall led to two other flats on the floors above. The Christies had sole use of the garden. There were no indoor toilet facilities, so anyone wishing to use the toilet or have a bath had to use the wash house that adjoined the Christie's kitchen and could only be reached by going through the garden – although it's difficult to know if anyone did. An elderly man called Kitchener had lived in the first-floor flat at the time that the Christies moved into Rillington Place, and Timothy and Beryl Evans would eventually rent the top flat. By early 1953 a new resident called Beresford Brown had moved into the top-floor flat, and he was eventually given permission by the landlord to use Christie's kitchen, after he and Ethel had mysteriously moved away on 20 March. In fact, Ethel was by then under the floorboards of the front room, and Christie was on the run.

Christie's final three victims were all sex workers: Rita Nelson, who was six months pregnant at the time of her death, and Kathleen Maloney, both of whom he murdered in January 1953; and Hectorina MacLennan, whom he killed on 5 March. Like many serial killers who evade detection for any length of time, the gap between his murders was becoming shorter. Len Trevallion, who discussed these murders with Christie after his arrest, was convinced that the women who died had come to Rillington Place in search of an abortion, and that Christie 'had devised a ghastly way of sedating the women'. This involved him having them sit in a specially adapted deck-chair, in which the canvas had been replaced with a criss-cross network of string – a terrible contraption that was found after

Christie's arrest. The woman would sit in the chair and then be encouraged to inhale Friar's Balsam – a strong-smelling remedy for catarrh – from a square glass jar with a screw-top lid. The lid had two holes bored into it, and a short and a long piece of rubber tubing passed through these holes. The short tube contained Friar's Balsam, but the long rubber tube, which passed over the back of the chair so that the poor victim couldn't see what Christie was doing, was connected to the gas tap. The Friar's Balsam would mask the smell of the gas. It has never been adequately explained how Christie avoided being gassed himself (perhaps he wore a gas mask), but quite quickly the unsuspecting woman would inhale the carbon monoxide, become unconscious and then, as Len Trevallion explained, 'the Christies would lift the front two legs of the deckchair on to the edge of the kitchen table, thus giving Ethel Christie easy access to perform the sordid operation'.

We do not need to accept Trevallion's conclusion that these operations were performed by Ethel (who was dead by the time Rita, Kathleen and Hectorina were murdered) to appreciate that this technique would render the women unconscious and expose their genitals. This was exactly the state Christie preferred his victims to be in before he could have sex with them. It is a moot point as to whether the women were already dead or dying at this stage – and so we might debate whether this meant that he was a necrophiliac – but, in any event, Christie would also strangle his victims, and again we have no real idea if this took place before, during or after inter-course. Undoubtedly he enjoyed the feelings of power that squeezing the life out of these women gave to him but, ever fussy and fastidious, it also disgusted him that when he did so his victims would urinate and defecate. As a consequence, Christie would put pieces of cloth between their legs, almost as if they were wearing nappies, which also meant that at their post-mortems his semen was still to be found in the vaginas of Rita, Kathleen and Hectorina.

The bodies of these poor women were not found until Mr Brown took over the kitchen. He immediately noticed a smell but was preoccupied by a search for a suitable place to fix brackets to support a radio. He tapped at the wall and discovered a place that sounded hollow, covered in wallpaper. He tore a hole in the wallpaper and flashed his torch inside. It turned out to be a tiny alcove, about two feet wide and five feet deep, which had perhaps once been used to store coal. However, it wasn't coal that Mr Brown saw but the bare back of a half-naked woman's corpse, with her head dropped forward, and so he rushed out of the house and called the police.

By half past seven on the evening of 24 March 1953 a variety of police officers, as well as Dr Francis Camps, the Home Office pathologist, and Chief Inspector Percy Law of Scotland Yard's Photographic Department had descended on 10 Rillington Place and were all crammed into the tiny kitchen. Photographs were taken at every stage of their investigation. The first woman, who was dressed only in a suspender belt, stockings, bra and blouse, was prevented from pitching forward out of the alcove because her bra strap had been tied to a tall cloth-covered bundle leaning against the wall. It was quite quickly established that she had been strangled and her wrists had been fastened together with a handkerchief tied in a reef knot. As she was being removed, semen leaked from her vagina. Between this first woman and the tall bundle was the body of another young woman, who was tied up in a blanket and lying on her back with her feet propped up against the wall. The blanket was fastened around her ankles with a sock and her head was covered with a pillowcase. Both the sock and pillowcase were tied with reef knots, and a vest had been placed between her legs. The tall bundle contained a third body. This woman was upside down, with her head beneath the body of the second victim. Her ankles had been tied with a piece of electrical flex and her head covered in a cloth, the ends of which were also tied around her neck; reef knots were again used for the flex and the cloth. She was wearing a blue cardigan and a fawn dress.

The first body removed was Hectorina's, and Camps inferred that she had been raped at the point of her murder; she was not pregnant. Kathleen had been lying between Hectorina and Rita, and she too had been asphyxiated and raped but she wasn't pregnant, although there were signs of a past pregnancy. The third woman had been six months pregnant and so we can confidently conclude that this was Rita, who had last been seen alive on 12 January 1953. The fact that neither Kathleen nor Hectorina were pregnant does not mean that Christie and/or Ethel were not at some stage back-street abortionists, as suggested by Trevallion, and it may well be the case that they were willing to accompany Christie back to Rillington Place – and trusted him enough to sit in the macabre deckchair and inhale what they believed to be Friar's Balsam – because they had used his, or Ethel's, medical services in the past.

After the murder of Hectorina, Christie abandoned Rillington Place, leaving all the dead bodies behind, rather than choosing to stay close to them. It's difficult to make sense of Christie's often illogical behaviour at this time, but it is tempting to see an element of secondary staging in how he disposed of Rita, Kathleen and Hectorina's bodies, hiding them in the alcove that he then simply papered over. It was inevitable that their bodies would be discovered, and that the police would be horrified by what they found.

We know a little about Christie's movements after he abandoned Rillington Place – seemingly he wandered aimlessly around London, often staying in cheap hotels. After a week, he was finally arrested on 31 March on the embankment near Putney Bridge, and hanged at HMP Pentonville on 15 July, after his plea of insanity had been rejected.

*

Our next, and much more recent, case study is of the murder of Hollie Kerrell by her estranged husband Christopher in the kitchen of her home in the village of Knucklas in Wales on Sunday 22 April 2018. It involves the first form of staging by a murderer, when physical evidence has been deliberately removed and the offender attempts to mislead or misdirect the police. I saw this in real time in Ipswich in 2006, when the serial killer Steve Wright deliberately left the body of Anneli Alderton, his third victim, in a cruciform position in an attempt to manipulate ideas about the motivation of the perpetrator. Hollie's murder also gives us a glimpse of the coercively controlling behaviour that some men will use to try to keep their partner within a relationship and, when they feel that they have lost that control, how they resort to murder as a deadly means of re-establishing their sense of power and being in charge.

Hollie had moved to Wales from Devon when she was a teenager and was twenty-eight when she was murdered. She was a talented make-up artist and sold beauty products online; she also ran a stall at a local market and several of her friends described her as a good businesswoman. She married Kerrell in 2013 and they had had three children to whom Hollie was devoted. However, Hollie and Kerrell's relationship was volatile. Hollie had always remained close to her mother and sister, and admitted to them that Kerrell had hit her in the past; it would later transpire that he had also been violent to a previous partner. Slowly but surely his domestic violence, often employing the everyday household objects that surrounded him, escalated. Hollie had attempted to leave Kerrell on several occasions, but he threatened to kill himself in front of their children if she did so. This was a dramatic means of trapping her in the marriage. By April 2018 Hollie had finally managed to end their relationship and Kerrell had returned to live with his mother on her farm, which was some twenty minutes away by car. Nonetheless he maintained contact with Hollie and continued to help with the children, but on Saturday 21 April they had had a public row in the street, and Kerrell had tried to drive over her mobile phone; he'd also broken her car keys.

Hollie sent her sister a text message at 9.55 a.m. on Sunday, the day after the argument, saying 'I'll message in a bit', but that was the last that anyone heard from her. This lack of communication was very unusual and so her sister reported Hollie missing the following day, and by Tuesday 24 April Dyfed-Powys Police had begun house-to-house enquiries in Knucklas. Later, a documentary about her murder, called

Murdered by My Husband, used footage from the body camera worn by a police officer who went to Hollie's own house on the Glyndwr estate to interview Kerrell, and so we not only see inside the house but we also get to observe and listen to Kerrell.

In the immediate aftermath of her murder Kerrell had texted Hollie's family and friends to ask if they knew where she was, and he went on Facebook appealing for help to find her. He said that they had had a row and Hollie had packed all of her clothes into a suitcase and abandoned the house and the children. Kerrell took the children to school on the Monday, all the time feigning concern as to what had happened to Hollie. In the body-camera video we see Kerrell approach the police officer who had come to interview him and ask, even before he gets out of the car, 'What's going on over here?' and offering to make a cup of tea. He was relaxed in his dealings with the officer; rather than anxious, he was eager to help: he wanted to please – all of this is a tactic of misdirection too. Inside the house, and specifically in the kitchen, Kerrell explains to the officer that 'I've asked like pretty much every house around here and they didn't notice or see anything.' We get to view the kitchen crammed with all of the flotsam and jetsam of family life, and when Kerrell opens the front door for the officer we also see the children's bikes parked against the garden fence, alongside his Vauxhall Astra. Earlier in their discussion Kerrell had pointed out to the officer that there were two sheds in the garden.

These details are of interest because we now know that Kerrell had murdered Hollie in the kitchen and then put her body in the boot of the Astra, before later driving to his mother's farm, where he buried Hollie's body in an isolated field. He didn't want to keep her body close to him, as Christie had with his last three victims, and was making every effort to ensure that Hollie would not be found – he wasn't simply papering over an alcove. Kerrell had arrived at the house, picked up a hammer from one of the sheds, and entered the kitchen as Hollie was making a cup of tea. The *heimlich* was about to become *unheimlich*. He hit Hollie over the head with the hammer, and then straddled her body and strangled her to make certain that she was dead. He was later to tell a detective that this had taken about ten minutes, and that during this time the three children had been playing outside. After he had strangled Hollie, he drank the still-warm tea that she had made for herself. After that he placed her body in the foetal position, wrapped it up in a *Thomas the Tank Engine* duvet cover, before putting her in the boot of his car. Kerrell had tidied the kitchen and made the children their lunch, and would visit two different supermarkets to buy a mop, bucket, bin liners and bleach – using Hollie's credit card to do so. He drove the children to his mother's farm and left them in the company of their grandmother before finding a suitable field to bury Hollie. He disposed of all of her clothing at a clothes bank.

These activities were deliberate attempts to manipulate – to stage – the crime scene. Not only had Kerrell buried Hollie's body to give credence to the story he had invented that she had disappeared and was 'missing', he also got rid of her clothing, thoroughly cleaned the kitchen and encouraged family and friends to help in the search for his estranged wife. He lied to the police in the hope of misdirecting them, telling them that they were dealing with a woman who had abandoned the family home, thereby preventing them investigating the case as a murder. Drinking the tea is also symbolic and *unheimlich*. The cup of tea had been Hollie's, but now it was his, as well as everything else in the kitchen and in their lives. The men who kill their wives don't 'lose it', but simply find a violent means to 'get it'. From now on it would be him who would make the children their lunch and drive them to school. He didn't want Hollie's body to remain in the kitchen as an evocative object; he wanted her gone. In that respect Kerrell was different from Christie. The kitchen had quickly become emblematic of the contested nature of their relationship, and killing Hollie allowed Kerrell to feel that he had regained the upper hand; that he had 'won' and was in charge. And, like a good host, it would even be him who offered the searching officer a cup of tea.

However, ANPR technology caught Kerrell driving to his mother's farm; CCTV captured him using Hollie's bank cards at the two supermarkets, buying the cleaning products that he would use in the kitchen; he was spotted and challenged by a dog walker immediately after he had buried Hollie's body, and she reported this encounter to the police; and he was seen disposing of Hollie's clothing at the clothes bank. The police duly dug up the field where Hollie had been buried and discovered her remains. Within six days Kerrell had confessed to murder and, as Detective Superintendent Anthony Griffiths, the senior investigating officer in charge of the investigation, put it, Kerrell 'told us in great detail' what had happened, which is why we know so much about this particular case. Even so, Kerrell still tried to manipulate his confession by claiming that the hammer that he had used to kill Hollie had already been in the kitchen. That wasn't true. He didn't realise that Hollie's penultimate text message to her sister had been 'He's just been in shed [*sic*] and got hammer', to which her sister had replied 'Ring the police! NOW!'

*

Our final case study is of a young man, and first offender, who went to even greater lengths than Kerrell to stage the crime scene in an effort to evade detection. Ellie Gould had celebrated her seventeenth birthday in February 2019 and was studying for her A levels. She hoped to go to university to read psychology and, as a keen horsewoman, had dreams of joining the mounted police after graduation. Just before her birthday she had started a relationship with Thomas Griffiths, her first boyfriend, and someone whom she had known since the age of eleven. Ellie's parents – Carole and Matthew – couldn't quite work out what she saw in Griffiths but, even so, he asked the couple if he could do work experience with their kitchen design business just days before the murder. Was this done to create another connection to the family, which would have made it more difficult for Ellie to have broken off their relationship, or simply an indication of his lack of self-awareness? In any event, Ellie felt that their relationship had become 'suffocating' and, as she also wanted to concentrate on her studies, she broke up with Griffiths on Thursday 2 May 2019 – the day before her murder.

On the Friday, Griffiths was dropped off at school by his mother but, almost as soon as he arrived, he emailed his teachers to say that he wasn't feeling well and caught a bus back to his home in the village of Derry Hill. Did he go to school expecting to find Ellie there too, and feigned sickness when he realised that she was absent? After he had arrived back home, when he was getting changed into a black hooded top and jeans, his mother unexpectedly came back to their house. Griffiths hid in his wardrobe until she left, so that she wouldn't discover that he was absent from school. He then illegally drove his Ford Fiesta (he was learning to drive) the seven miles to Ellie's house, where she was spending the morning studying; a friend called Ellie Welling was due to come by and pick her up to go to school later that day. A neighbour saw a young man matching Griffiths's description arrive at Ellie's house around 10.30 a.m. Ellie's father Matthew described what he discovered when he arrived home from work at approximately 3 p.m., in a TV show about the case:

So I pull up in the drive, and Ellie's car – a small red car she was learning to drive in – was on the drive. I walk in the house and go into the kitchen, put my phone and wallet on the table, and out of the corner of my eye I see Ellie's legs on the kitchen floor. ['There's an] island unit in the middle and her legs [were] just poking out from the side of it. My first thoughts were that she's fallen, banged her head and hurt herself. I bent down to see if she was okay and she was cold; she was very cold; stiff. I couldn't really move her. I thought she'd climbed up onto the worktop to get something out of the cupboard and fallen and banged her head. Then I take two and I see there's a lot of blood splatters around that end of the kitchen which wouldn't have come from a fall. But I couldn't compute then what had happened. I was panicked. And so I immediately rang for an ambulance and yeah, they tried to tell me how to resuscitate her and I told them it was pointless as I believed she was dead. Yeah – it was horrific.

Ellie was lying face-down in a pool of blood, and there was a knife in her neck. At first Matthew thought there had been a dreadful accident, and there was some discussion about how this might possibly have been a suicide, given that Ellie's hand was on the hilt of the knife. However, as is indicated by Matthew saying that he couldn't 'compute then what had happened', the crime scene had been carefully staged by Griffiths to disguise what had actually taken place. We now know, from what he has disclosed, that Griffiths came into the house and argued with Ellie – presumably about the break-up of their relationship, although his motivation has never adequately been explained. He had tried to strangle her, but when she fought back, leaving scratch marks on his neck and face, he grabbed a kitchen knife and in a frenzied attack stabbed her thirteen times in the neck, before trying to make these wounds appear self-inflicted. Griffiths did not panic, but carefully cleaned the knife and then put it back into one of the wounds in Ellie's neck, before placing her hand on the hilt. This was the scene that Matthew was to discover when he returned home that afternoon.

We know from his phone's GPS data that Griffiths spent at least an hour in the kitchen trying to clean up the crime scene before he drove back home. He cleaned his black Vans shoes in the sink, and the cloths that he used to mop the floor were put into a black bin liner, which he took with him. He then used one of Ellie's fingers to unlock her mobile phone and, posing as her, texted Ellie Welling to tell her not to bother picking her up. Ellie would later say that she didn't find that so unusual as they both hated history, and that would have been their lesson that afternoon. Griffiths then left, and CCTV from a bus caught him on his way back to Derry Hill at 11.56 a.m. Once he had arrived home, he put the black hooded top and jeans into the washing machine, and hid the bin liner containing the bloodied cloths in woodland about a ten-minute walk from his house. A neighbour spotted him on his return from the woods, commented on the marks on his face and gave him a lift to school. At about 3 p.m. Griffiths, perhaps alerted by the neighbour's concern, texted a number of his friends on a group chat to explain away the marks. 'You know me and Ellie are going on a break,' he wrote, and continued, 'I have been so anxious and nervous about everything lately and I don't know who else to talk to X.' Showing how important these friends were to him, he added, 'I've also not told anyone this but I've been kind of hurting myself by scratching my neck quite hard.' Like a 'new man', he is making himself appear vulnerable by being able to talk about his mental health, while all the time this was merely an elaborate ruse to hide his old-fashioned, toxic masculinity.

The fact that his murderous assault on Ellie took place within the kitchen underscores how this contested space heightened their different agendas and motivations. Ellie wanted to study, end their relationship and move on. Griffiths, on the other hand, wanted to keep Ellie in her place – not only in a relationship with him, but also by prioritising Griffiths and therefore shaping her ambitions accordingly. The kitchen acted both as a site of murder and as a ghastly metaphor for time: their past, the present and their different hopes for the future.

These are criminally sophisticated behaviours for a first offender, and someone who was only seventeen when he committed the murder. Not only did Griffiths stage the crime scene to the extent that it was initially believed to have been an accident or a suicide, but he also tried to dispose of evidence that would be forensically incriminating and attempted to establish an alibi for the scratches on his face and neck. Later that day he would text Ellie, making it appear that he had never been to her house. Nor was he concerned about staying close to a dead body – his former girlfriend, whom he had stabbed to death – or, rather chillingly, about putting the knife back into Ellie's neck or, because he didn't know the code, using her finger to open her phone.

We have to consider whether his murder of Ellie was premeditated. While some behaviours, such as changing out of his school clothes, imply that he knew what he was going to do, the fact that Griffiths used a knife from Ellie's kitchen suggests that it was not premeditated: he had not brought a weapon with him. We will never know what really motivated Griffiths to take Ellie's life, but might the most likely scenario be that he had gone to her house to try to convince her to get back together again, and felt unable to cope when she rejected that offer? We all have to face rejection at some time in our lives, but Griffiths appears to have been so emotionally immature that he was unable to manage being rebuffed. If that is the case, then it makes him very unusual and dangerous, otherwise there would be many more young people ending up dead after a relationship that they had valued came to an end.

Griffiths was charged with Ellie's murder on 6 May, after it became clear that he had visited Springfield Drive – through being caught on CCTV and mobile phone records – and his inability to adequately explain the marks on his face and neck, despite his claim to have been self-harming. He was also linked to the crime scene through blood that was found on his shoes and, despite his best efforts, the police discovered the black bin liner in the woods. He would plead guilty of murder at Bristol Crown Court and was sentenced to life imprisonment with a minimum term of twelve and half years. However, because he was under the age of twenty-one at the time that he killed Ellie he could not be given a whole-life tariff. Carole Gould has since campaigned for there to be an 'Ellie's Law', which would enable young offenders to be treated more like adults if they have been convicted of serious crimes such as murder. This idea was contained within the Police, Crime, Sentencing and Courts Bill, which was introduced into parliament on 9 March 2021 and, with the passage of the Bill, the new 'Ellie's Law' means that a teenage killer could face a sentence of up to twenty-seven years.

*

There are more than sixty years between the final three murders committed by Reg Christie and the murder of Ellie Gould by Thomas Griffiths. During this time how we use our kitchens has changed drastically. The Christies seem to have rarely used their small kitchen at all, and when they did, there is every likelihood that it was for illegal abortions. That's hardly a usual function – then or now. Considered in this way, we can see the specially constructed deckchair and the deadly glass jar with its tubes that would fill with carbon monoxide as a grotesque echo of all the gadgets that would fill more modern kitchens in the decades to come – the juicers, microwaves and espresso machines. These might not be used to kill, but they make just as much of a statement about the function of the space. In his informal clinic, Christie was able to indulge his sexual interests and fantasies to have sex with women who were unconscious and inert, women who were unable to speak and fight back, and, ultimately, it was a place where he could kill them. Storing the bodies of Rita, Kathleen and Hectorina in the alcove indicates that he wanted to keep these women close to him, although we also have to consider the possibility that in such a small flat he might simply have run out of places to dispose of the bodies of his victims. He'd filled up the garden, used the washroom, and so now he was using the alcove. This instrumental reasoning has some merit, but we also have to remember what Christie himself said about burying Ethel under the floorboards: 'I think in my mind I did not want to lose her.' This seems to me to reveal much more than a lack of a suitable place to dispose of her body, or the bodies of his other victims – if only because the smell of decaying flesh would have quickly filled the house.

And why did he kill Ethel? It was clearly no 'mercy killing', as Christie claimed, and while it can never be adequately explained, does it not also remind us that some men will end the lives of their wives or partners if they believe it suits their own best interests? Murder becomes for them the ultimate way of expressing their own needs, authority and dominance. Ethel had outlived her usefulness to Christie, and so he no longer needed her in his life. In any event, it's hard to escape the conclusion that she had only ever been a prop in his performance of respectability, and when he no longer wanted to play that part he got rid of her. But also,

Ethel was like an old toy that many of us find hard to part with, and so we store it away and occasionally dig it back out, if only to remember when it had once been a crucial and indispensable comfort.

Within the time frame of our case studies, kitchens have developed into the space where we now 'live our lives', although it is of course ironic that it is sometimes the space where the lives of women, rather than men, are ended. In that sense, there is a depressing continuity between these three case studies, as the oppression of this toxic form of domesticity has also altered and shifted shape, and can easily, when the occasion demands, accommodate murder. The kitchen might have moved to being centre stage but that doesn't mean that the chances of women dying there have lessened. If anything, murder is more, and not less, likely.

We see this in the murders of Hollie and Ellie, where it seems clear that their former male partner could not come to terms with these women wanting to live their lives. Theirs may have been a very different existence from Ethel Christie, with the improved aspirations and life chances that have been won by women in late modernity, but the issues that they faced seem stubbornly persistent. Hollie was a talented businesswoman and Ellie wanted to go to university. However, rather than celebrate these qualities and ambitions, the men they encountered seem to have been threatened by them. Christie may have used carbon monoxide to render the women he met inert and compliant, whereas Kerrell and Griffiths tried to use threats or pleas, and other forms of coercively controlling behaviour, but the end result was still the same: they needed Hollie and Ellie to behave in ways that they alone wanted to determine. When it became clear that this could not be achieved by any other means, both turned to murder.

It is easy to see the filthy and fussy in Christie, both as a man and how he committed his crimes. As I have drawn attention to, the public and private Christie were two very different people; he was a 'house divided', with a personality that could be both fastidious and transgressive at the same time. In fact, that's why he stands out and continues to fascinate us, as much as he assaults our sensibilities. With Christie – and with other serial killers – they appear to be monstrous 'others', not really like us at all. That's always a comforting but mistaken thought: we should remember that Christie was a War Reserve constable and a former assistant Scout master, and so he was hardly some alien other who was not part of our community. However, while his serial crimes do set him apart, is he really so different from Kerrell and Griffiths?

Kerrell happily played the part of the anxious, if estranged, husband, and Griffiths went to some lengths to present himself as self-harming. Christie was to claim that he was insane, whilst Griffiths wanted to appear depressed. Both were quite happy to stage the crime scenes of their victims and to stay with their bodies. Does not Kerrell wrapping Hollie's body in a *Thomas the Tank Engine* duvet cover, while his children played outside, have a moral equivalence to the makeshift nappies that were used by Christie on his victims? Does the fact that Griffiths re-inserted the knife in Ellie's neck and used her finger to open her mobile phone after she was dead not make the same assault on our sensibilities as Christie's necrophilia? I think that they do, even if these behaviours have been interpreted as 'normal' and explicable, rather than the more obvious gothic and macabre behaviour of Christie. Kerrell and Griffiths were equally adept at playing a public role, while their private reality was something altogether different, and so how they behaved before, during and after they had killed is for me just as monstrous as the behaviour of Christie, even if thankfully they were only able to murder once, rather than repeatedly.

*

The kitchen was once physically separated from other rooms in the house through fear of fire. Today, the kitchen has become central to the design of houses, and integral to how and where we live our lives. It is now so much more than the room where we eat and drink; it is the place where the kitchen-sink drama of our existence unfolds on a daily basis, and that reality has proven to be more deadly than the threats once posed by fire. Is it therefore any wonder that the kitchen has also become a site of murder?

Even by what it says on the wonky old clock given to me by my mother, I know it's time for us to leave the kitchen and its often noisy, public activities, and 'climb up the wooden hill to Bedfordshire'.

CHAPTER FOUR

The Bedroom

'What have we here? A Man or a fish? Dead or Alive? A fish. He smells like a fish, a very ancient and fish-like smell, a kind of not-of-the-newest poor-john. A strange fish! Were I in England now, as once I was, and had but this fish painted, not a holiday fool there but would give a piece of silver. There would this monster make a man. Any strange beast there makes a man. When they will not give a doit to relieve a lame beggar, they will lay out ten to see a dead Indian. Legged like a man and his fins like arms! Warm, o' my troth. I do now let loose my opinion, hold it no longer: this is no fish, but an islander that hath lately suffered by a thunderbolt.'

Trinculo encountering Caliban in *The Tempest*,
Act 2, Scene 2

August 2020 and the first time I had been on a train for several months – I have to admit that I was slightly nervous. Life could cautiously 'open up' again, the government assured us, but Milton Keynes station had been all but deserted and, when the train arrived – on time – it was practically empty. No more than a handful of passengers. Everyone was wearing masks and we all sat at a suitable distance apart, timidly checking each other out nonetheless. I'm not quite certain what it was that we thought we might see. We seemed to be together and alone at the same time, in a shared experience of obedient isolation. Ominously no one came to check our tickets. Once I began to relax, though, I started to feel rather comforted by all of this, and later thought that the whole experience was actually much nicer than the usually late-running, chaotic, overcrowded, cheek-by-jowl trains that I remembered from before Covid-19 had taken hold of our lives. And, joy of joys, we even arrived in London on time.

I hadn't yet plucked up the courage to take the Tube, and so I got into one of the many taxis that by then forlornly ringed Euston in a circle of cabbie despair. 'Where have you come from?' the driver asked, even before I had the chance to tell him where it was that I wanted to go to, as if a customer was an exotic creature or, perhaps, someone to be feared. 'Not so far,' I replied, 'Milton Keynes,' and then I asked him, before he could go off on one about concrete cows or roundabouts, 'What's life been like for you?' The driver looked at me in his rear-view mirror and said, as if it were explanation enough, 'It's all changed.'

The ride to the Victoria and Albert Museum was quick, which, like the prompt and empty train that I had travelled down on, was another advantage of the impact of Covid-19 on our existence at that time. The journey was so quick, in fact, that I arrived before the time slot I had booked, but museum staff just seemed pleased that the public were visiting again. 'Don't worry,' the guide who checked my ticket said when I pointed out that I was early, 'we can fit you in.'

I left my coat in the cloakroom and made my way to the information desk.

'I want to see the Great Bed of Ware,' I said, smiling at the woman behind the desk. She looked blankly at me, and I thought for a moment that the exhibit was no longer on show, or that she hadn't understood what on earth I was talking about. I was going to repeat my request when a look of recognition slowly started to appear on her now-smiling face, and she replied, 'Do you mean the big bed?' I nodded, and five minutes later had located the reason for my trip to London.

The Great Bed of Ware dates back to at least 1596, according to the guide pinned to an information board on the wall in the V&A, when a traveller recorded it being located in an inn at Ware in Hertfordshire – possibly as a gimmick to attract customers. It has been famous ever since because of its enormous size, and the number of people it can hold. There are records of twelve people sleeping in the bed together, although it is more commonly described as being able to hold four couples at the same time. Shakespeare refers to the bed in *Twelfth Night*, published around 1601, and as late as the Victorian period it is name-checked by Charles Dickens. To my modern eye this ornately decorated four-poster bed, with a thick canopy on top, looked rather lumpy and uncomfortable, although it was the size of a small boxing ring.

Even if the bed was an advertising tactic, its size hints at how the more public sleeping arrangements of the Tudors and Stuarts were very different from our own, where bedrooms have become an intimate and private sanctuary. That sanctuary has become embedded in our unconscious from childhood, and so we have come to associate bedrooms and our beds with the places where we once were tucked up and read bedtime stories by our parents, before going off to sleep by ourselves, with only a night light for company. It wasn't really allowed – unless you very sick or scared – to sleep in your parents' bed. Our ancestors, on the other hand, lived in communal societies and so thought nothing of sleeping in the company of their children or others – even bedding down with strangers for the night – and giving rise to a whole array of phrases, still commonly used, about sleeping and beds. We 'hit the hay', as that was what mattresses were once filled with, or the 'sack', which was the type of material that was used to contain the hay; 'strange bedfellows' is a sixteenth-century saying that describes how circumstances can bring together very different people. Indeed, in *The Tempest* Trinculo is going to shelter from a storm with Caliban – man or fish? – because 'misery acquaints a man with strange bedfellows'.

I want to look into this idea of 'strange bedfellows', the 'strange fish' that Shakespeare describes, and the confusion more generally that permeates this initial encounter in the play, as well as the cultural move from the public to the private in our sleeping arrangements. The case studies that illuminate this are: the murder of Joseph Nattrass by Mary Ann Cotton in April 1872, at 20 Johnson Terrace in the village of West Auckland; the murder of Alida Goode by Lee

Baker at 6 Shenton Road in Bournemouth on 28 July 1985; and finally the murder of Alice Rye in Poulton Road, Spital by Kevin Morrison in December 1996. I have again chosen a serial killer, although this time a female murderer and one of her male victims from a case that dates back to the mid-nineteenth century. Mary Ann Cotton's is the oldest case study in the book, but it gives us a glimpse of a time when it was still socially acceptable to have visitors in a bedroom – even when there was a sick occupant. It allows us to consider the activities of a serial killer who had escaped being apprehended for decades, and so was practised and confident within her killing cycle, and also how rooms within our homes have evolved over time. The 'strange bedfellows' will become all too apparent within the two more recent case studies, and I will use the first of these to introduce the rarely discussed idea of an individual having a catathymic crisis as an explanation for why some murders occur.

*

Given that her case is relatively unknown, and certainly not as well-known as those of other female serial killers such as Rose West, Beverley Allitt and Myra Hindley, it might be helpful to offer some biographical background about Mary Ann Cotton. She was born in 1832, in the small pit village of Low Moorsley in the north-east of England, and brought up in Murton in County Durham. It was at the Methodist chapel in Murton that Mary Ann once taught a Sunday school class. Her parents were Margaret and Michael Robson, and her father worked in the local pit. However, he was killed in a pit accident in 1842, and her mother soon remarried another miner called George Stott. At the age of twenty, Mary Ann married a thirty-five-year-old labourer called William Mowbray (she would acquire the surname Cotton from her last, and bigamously married, husband Frederick in September 1870), and the couple moved to Cornwall. However they returned to the north-east some four years later with their first child, John Robert Mowbray. The Mowbrays added further to their family and by 1858 they had two daughters, Margaret Jane and Isabella. John Robert died within a year and Mowbray in January 1865, with the cause of both deaths listed as gastric fever. As a result of her first husband's death, Cotton received £35 insurance money from the British Prudential – £4,500 in today's money.

After Mowbray's death Cotton moved with her two surviving children, Margaret Jane and Isabella, to Seaham Harbour, which was a coal port. It was here that she met her lover Joseph Nattrass, but he subsequently married another woman and moved away to work in a nearby colliery. Around this time Margaret Jane died of gastric fever and Isabella was taken in by Cotton's mother. Cotton was thus by herself, and moved to Sunderland, where she worked as a nurse at the Sunderland Infirmary in Chester Road. This nursing background must have given her some local standing – it certainly made her comfortable around doctors and she understood how they worked and what they might look for in a diagnosis. One of her patients was thirty-two-year-old George Ward, an engineer and a single man. On his discharge he married Cotton, although the marriage does not appear to have been a happy one, and no children resulted from their relationship.

Ward died in October 1866 and a month later James Robinson, a shipwright at a small yard on the River Wear, advertised for a housekeeper to look after him and his children, following the death of his wife. Cotton secured the job, and within a matter of weeks one of Robinson's children had died of gastric fever. By March 1867 Cotton was pregnant with Robinson's child, but she was called away to look after her mother. Mrs Stott was dead within nine days of Mary Ann coming to look after her and this created a minor scandal, as Cotton had predicted her mother's death to neighbours. Cotton then returned to Robinson with her eldest daughter, Isabella, and within a month two more of Robinson's children died, quickly followed by Isabella. All three children were seen by their doctor and seemed to have had the same symptoms: rolling about the bed, foaming at the mouth and retching. The cause of death listed on all three death certificates was gastric fever. Cotton and Robinson married on 11 August 1867, by which time Cotton was five months pregnant. Their child, Mary Isabella, was born in November 1867, but was dead by February of the following year. At around this time, Cotton gained employment at Sunderland's new Royal Infirmary. However, she and Robinson split because of disagreements over money – Cotton had forged one of her husband's bank books – and perhaps also from an earlier argument over whether Robinson should take out life assurance. Cotton had tried to insure Robinson, but he had discovered this and prevented it from happening. Robinson later moved in with his married sister and never again spoke to his wife, although they were never formally divorced.

In early 1870, Mary Ann was introduced to Frederick Cotton, who lived in a small, isolated mining community some six miles west of Newcastle. Frederick's wife had died of consumption in December 1869 and the following September he bigamously married Mary Ann, at which stage she was pregnant with Frederick's child. The couple moved to West Auckland with their baby, as well as two boys from Frederick's previous marriage, ten-year-old Frederick and seven-year-old Charles Edward. Frederick Cotton Senior died suddenly of gastric fever after a year of marriage, and three months later Joseph Nattrass moved in as a lodger, his own wife having died. Cotton had meanwhile been asked to nurse an excise officer by the name of John Quick-Manning who lived in West Auckland and who had contracted smallpox, and they soon formed a relationship. There was talk of marriage, and in the space of three weeks between March and April 1872, as if she was preparing for this eventuality, Frederick Cotton Junior, the baby Robert Robson Cotton and Nattrass were all dead. The only other person left in Cotton's household was seven-year-old Charles Edward, and it was his death – which Mary Ann also predicted would happen – on 12 July 1872 that was to lead to her arrest, conviction and execution.

Cotton had attempted to get Charles Edward fostered by an uncle, although this proved to be impossible. On 11 July she told Thomas Riley, an assistant overseer of poor relief in West Auckland, that she would like to put Charles Edward in the workhouse. Riley refused, and so Cotton complained that the boy's presence in her house was preventing her from taking in a respectable lodger. The following day Charles Edward was dead. Riley was suspicious and approached the local police. An inquest was held on 13 July, at which the local doctor, who had previously treated Charles Edward, suggested that the boy had died of natural causes. Riley refused to accept the verdict. The inquest was reported in the *Newcastle Journal* and, perhaps because of the publicity, or Riley's persistence, a chemical analysis was undertaken of the contents of Charles Edward's stomach, which demonstrated that the boy had died of arsenic poisoning. This finding would result in the exhumation of the bodies of other family members, and that of Joseph Nattrass, and it was discovered that all of them had been poisoned. At the time of her arrest on 18 July, Cotton was pregnant with Quick-Manning's child, and Mary Ann gave birth to their daughter in prison. Cotton was executed in Durham Gaol in March 1873.

Given the lack of reliable records from this period, it is difficult to be precise about the numbers of people that Cotton murdered, although a conservative estimate is seventeen, including a number of her own children and step-children. Joseph Nattrass was to be her penultimate victim and, by the time Mary Ann came to murder him, she had almost perfected her modus operandi. We actually know a great deal about the circumstances in which Joseph died as Cotton invited several of her neighbours into the bedroom of 20 Johnson Terrace, where she was supposedly nursing her former lover back to health, and those neighbours witnessed what she was doing. We might reflect that the culture surrounding bedrooms at this time was different from our own, and it is this difference which allows us to view a serial killer. One such neighbour who was invited inside was Jane Hedley, who would later give evidence about what she saw when she went into the bedroom:

I lived at West Auckland and was very friendly with the Prisoner. I assisted her about her house backwards and forwards. I assisted during the time of the illness of Joseph Nattrass. I saw him several times during the illness. The prisoner waited on him and was constantly about him. I saw no one else wait on him. The Prisoner gave him everything he required. Nattrass was several times sick and purged. This [*sic*] was occasionally he complained of pain at the bottom of his Bowels. I saw him have fits, he was very twisted up and seemed in great agony. He twisted his toes & his hands & worked them all ways. He drew his legs quite up. He was throwing himself about a great deal & the Prisoner held him & had to use great force. He was unconscious when in the fits. After the fits were over he sometimes said it was a very strong one and sometimes said it was not. Robert Robson Cotton died on the Thursday before Easter & was laid out in the same room where Nattrass was.

On the Friday before Nattrass died I was in the Prisoner's house with Dr Richardson, Nattrass & the Prisoner. Dr Richardson asked him if the pain had left him. He said no. Dr Richardson then said if he could stop the purging he thought he would get better. Nattrass said it is no fever I have. The doctor said if he knew better than him it was no use his coming. He then asked Nattrass if he had taken the medicine & he said no. I was present just at the time of Nattrass's death. He died in a fit, which was similar to the previous ones. The Prisoner was holding him down. I did not say anything about Nattrass having proper support. I have seen her several times give him a drink.

On the Thursday before Nattrass died the Prisoner told me that Nattrass had said she, the Prisoner, was to have his watch and Club money, as she had been his best friend. On the same day the Prisoner asked me to get a letter written for the Burial [*sic*] money from the Club of the deceased. I lived about half a dozen houses from the Prisoner at this time. Shortly after Nattrass's death, namely about a week, the Prisoner was in my house assisting to clean. She sent me to her house for a pot that stood on the pantry shelf. She said there was soft soap and arsenic in this pot. I went for and got this pot and showed it to the Prisoner. She said it was the right one & what she got to clean beds with. I got the pot from the top shelf in the pantry of the Prisoner's House and which was the place where the Prisoner told me.

There is a great deal to consider in Jane's testimony, even if it was constructed under oath during questioning at the magistrates' court with the sole purpose of convicting Cotton. Her account is evidence for the prosecution, and as such we see an emphasis on specific topics, for example Cotton's access to and possession of arsenic, and the fact that Jane had seen her give Joseph a drink 'several times'. As Mary Ann never gave any evidence we have no 'defence' to consider, but, bearing all of this testimony in mind, we can begin to glimpse how a female serial killer managed to gain a hold within the community where she lived, and then how she went about murdering her victims. Sadly Jane's testimony also allows us to see a little of the pain that these victims suffered before they died.

It is interesting that Jane described herself as 'very friendly' with Mary Ann. In other words, good friends rather than just friends, even though Cotton had only moved to West Auckland a matter of months previously – and there is no evidence that the two were acquainted with one another prior to that move. This seems to hint at Mary Ann's ability to impress and seduce, and how plausible she must have been to the other women who lived in these communities, perhaps because of her background as a nurse and a Sunday school teacher. There's a foreshadowing here of Reg Christie – the most respectable man in Rillington Place – and without doubt the roles she had once performed would have made Mary Ann appear different, capable and more worldly than her contemporaries. She also seems to have employed Jane as a cleaner, although I am uncertain how she could have afforded to pay for this service. After her arrest there were a number of local press reports that suggested Mary Ann owed money at various stores in the towns and villages where she had once lived, and so perhaps there were cleaners who were owed money too. However, she also seems to have cleaned for Jane, so it is perfectly possible that there were informal, reciprocal arrangements between good friends, which bound them together. Those bonds might have also in the past ensured silence, or engendered a scepticism that Mary Ann could be a murderer.

This account also allows us to view Mary Ann as an experienced serial killer and how the bedroom was the preferred site for her murders – even if it was a more public space than contemporary bedrooms and therefore visitors, as well as the intended victim, had to be managed. She has Joseph challenge Dr Richardson about his illness and his treatment, although she herself does not question the doctor's judgement. She wanted Dr Richardson on side when it came to assigning a cause of death, and so she allows Joseph to say 'It is no fever I have' – which, as it happened, was actually true: he was being poisoned. Rather peevishly, Dr Richardson is forced to reply that if Joseph knew better than he did 'it was no use his coming', although during what must have been a tense exchange Mary Ann makes no comment. I get the sense that Mary Ann would have been encouraging Joseph behind the scenes to think that doctors were useless, and that the medicine that he had been prescribed would not make any difference to his fate. Of course, by downplaying Dr Richardson's skills she was by implication also elevating her own abilities as a nurse and carer. This strategy obviously worked, as Joseph described her as his 'best friend', and after his death he left Mary Ann his watch and his savings – his 'Club money', and Dr Richardson never suspected foul play.

Another feature of Cotton's abilities as a killer can be seen in Jane's evidence: how attentive she was to Joseph's needs, blurring the line between the public and the private about what we might expect between men and women in the bedroom. Jane notes that Mary Ann was 'constantly about him' and gave him 'anything he required'. Obviously, this was also important for the prosecution to establish, as they wanted to demonstrate that Cotton alone could have carried out the killing. However, it also shows us that Mary Ann was carefully controlling who had access to Joseph and, perhaps because Jane was impressed by Cotton's background as a nurse, she did not think to ask why Joseph wasn't getting 'proper support'. As a result Mary Ann was able to ply him with drink, which undoubtedly contained the dissolved arsenic, while all the time appearing to those who visited as if she was being attentive and caring. In other words, Cotton was performing

Victorian femininity, although she was actually engaged in murder.

It is clear from what Jane says that Mary Ann held Joseph down in his bed as he was having his fits, and that he was visibly in agony – he was 'twisted up'. Cotton was responsible for that agony, and it is interesting to speculate how this might have made her feel. Did she enjoy this physical control over her victims? No matter how difficult it is to prove definitively, it is legitimate to consider whether Mary Ann was a sadist and, like Brady and Hindley, who took photographs of their victims which they were happy to display, perhaps having neighbours like Jane observe what she was doing added to her perverted pleasure. She controlled who had access to Joseph; controlled him physically; and, in the most grotesque way, she also controlled him psychologically. There is no better evidence of that psychological manipulation than the body of her dead child – Robert Robson Cotton – being left in the same bedroom as Joseph; his corpse was an awful foretaste of the fate that was about to befall Joseph too. He must surely have realised that the failure to bury the dead baby was because his 'best friend' had calculated that he hadn't that much longer to live, and so she could save on funeral costs. Rather than paying for two, it would be much cheaper to have one instead. And, almost unbelievably, when the end did come, Joseph died while being held down by Mary Ann.

Finally, Jane's testimony provides us with an account of where Cotton kept the arsenic that she used, and how she used it: to clean beds, or at least that is what she claimed. This was clearly important for the prosecution to establish, although Jane was never actually asked to give evidence at Cotton's trial at the Durham Spring Assizes as Joseph's murder was left on file, after Mary Ann had been found guilty of murdering her final victim, Charles Edward Cotton. As this was a capital offence for which she was to be hanged, there was no need to try her for any other cases. However, from what Jane reveals, we know that Mary Ann kept the poison in her home in a pot on the top shelf of the pantry at 20 Johnson Terrace. We know that she was attentive to her victim, plied him with liquids in which the arsenic was dissolved and, as a result of his illness, was able to extract from him monetary and other more psychological advantages; she did not question the doctor's judgement; and that she physically controlled Joseph as he writhed in agony in his bed – an agony which would culminate in her former lover's death and that she was happy for her neighbours to view. Like the serial killers that would emerge in the years to come, that visibility – no matter how illogical this might seem – was all part of the thrill. The visibility of what she had done was a demonstration of her power and control.

That the murder should be seen and viewed by others was an important dynamic in our next case too, although it occurred over a hundred years after Mary Ann had been executed, and when our use of bedrooms – and the culture that surrounded them – had changed dramatically.

*

In October 1983, when he was sixteen years old, Lee Baker started a relationship with Caroline Goode, although quite quickly both her mother Alida Goode and Caroline's best friend Helen Longhurst thought that Baker was an unsuitable boyfriend because he was so controlling and unpredictable. However, their relationship was to last until

April 1986, and only ended after Baker punched Caroline in the face and broke her nose. At first Baker seemed to take the end of the relationship well, but he secretly brooded over the next few months, and then became determined to exact what some would later describe as his revenge for the break-up – particularly on Alida and Helen. So, on Monday 28 July he went to Alida's house on Shenton Road in Bournemouth and, after being invited in for a cup of tea, while they were looking through photographs in the sitting room, Baker stabbed and killed Alida. He dragged her body towards the bedroom but, perhaps because he was unable to carry the whole body up the stairs, he proceeded to decapitate Alida and then put her head in Caroline's bed. As odd as all of this is, what happened next was even stranger.

Baker posed Alida's head on her daughter's pillow, tucked the bedclothes right up to her chin as if everything were normal, and then arranged various cuddly toys around her. Later, when he was in custody, Baker said that he wanted Caroline to find the head, but explained that he had left it 'somewhere nice'. This extraordinary statement has to be contrasted with the macabre reality of these strange bedfellows and staging behaviour: was this a cuddly toy that was intended to bring comfort, or a severed head that was meant to shock? We can perhaps also glimpse in this statement his immature thinking. His was the reasoning of a little boy who had been rejected by his mother at eighteen months, which meant that he had spent most of his life in care, and so we have to infer that the 'somewhere nice' comment was what he had once associated, or come to believe was associated, with beds and bedtime. In his troubled mind, this staging was perhaps both reassuring and appalling, and channelling dissonant emotions that he must have experienced when he was a child.

After he had finished with Alida's head, Baker went back downstairs, shot the family dog with a crossbow, and then set a small fire in the living room. This latter behaviour is somewhat inconsistent, given that he wanted Caroline to discover her mother's decapitated head, and setting a fire could potentially burn down the house, destroying all the evidence of his carefully constructed crime scene. However, the fire didn't really take hold. As he cycled away from the house, Baker encountered Caroline and, while there are disputed claims as to their exchange, one version suggests that he said: 'Your mother's head is in your bedroom and I've killed your dog. That will teach you a lesson.' He made no attempt to harm or kill Caroline, although he did then cycle on to Helen Longhurst's house and attacked her – leaving her for dead, although thankfully she survived. Thereafter he went on a spree, attacking people at random, including Clive Rattu, whom he stabbed to death, and using his crossbow to shoot at a German student called Rene Weigel, although he was not badly hurt. Baker later claimed that he had then wanted to set fire to a local petrol station and kill as many people in Bournemouth as possible. He may also have wanted to have committed 'suicide by cop', although he seems to have run out of steam, and so never set the petrol station alight. He slept rough overnight, and was easily arrested the following morning. The police officer who interviewed him found Baker emotionless, but he did respond to the questions put to him. The officer thought that he was honest, although he suggested Baker was insensitive to what he had done, and only got distressed – and fell silent – when he was asked to explain why he had decapitated Alida.

Baker was found guilty of murder at Winchester Crown Court in June 1987, and was given two life sentences. I encountered him at two different prisons while he was in custody, and spoke with him at some length on a number of occasions, given the various extraordinary elements to his crimes – most obviously the decapitation of Alida, which, at that time, was a relatively uncommon post-mortem behaviour. I discovered that he was a talented artist but egocentric, and held fixed views that emanated from a 'black and white', controlling personality. All that having been said, Baker was not a difficult person to talk to, and in the main I enjoyed our exchanges. I also discussed his case on a regular basis with the forensic psychologist who was working closely with him, and who was also trying to make sense of what Baker had done. We both noted the importance of his early childhood experiences, and how this had been characterised by rejection by his mother, rather than attachment – long considered an important psychological component since the British psychoanalyst John Bowlby's original formulation for a child to feel safe and loved. However, I still struggled to understand what might have motivated him to murder Alida, and how his reaction to the lack of 'attachment' in his own life had been to remove her head; he'd 'severed' rather than attached, although not his mother's head but the mother of his girlfriend. Nor did I understand how, after the spree, he returned to almost being 'normal' again. It was then that I first heard about the 'catathymic crisis'.

This concept was introduced in 1912 by the Swiss

psychiatrist Hans W. Maier as an explanation for crimes committed as a result of a psychological reaction that overwhelmed the perpetrator, and which was connected to an underlying complex of ideas. *Kata* and *Thymos* is Greek for 'in accordance with emotions'. Since this original formulation the concept has been used to explain different forms of violence, but all seem to have been the result of a latent and unconscious motivation that results in what has been described as an 'emotional explosion'. This explosion could last for a few minutes, or even a day or two, and then suddenly stops. When that happens, the perpetrator once again appears 'normal'. The victim – whom the perpetrator might or might not know – triggers and then brings to the surface some unconscious meanings for the offender, and the violence that then takes place is not so much about revenge, but is instead a means by which to resolve this deep-seated and often previously unexpressed unconscious conflict.

The German-American psychiatrist Fredric Wertham posited that the catathymic crisis has five stages. First there was an initial thinking disorder, which has been built on some unconscious, precipitating event or circumstance; next, the development of a plan when the violent act emerges into consciousness; extreme emotional tension culminating in the violent crisis, when the violent act is committed; then a return to superficial normality when the emotional tension seems to subside; and, finally, insight and recovery, with the establishment of an inner equilibrium. Wertham also suggested that the catathymic crisis could be 'acute' – triggered by a sudden and overwhelming set of emotions which have a deep significance for the perpetrator – or 'chronic', which would be characterised by a build-up of tension over time, correspond-ing feelings of frustration and a sense of helplessness.

The forensic psychologist working with Baker was convinced that Alida's murder, and what Baker then did with her decapitated head, was related to his own unconscious and deep-seated sense of grievance against his own mother. If this is so, it helps to make sense of why he had attacked Alida rather than Caroline. His was a chronic catathymic crisis, which explains why it took some months before he reacted to the break-up of his relationship, rather than an acute crisis, which would have meant that he would have reacted immediately. In other words, there was a build-up of tension before he felt compelled to act. Tucking Alida's head up in Caroline's bed – and we should remember that he described this to the officer who interviewed him as leaving it 'somewhere nice' – would again seem to be about his own unconscious need to remember himself being tucked up in bed, and how bedtime was a space and a time when parents read their children comforting stories before they went off to sleep. Perhaps that had not happened in his childhood, or, if it had, not to the degree that seems to have given Baker com-fort. It also seems significant that Alida invited Baker into her home and gave him tea, and was showing him photographs before he attacked and killed her: she was being friendly; she was behaving as a mother might act. His apparent return to normality the following morning was also consistent with the final stages of a catathymic crisis. After the explosion of emotions has erupted, and when previously unexpressed feelings have been able to make their way to the surface to be acted upon and, in that sense, resolved, the crisis subsides. Of course, the price that was paid by expressing and seeking to resolve those feelings was high – Baker killed two people and injured two others.

*

The final case study develops some of these themes and, while it does not use the idea of the killer having a catathymic crisis, it does return to the broader subject of how murders within bedrooms, and their public/private culture, can have more extreme and confusing elements than those that happen within other murders in different rooms of the house.

Alice Rye was seventy-four when she was murdered in a back bedroom of her detached home on Poulton Road, Spital, on the Wirral, on Tuesday 10 December 1996. A regular churchgoer and stalwart of the Women's Institute, Alice had been widowed for ten years and was living by herself at the time of her death. She was described by her friends as being 'elegant', 'dignified', and as 'a woman with poise'. She had three children, and had been planning to spend Christmas with one of her daughters. The day after the murder a concerned neighbour called Geoffrey Howarth noticed that Alice's garden gate was open, and so went to check that everything was all right. Because of this neighbourly deed, it was Geoffrey who discovered Alice's body. The sight that greeted him was truly horrific.

The crime scene photographs show that Alice had had her hands tied behind her back and she was naked from the waist down – in fact, the police later discovered that her underwear was missing from the house. Her upper clothing had been pushed up, and she had been stabbed twice in the chest; one of these wounds had punctured her heart. There were also stab wounds to her back. A towel had been pushed into her mouth, and around her neck was a loosely tied piece of cloth. It was obvious that she had been tortured and sexually assaulted. All of this was gruesome enough but, most chilling of all, Alice's killer had placed a kitchen knife in each of her eyes.

This particular detail about what happened to Alice was not released to the public, and it would later transpire from the pathologist's report that this had been a post-mortem behaviour on the part of her killer. In other words, Alice was dead before her murderer had placed a knife in each of her eyes. The killer was staging the crime scene and creating a grotesque *tableau vivant*, or more accurately, a *tableau mort*. The killer wanted to shock and, even though I find that most photographs have a flattening effect, the image of what he had done certainly has never left me, and I believe that was exactly what he had intended.

The crime scene photographs were like gothic still lifes. They captured Alice's inanimate body but rendered her both human and less so at the same time. Elements of this still life – like all still lifes – had been consciously placed to catch the viewer's eye; to startle, amaze and sometimes to horrify. I remember that the detective who was to show me the first of the photographs tried to prepare me for what I was about to see, and I can only imagine how those who first came across the scene must have reacted. It was a small act of professional courtesy and I was grateful for his kindness, although, for me, photographs never seem to capture reality but just a version of what reality might or might not have been like. Perhaps I have simply steeled myself over the years: this was not Alice Rye I was looking at, but Alice's body, which had been consciously moulded – staged – by her killer to create the effect that he wanted us to see. In that sense, her murder wasn't all that he wanted to achieve, and the horrific crime scene he constructed seemed to demand an audience; he wanted us to view what he had done and understand the story that he was telling.

The crime scene more generally had been well controlled and organised by Alice's killer; he – we are again dealing with male violence – had been methodical and careful, and therefore, despite the shock that her murder had created in the local area, the police made little headway in their investigation. No one had seen or heard anything that was of any assistance. It was also interesting that very little of value had been taken from the house, suggesting that the motive for the crime was unclear, and also preventing another strand of the investigation from moving forward: no stolen goods from the house appeared on the market. A £5,000 reward was eventually offered for information about the crime in the hope of generating leads and then, in May 1998 – nearly eighteen months after Alice's murder – a police informant called Kevin Morrison came forward claiming that he knew the identity of Alice's killer. Morrison said that one of his friends, Keith Darlington, was the murderer, and proceeded to give the police information about what Darlington had told him about Alice's death, almost as a way of demonstrating the veracity of what he was saying. However, Morrison knew too much – specifically, all about the knives that had been placed in Alice's eyes after she had been killed – and it was soon obvious that he, rather than Darlington, was the murderer. A search of his caravan and a lock-up garage that he rented in Ellesmere Port yielded DNA evidence connecting Morrison to the crime scene, and the police also found Alice's missing underwear (along with some belonging to other women) in the garage. Most significant of all, Morrison's DNA was on Alice's underwear, and we can presume with some confidence that her knickers were stolen as a form of trophy-taking.

At the stage when Morrison was still trying to blame his friend for the murder he offered the police an explanation of the dynamics of the crime, which is probably the closest we can get to the reality of what had happened. His account also allows us to make sense of some of the more bizarre aspects of the case. Morrison suggested that the electoral roll had been used to identify elderly, wealthy women living alone in detached properties, and his friend had conned his way into her home. Alice had been marched upstairs at knifepoint, and her killer had demanded to know the PIN of her bank card. She refused to give this information, and so her killer pushed the towel into her mouth and dripped water onto it as a slow form of torture, but Alice would still not reveal her PIN. Her killer had then started to choke her. The more sexual elements of the murder were only briefly discussed, but later, when Morrison was asked about the knives in Alice's eyes, he said: 'I watch *Cracker*. They're going to do a psychological profile on this guy and they won't be looking for me – they'll be looking for a nutter.'

In other words, we know that this post-mortem behaviour was deliberately intended to direct the police's gaze elsewhere. This staging had a different motivation from how Baker had posed Alida's head in her daughter's bed, even if both crime scenes were characterised by strange bedfellows – a decapitated head surrounded by cuddly toys, and kitchen knives placed in the eyes. Morrison had indeed succeeded in deflecting attention, and so of even greater interest is why he then chose to bring the focus of the police's investigation onto himself. Was he simply being too clever? Did he really believe that he could blame a friend for the crime? We might also question whether accusing Keith Darlington was merely a device intended to allow Morrison to confess. Whatever his motivation might have been to come forward, his willingness to discuss Alice's murder offers us a valuable insight into what happened to her, and also raises other issues such as how much offenders are influenced by what they see on their TVs or at the cinema. This was clearly a case where life had imitated, or at least been influenced by, art.

The knives placed in Alice's eyes relate to this chapter's main theme, but Morrison's choice of the back bedroom, rather than the one in which Alice usually slept, is also significant. The bedroom where she was murdered could not be observed from either the front or the back of the house, and afforded her killer the opportunity to take his time with Alice; it was private. He used the privacy and sanctuary that we have come to associate with bedrooms for a more monstrous end, as he clearly understood that it would be easier to torture Alice there than downstairs in the sitting room, or in the kitchen.

However, what's of interest about all three of these case studies is that despite the bedroom's privacy – especially in the two twentieth-century case studies – the killers all still wanted to be seen. Mary Ann Cotton invited neighbours into the bedroom where she was supposedly nursing Joseph Nattrass; Lee Baker revealed what he had done to his former girlfriend when he passed her in the street; and Kevin Morrison gave a pseudo-confession to the Merseyside Police.

How are we to make sense of their desire for this visibility? I have suggested that a catathymic crisis perhaps best explains Baker's behaviour, but there seems to be different motivations for both Cotton and Morrison's willingness to be observed as killers, to the extent that they might be seen to have been channelling the bedroom's historic public, rather than private, role. However, leaving the culture of bedrooms to one side, we would do well to remember that Cotton was at the end of her killing cycle, and I get the impression that by that stage she simply didn't understand how bizarre her behaviour had become and didn't realise she was in fact killing in plain sight. This wasn't about her overcalculating her skills as a murderer, but merely reflects that she had become fully embedded in a parallel universe with a different moral code to our own; a universe in which it was acceptable not to bury a dead child.

Morrison, on the other hand, does make a calculation in deciding to come forward with information, but I sense that he understood the risk he was taking. Perhaps it was the risk that gave him a perverted enjoyment. He needed to feel that he was getting the better of the police and, even if their investigation had run cold – he had literally got away with murder – that in itself didn't deliver the long-term psychological benefits that he craved. The staged crime scene was a 'come on and catch me'; it was a provocation from someone who thought of himself as bold and daring. There was much more going on in his trip to the police station than any hopes he might have had for claiming the £5,000 reward, or blaming a friend, and these psychological motivations also help to explain why very little of value was stolen from Alice's house. Robbery doesn't seem to have been the motive at all, but rather the sexual pleasures that, for him, came from misogyny, torture and sadism. Of course, in coming forward, Morrison could also think of himself – and be seen – as a 'criminal mastermind', rather than a sexual predator who preyed on an elderly woman. In that aspect he is like Ian Brady, who saw himself as a cool anti-authority, bank-robbing philosopher-villain, but who was in reality abducting and torturing children.

Compare these murders to the clinical doorstep hits or the relatively clean kitchen murders described in the previous chapter. What seems obvious is that murders in bedrooms, and especially in these three cases, are more bizarre and extreme than the other murders that I have described thus far. By extreme I not only mean that these killers have breached the sanctuary of the bedroom but also that by harnessing that privacy, and then perverting it in grotesque ways that were not possible in kitchens or in sitting rooms, they took murder to a different and outrageous level. In a bedroom the killer could spend longer with a victim, take their time and savour the moment; they could let their fantasies flower and be made real; they could be more intimate, even sexual. It's strange to think of murder as intimate, but both Cotton and Morrison engaged in sexual behaviour with their victims – behaviour that is usually seen as belonging in the bedroom – and so sex and death become inextricably linked. Not so much *la petite mort* of orgasm, but rather the finality that comes when life itself is irrevocably stolen. That too is an echo of our history with beds and bedrooms: they were places where we were born, and where we would take our last breath.

Let's also look again at Morrison's allusion to the popular British TV series *Cracker*, about a fictional criminal psychologist who helped the Greater Manchester Police, and what he says about the type of person that would put knives in the eyes of his victim. It was, of course, Morrison who was the 'nutter' – he was describing himself – although he perhaps didn't appreciate the picture that he painted for the police was a self-portrait. In many ways he must have been having an unconscious dialogue with himself, as much as he was speaking with his police handler. For me it is much more likely that his self-dialogue began before he started to kill Alice, and had been created in his adolescence. As I've suggested, there's clearly an element of sexual fantasy here, but to be able to even imagine the scene he would go on to enact implies that aberrant thinking characterised his personality and behaviour long before he knocked on Alice's door. I get the distinct impression that he had fantasised about placing knives in the eyes of a dead woman for a very long time, and that they were a fetish without which he was unable to feel sexually competent. Indeed this also helps to explain the stealing of Alice's underwear, and the misogyny and sadism of the crime scene more generally. For a woman who had been described as 'elegant', 'dignified' and 'poised' in life, the ghastly way in which Alice was murdered and then posed thereafter must have heightened Morrison's pleasure. If my suggestion is accurate, it also implies that he might have known who she was long before he undertook his research about wealthy widows living by themselves in detached houses. Sadly, Alice's murder is so extreme we also have to accept the possibility that this was not Morrison's first violent crime, and that there may be others for which he is responsible.

*

When Trinculo first encounters Caliban he is uncertain if he has stumbled across a man or a fish, and even if the creature is dead or alive. Confusion is at the heart of their initial encounter, and a similar confusion has been at the heart of these three case studies. Jane was uncertain whether she was watching Victorian femininity being performed by Mary Ann, or a murder being committed; the 'somewhere nice' where Baker had casually left the head of his former girlfriend's mother was tucked up in bed, surrounded by cuddly toys; and the knives placed in Alice's eyes were either the deviant fantasies of a madman or the rational calculation of a skilled offender to throw the police's investigation off track.

The bedroom as a space contributes to this confusion. Is it still a public space, as symbolised by the Great Bed of Ware, or a private sanctuary that only those who are intimate with the occupant are allowed to enter? And, if the latter, why did all three killers seem so eager to be seen or identified within that space? They had penetrated that sanctuary, and now wanted the attention they believed should come with that breaching. That's confusing too. All of this seems to add a different layer to each of these murders – a layer that does not appear within our case studies of murders that have taken place in other rooms. If the unexpected role of the kitchen in our history of murder has been to accommodate the most likely weapon used to kill another human being, the bedroom emerges as the space in the house where the extraordinary fantasies of the murderer can be made real. A space where we think of ourselves as especially safe and protected can all too easily become a site of danger. Whether in the past or today, it is in our beds that we sleep and then dream, and so perhaps it's no surprise at all that the bedroom has produced murders that are the stuff of nightmares.

CHAPTER FIVE

Stairs, Attics and Cellars

'Fair is foul and foul is fair: Hover through the fog and filthy air.'

Macbeth, Act 1, Scene 1

I quoted from *Macbeth* earlier in the book, when considering the doorstep and the role that this liminal space plays in facilitating murder. I quote from *Macbeth* again here because the enduring motif of Shakespeare's Scottish tragedy captures the most obvious theme within this chapter: namely, that appearances can be deceptive, and not everything is as it seems. The three witches who utter 'fair is foul and foul is fair' embody that motif: are they female or male? Are there three of them or just one? And can they be trusted? The warning throughout the play is that we can't trust our senses – appearances and reality might be two very different things if harnessed in support of 'vaulting ambition, which o'er leaps itself'.

That ambition, in Macbeth's case, was his desire to be

king – something he had never considered until he met those three witches. His previously fair demeanour quickly becomes foul after their encounter, and so he appeared to be the perfect host to Duncan, only to abuse that hospitality to facilitate murder. In fact the word 'hospitality', as well as 'host', 'hostage' and 'hostility', all come from the Latin *hostis*, which can mean both 'guest' and 'enemy', and so there has probably always been an ambivalence about how we are supposed to react when strangers come calling. Poor Duncan describes Macbeth's castle as having 'a pleasant seat; the air nimbly and sweetly recommends itself unto our gentle senses', only to be murdered there a few hours later.

The presence of the three witches ensures that there is a supernatural atmosphere throughout the play, and questions of good and especially evil are discussed. A number of characters share their views, and perhaps Banquo is the most relevant to this chapter. For example, he warns Macbeth not to be taken in by what the witches are saying because 'oftentimes, to win us our harm, the instruments of darkness tell us truths, win us with honest trifles, to betray's in deepest consequence'. The witches offered one small truth – an 'honest trifle' – so they could trick Macbeth into believing other things and 'win him to his harm'. However, Macbeth does not listen to Banquo's good advice, and later goes on to kill him too, viewing Banquo as a threat to his throne.

I want to use these ideas that we should not be won by 'honest trifles', that appearances can be deceptive and therefore we must look much more deeply to truly understand the thoughts and actions of people. Macbeth as a character always seemed unable to find a secure identity, and while the murderers in my case studies were not trying to become king, they too had difficulties with reconciling who they were and what it was they wanted to achieve. They might say one thing but behave entirely differently. Liminality is also again key in a chapter discussing stairs, attics and cellars. These are, after all, liminal parts of a house – they are not the rooms we inhabit regularly but instead we pass through them, or use them as storage (unless, of course, the attic or cellar has been converted into an additional room, changing its purpose). They are part of the house, but usually separate from it at the same time.

The uncertainty fostered by the liminality of these spaces already runs deep in our unconscious, which is why I suspect film directors always seem so keen to employ the idea of danger lurking in the attic or cellar. We know deep down that that is where the killer is likely to be hiding, where evil will be found, and yet we are still always keen to go there as a viewer, perhaps screaming at the screen. We know the truth, but we choose not to know it, and so we convince ourselves that we don't actually know what we are about to discover. From *The Birds*, *Shallow Grave*, *Flowers in the Attic*, *Sinister* and *Black Christmas* to *The Changeling*, *The Skeleton Key* and *Red Dragon*, the attic emerges as the dusty space to hide inconvenient children, vengeful crows, ghosts, appalling abuse and demonic rituals. The cellar performs a similar function in *The Amityville Horror*, *The Evil Dead*, *The Conjuring*, *The Cabin in the Woods* and *The Silence of the Lambs*. The best mainstream movies, in other words, have been playing around for years with the drama that is created when the ordinary and everyday turns out to be terrifying and the homely becomes unhomely.

Attics and cellars are the hidden areas of the home, and what connects them – even if they are the spaces that are physically at the greatest distance from each other within a house – is that they are where we collect unwanted, or temporarily unwanted, things; they are where we accumulate, stockpile and also forget what we have left there. This is especially true of houses in the country, where historically foodstuffs would have been stored away in the spring and summer, until they were ready to be eaten in the winter. Of course there have also been times when we have sought shelter and safety in the cellar, or in the attic (think about poor Anne Frank), but attics and cellars are now much more likely to be the places where we make things disappear from public view, rather than where we seek sanctuary. That disappearance, as far as murder is concerned, might have been caused by a range of emotions – from shame, disgust and a fear of exposure to those inspired by more perverted fantasies. We might equally ask why, if someone is truly disgusted or ashamed by what they have done, they would want to keep hold of what it is that makes them feel this way.

This chapter will look at the murder of Florence Little by Harold Jones at 10 Darran Road in Abertillery, Monmouthshire in July 1921; the murder of Tia Sharp in August 2012 by Stuart Hazell at the home of Tia's grandmother, 20 The Lindens, New Addington; and five murders committed by Fred and Rose West at 25 Cromwell Street in Gloucester: Carol Ann Cooper, Lucy Partington, Therese Siegenthaler, Shirley Hubbard and Juanita Mott. Though it has been impossible to visit 25 Cromwell Street and 20 The Lindens as the houses have been demolished, I have been in the loft where Jones hid the body of Florence Little. As a general rule I prefer to visit the sites where a murder has taken place – it's often surprising, the detail that you can discover that doesn't get described in newspaper accounts – but in relation to Hazell, and especially the Wests, so much has been written about what they did that I felt that all the relevant information had been collected. But let's start with how we might get to the attic or the loft: the stairs.

*

When I was a schoolboy I became rather obsessed with the Defenestration of Prague in 1618, largely because 'defenestration' was such an interesting word – from the French for window. Defenestration literally means to push someone out of a window to their death, and while those defenestrated in Prague actually survived their fall (though the event was supposedly the origin of the Thirty Years' War), other victims such as William Douglas, 8th Earl of Douglas, thrown out of a window of Stirling Castle by King James II of Scotland in 1452, have not been so lucky. I could find no recent British cases of someone being killed in this way, perhaps because the design of modern windows has radically changed since the Middle Ages, although there are contemporary examples in China, Canada and Russia. However, while reading through various newspapers, secretly hoping for a recent British defenestration, I became increasingly aware of a number of people being pushed down stairs to their deaths. There is no technical term for this method of killing, so I am going to propose one, partly inspired by the word 'defenestration'. Again using French as my source, let's employ the term *descendre mal* – literally 'to descend wrongly', with 'mal' also suggesting malevolence or malice.

It was perhaps the Netflix documentary series *The Staircase* that brought *descendre mal* to a more popular audience. The series followed the case of the American novelist Michael Peterson, who telephoned the police to report that his wife Kathleen had fallen down the stairs of their Durham, North Carolina home after she had been drinking and had consumed Valium, and had died as a result of her injuries. Peterson claimed that he was out by their swimming pool at the time of his wife's fall. Was everything as it seemed? Was this really a tragic accident, or had Kathleen been bludgeoned to death and the crime scene staged to look like an accident? There were no witnesses and so all that the police had to make an assessment about what had happened was what they were told by Peterson, toxicology reports in relation to what Kathleen had consumed, and various other medical and forensic tests – such as blood spatter analysis – that could be conducted.

The US authorities certainly thought there was something amiss, and in 2003, two years after his wife's death, Michael Peterson was found guilty of killing Kathleen and sentenced to life without the possibility of parole. However, Peterson was granted a new trial in 2009, after the judge ruled that a crucial prosecution witness gave misleading testimony, and so he was released. At his second trial, which didn't take place until 2017, Peterson entered an 'Alford plea' to the voluntary manslaughter of Kathleen, which meant that he accepted sufficient evidence existed to convict him of the offence, but he still asserted his innocence. This plea was accepted and the judge sentenced him to a little over seven years in prison, although given that he had already served more than that inside Peterson did not spend any further time in jail. Was this foul, or fair? Had appearances deceived and a guilty man escaped a life sentence?

These same dilemmas are repeated in the many British cases of *descendre mal*. Linda Rainey was pushed down the stairs to her death in South Market Road, Great Yarmouth by her friend Rosalind Gray in a row over money. The two women had discussed going on holiday together, and Linda had paid Gray £200 as a deposit on a five-star holiday to Morocco. However, when they went to Luton airport the pair were turned away as their flights had not actually been booked, and Linda demanded her money back from Gray. This financial dispute seems to have been the source of a bitter disagreement, but this might have never come to light had there not been a witness – Emma Walker – who came forward to inform the police that she had been drinking with Linda, Gray and Adrian Lawrence, the owner of the flat where the incident took place, and that she had seen Gray push Linda down the stairs. When the ambulance arrived, Emma had been ushered into another room, as she couldn't be trusted by the other two to keep quiet about what had happened, which Gray and Lawrence had made out was a terrible accident. Emma's conscience got the better of her, though, and she and one of her friends contacted the Norfolk Police. As Detective Chief Inspector Mike Brown said after Gray had been sentenced to thirteen years for manslaughter, 'without their [Emma and her friend's] honest and consistent account of the circumstances leading up to and during the days after the incident, we may not have ever known the truth behind Linda's untimely and tragic death'.

Michelle Morris was rushed to hospital in May 2020 after

she fell down the stairs at her friend's house in Ramskir View, Stainforth, and died three days later from her head injuries. An inquest into her death at Doncaster Coroner's Court heard that Michelle had been at the house drinking with three of her friends. She had arrived in the morning, before going upstairs to rest in a bedroom and sleep off the effects of the alcohol. It was when one of the friends went to rouse her a few hours later that Michelle had fallen down the stairs. The court heard that it had been alleged that one of the friends was at the top of the stairs when Michelle had fallen and that he had pushed her, although no one had witnessed this. This was strenuously denied by the man concerned, and each of the friends reported that Michelle had been drinking and was 'wobbly on her feet'. At one stage all three were arrested on suspicion of murder, although they were all later released with no further action being taken. Louise Slater, the coroner, still recorded an open verdict as she had been unable to rule out either an accident or death through 'third-party involvement'. She explained her findings further:

There are two people who know what happened that day and sadly one of those isn't here with us any more, and that is Michelle. I have to be satisfied by at least 51 per cent on my conclusion and with the evidence I have I cannot say on the balance of probabilities that I could say [her death] was an accident or anything else. The evidence does not allow me to determine that Michelle died as a result of an accident because the evidence does not persuade me over the 51 per cent mark. Similarly I cannot rule out third party involvement, so I have to record an open conclusion.

There is more certainty about what happened to David Thomson, just a month before Michelle died – during the first coronavirus lockdown – when, as a result of an argument in a shared house in Dorchester Road, Weymouth, he was pushed down a flight of stairs by Mark Bosworth and died the following day from the head injuries he sustained. Bosworth, who admitted to the police that alcohol may have 'clouded his judgement', admitted to pushing David but said that he hadn't intended to cause him lasting injuries. Bosworth was convicted of manslaughter and sentenced to six years' imprisonment.

There are many other examples of *descendre mal*: Kevin Syms was convicted of murdering taxi driver Nicholas Tame after he became jealous of his relationship with Joanne Parkhouse-Thomas; Frederic Pallade was killed by his partner Andrew Jones after the pair had been drinking at their home and got into a disagreement which culminated in the *descendre mal*. Jones would later be convicted of manslaughter, but there is also an indication from press reporting at the time that he had been domestically abusing Frederic. Alan Evans was jailed for life at Warwick Crown Court after pushing his wife Louise Evans down the stairs after she found out about his affair. Evans staged the crime scene by placing an uncoiled vacuum cleaner hose at the top of the stairs and a skipping rope near to Louise's body. This is an example of 'primary' staging – that which is intended to deliberately disguise the true nature of what had happened. Detectives became suspicious as Louise's injuries were inconsistent with having tripped and fallen, and the police also discovered various incriminating text messages between Evans and his lover on his mobile phone.

As is clear from these vignettes, there is often a debate as to whether a death caused by *descendre mal* should be viewed as murder or manslaughter, the two most serious offences that you can be charged with, although differentiating between the two can sometimes be difficult. Manslaughter – which might be 'voluntary' or 'involuntary' – can be committed in one of three ways: voluntary manslaughter is where there is a loss of control, a suicide pact, or the offender has diminished responsibility; involuntary manslaughter is either conduct by the accused person that was grossly negligent given the risk of death or conduct that takes the form of an unlawful act involving a danger of some harm that resulted in death. Murder, on the other hand, is when the culprit intends to kill or cause grievous bodily harm, and so the difference between the two offences comes down to the issue of responsibility and intent: did the accused intend to kill the victim? Can the person who has been accused be held responsible for their actions?

These differences between murder and manslaughter are why we see within the vignettes references to the perpetrator having been drinking heavily so that their judgement was 'clouded', that the victim was 'wobbly on their feet', or that the *descendre mal* resulted from an argument. What happened hadn't been planned, and so there was no intent to take the life of the victim – in other words, this wasn't murder but manslaughter. There are no difficulties in determining what happened in the first of our case studies – this was murder.

*

Cromwell Street in the 1990s had seen better days. Close to the centre of Gloucester, the street was a narrow Victorian terrace that must have been sought after at one stage but had long ago been split into low-rent flats that catered for students, the unemployed and a flotsam and jetsam of assorted others who were mostly down on their luck. Number 25 was unusual in that it was still complete, and so was relatively spacious. It had two upstairs floors and, according to the journalist Howard Sounes, who was the first to attach the phrase 'House of Horrors' to it, 'a ground floor, all with open marble fireplaces'. There was also a doorway below street level that led to a cellar. As an end of terrace, the house was larger than the adjoining houses and also had a garage, which was reached from the front of the house by a narrow drive that separated it from the Church of the Seventh Day Adventists next door. At the back of the house was a long, narrow garden. From the front could be seen three net-curtained sash windows – one for each floor – and at pavement level a black wrought-iron railing on top of a small brick wall. On the wall of the house itself there was a wrought-iron sign that said '25 Cromwell St', which had been made to match a set of gates.

The house was also unusual in that Fred and Rose West had lived there since 1972, making them among the few stable residents of the street. They paid their mortgage, sent their children to school and Fred, a builder, was always willing to help out with any odd jobs for neighbours. There were local rumours – Rose was said to sell sexual services – and Fred was known to make lewd comments, but this was all put down to eccentric behaviour rather than something that needed to be taken too seriously. In fact, the Wests were so completely embedded in the life of the street that Chief Superintendent John Bennett remembers that at the start of his investigation into the disappearance of the Wests' eldest daughter, Heather, which involved digging up their back garden, one angry neighbour shouted at him: 'The Wests are a lovely family. He's done nothing [wrong] and there's nothing in the garden.' However, fair really was foul; very foul.

The back garden of Number 25 not only contained the body of Heather West, who had been missing since June 1987, but also those of Lynda Gough, who had moved to Cromwell Street in April 1973, Shirley Robinson, who went missing in April 1978 when she was six months pregnant, and Alison Chambers, who disappeared in September 1979. Lynda, Shirley and Alison had all at some stage lived with the Wests – Alison, for example, had told her mother that she was working as a nanny for the family. However, in this chapter I am not concerned with the victims that the Wests buried in their back garden; for now, I'm only interested in how they used their cellar. It was there that the bodies of Carol Ann Cooper, Lucy Partington, Therese Siegenthaler, Shirley Hubbard and Juanita Mott were discovered. With the exception of Juanita Mott, who had lived at 25 Cromwell Street and went missing in April 1975, none of the other women had been to the street before and had instead been picked up by West (perhaps in the company of Rose) as they waited at bus stops, or as they hitch-hiked. Is there some significance that these women's bodies ended up in the cellar, as opposed to being buried in the garden? West had already buried Lynda Gough in the garden, so why did he then choose to bury Carol Ann Cooper in the cellar of the house in November 1973, and continue to use this space until disposing of Shirley Robinson's remains in the garden five years later? His choice of deposition site seems to hold a deep psychological truth, rather than simply having been chosen for instrumental reasons.

I believe the answer to this lies in my hypothesis that the Wests' victims can be divided into three different groups: family and pseudo-family; 'the seduced', who had been in care at Jordan's Brook House in Gloucester – a former approved school that cared for 'delinquent girls', and who saw in the Wests an idealised family, with a 'pleasant seat', that they could attach themselves to; and 'the snatched', who ended up in the cellar.

The first of the snatched victims was Carol Ann Cooper, known to her friends as Caz. Her parents divorced when she was four, and her mother died when she was eight. Thereafter she lived with her father for a time, but when this did not work out she was placed in a succession of children's homes, and from the age of thirteen she had been living at the Pines Children's Home in Worcester. Caz was pretty, intelligent, tall and strong but she didn't like any of the residential homes that she had been sent to – including the Pines – and she regularly absconded, slept rough and seems to have survived by shop-lifting. In late 1973, when she was fifteen years old, she started a relationship with a boy called Andrew Jones. On a November Saturday they went to the Odeon cinema in Gloucester, had fish and chips and went to a pub, where Caz had a soft drink. Afterwards Andrew walked her to the bus stop and gave her the fare back to the Pines. He waited with her until the bus arrived, and that was the last time he ever saw his girlfriend.

Six weeks later, West snatched Lucy Partington.

Lucy had been visiting a friend in Cheltenham called Helen Render and the pair had discussed where Lucy thought that she might like to continue her studies after completing her undergraduate degree at Exeter University, and whether Lucy should apply to the Courtauld Institute in London to undertake a masters in medieval art. Her life, in other words, was very different from that of Caz Cooper. Lucy was serious, artistic, musical, religious – she had recently converted to Catholicism – resolute, and wrote poetry. After speaking with Helen she left her friend with a completed application form in her hand to walk the short distance to the bus stop. Lucy never posted the application to the Courtauld and she never boarded the bus home. It would be twenty-one years before her body was found in the cellar of 25 Cromwell Street.

Shirley Hubbard was, like Caz, seen boarding a bus, although in her case in Worcester rather than Gloucester. She had lived in children's homes from the age of two but was eventually fostered by Jim and Linda Hubbard, who lived in Droitwich. At fifteen Shirley ran away from home and was found sleeping rough with a soldier in a field some five miles outside of Worcester. Around this time she decided to also tattoo 'Shirl' on her forearm. At the time of her death, she was seeing a boy called Dan Davies, and in November 1974 she and Dan spent the afternoon walking around Worcester and he waited with her until she boarded the bus back to Droitwich. Shirley never made it home.

The final two snatched victims were Therese Siegenthaler and Juanita Mott. Therese was born and raised in Switzerland but in 1974, aged twenty-one, she was studying sociology at Woolwich College and living in digs in Deptford. That April she set out to hitch-hike to Holyhead in order to catch the ferry to Ireland and meet up with a friend. We do not know where she was picked up by West, but her body was eventually found in the cellar beside her fellow student Lucy Partington. Juanita Mott's father was a US serviceman who returned to Texas without his wife or daughter, and her mother then found Juanita difficult to handle. As a result she was taken into care on a number of occasions, and at fifteen she left home, eventually moving to Cromwell Street. She was convicted of theft and spent some time in Pucklechurch Remand Centre in Gloucester, and after being released found herself work in a local bottling factory. By 1975 she was living with a friend of her mother in the small town of Newent and would hitch-hike into Gloucester to see friends. The day after she went missing, Juanita was supposed to be looking after the Newent friend's children and it may well have been the Wests' fear that her disappearance would be reported that led to her being buried in the cellar because it was a more secure deposition site. In fact, Juanita was the only one of these 'cellar girls' *not* to be reported missing.

These women are linked in a number of ways – most obviously that they used public transport or hitch-hiked to get from one place to another. They are also linked in a more tragic way, in that their naked bodies were discovered in the cellar of 25 Cromwell Street, with none of their personal possessions ever being found. We know that there are more gruesome connections too in relation to how they died, largely as a result of the forensic work that was carried out by the Home Office pathologist Professor Bernard Knight, who supervised the digs in the garden and in the cellar. A few details will suffice. Shirley had been decapitated, and when her skull was found in 1994 it was still encased in a hood mask. The mask had two holes, through which had been inserted plastic tubes. Clearly this had been done to keep her alive for as long as possible, and was part of the torture that she had had to endure prior to being suffocated. John Bennett remembers that when Knight realised that every part of Shirley's head and face had been covered, 'even the Prof was momentarily lost for words'. Caz's decapitated skull was bound with surgical tape, and her dismembered limbs were tied with cord and braided cloth; she may well have been suspended from one of the wooden beams that supported the ceiling prior to her death. Lucy had been decapitated and dismembered, and her remains crammed into a shaft between leaking sewerage pipes along with a knife, rope, some masking tape that had been looped round her skull and two hair grips. Juanita had been decapitated and appeared to have been hog-tied from her arms to her legs and different pieces of material had been wound around her skull from the top, down below the jaw and then round to the back. Therese had been gagged and bound before being decapitated and dismembered but, as with the other victims, many of the bones from her hands, her feet and her two kneecaps were missing.

It is clear even from these briefest of details that this space operated as a dungeon and torture chamber, though over a decade later in the summer of 1987 it would be converted into a bedroom for Rose West's younger children. Thereafter, the five graves jostled together in a circle beneath a concrete surface covered in linoleum, and children's drawings and cartoons were now displayed on the cellar walls. Fair was hiding foul, and this new function as a bedroom might be why no further bodies were buried there. Fred had first converted the cellar just after Caz had disappeared in November 1973, digging down past the foundations so that it was then possible to stand up in the space without hitting your head. Howard Sounes writes that West had drilled some holes in one of the heavy beams that acted as a support, and fixed hooks into them so that he could suspend the heavily bound and gagged bodies of his victims. West never spoke about the sexual torture of his victims – scandalously claiming that they had all been willing sexual partners – but there is no doubt that he and Rose were predatory, sexual sadists who were interested in life-threatening forms of bondage, such as breath control, dismemberment and decapitation. The missing bones of the women may also have been taken by the couple as trophies.

Sexual torture was not so prevalent in the victims who were found in the garden. Their bodies had also been dismembered (although that in itself is not an act of sadism) and several of their bones were missing, and while a belt was fastened under the skull of Shirley Robinson, there were no grotesque masks with breathing tubes of the type that had been wrapped around the head of Shirley Hubbard. The sadism that we can detect in the cellar was of a more marked degree, and suggests what the full expression of the Wests' fantasies was like. The women they snatched seem to have been more valuable to them as victims than those who were buried in the garden. Above all, it was the cellar that served to make their fantasies come to life. They did not want their victims to die quickly but to be conscious for as long as possible because it was their suffering that satisfied the Wests' sexual needs. The majority of the victims were strangled or suffocated, and it is likely that they would have been allowed to drift out of consciousness only to be revived by the Wests so that their awful, sadistic torment could begin again, and again.

That's what the Wests enjoyed, and keeping these victims close and within the house – beneath the beds of Rose's children – was not only a way of trying to ensure that their bodies would never be found (and we should remember that with the exception of Juanita all the others had been reported as missing) but was also an exciting aide-memoire for what they had done, in much the same way that Brady and Hindley took photographs of themselves standing on the graves of their victims on Saddleworth Moor, and then put those photographs on their mantelpiece. The cellar was an instrumental sanctuary for the Wests, as they didn't expect the police to ever uncover their crimes. However, it was also a place to stockpile, accumulate and forget who or what had been left there until they again wanted to remember their victims and relish what they had done to them; to remember a time when they were dominant and powerful and not just desirable but, well, irresistible. We should see in Fred's reluctance to talk about the sexual torture of his victims, and in Rose's outright denials, not so much shame or their fear of being exposed as predatory sexual sadists but merely their inability to express in words behaviours that were the stuff of their dreams and fantasies, and of our nightmares. Of course it's important to remember that the Wests are outliers – they are at the extreme end of murder, and you are much more likely to be pushed down the stairs in a drunken stupor or stabbed by an enraged lover than be picked up by a serial killer as you hitch-hike around the country.

*

Harold Jones was a fifteen-year-old assistant at Mortimer's Stores, a seed shop in Abertillery, Monmouthshire. He was also a sexual sadist who murdered two young girls within the space of six months. His first victim was an eight-year-old called Freda Burnell, who had been sent to Mortimer's Stores to buy poultry seed by her father, at around nine in the morning on 5 February 1921. Freda never returned home, and her body was discovered in a lane behind the shop the following day. She had been hit over the head, strangled – the cord was still around her neck – her arms and legs were tied, and there was evidence of attempted rape. Jones was a suspect as he confirmed that Freda had indeed visited the shop – an 'honest trifle' – but, he claimed, she had left to check with her father if the poultry seed that they stocked was the right type. Jones vehemently denied that he had killed Freda, and while his story did change under questioning there was no physical evidence to connect him to the crime. However, he was later charged – partly as a result of the work of Scotland Yard detectives who came to advise the local police – as Freda's handkerchief was discovered in the shed belonging to the store and only Jones and Herbert Mortimer, the shop owner, had keys to the shed.

At his trial at the Monmouth Assizes on 21 June 1921, Jones was found not guilty of Freda's murder, largely because of an alibi provided by Mr Mortimer, who also spoke of Jones's good character. His acquittal turned him into something approaching a local celebrity. That day, after a private reunion with his mother and father, he was taken to a restaurant by a group of the townspeople for a celebratory meal. During the celebrations Jones stood on a table and addressed his supporters:

'I thank you all. I do not hold a grudge against the people of Abertillery for the horrendous ordeal I have been put through.' He was then driven back to Abertillery in an open-top bus adorned with flags, accompanied by a brass band, with the cheers of the public ringing in his ears. Most people simply couldn't accept that it was possible for a fifteen-year-old boy to commit murder. One of those to greet him was his neighbour George Little, who said to Jones, 'Well done, lad. We knew you didn't do it.' Seventeen days later, George's eleven-year-old daughter Florence was murdered.

Florence lived with her family on Darran Road, three doors away from Jones, and was out in the street playing hopscotch when she taunted him that he had got away with murder. Inviting Florence into his house, Jones then bludgeoned her with a broom handle before cutting her throat with his father's pocket knife and bleeding her out over the kitchen sink – to the extent that there were barely two teaspoons of blood left in her body. Jones then cleaned the sink and the kitchen floor, and dragged Florence back through the house before hiding her body in the attic. He bathed and later calmly assured Florence's increasingly anxious parents that he had indeed seen her but didn't know where she had gone to after she had knocked on his door. The following day Superintendent Henry Lewis and a constable searched Jones's house and, noticing that there were bloodstains on the latch of the attic trapdoor, soon discovered Florence's body. Jones was duly arrested and pleaded guilty to Florence's murder, later admitting to having killed Freda Burnell too – a result, he said, of his 'desire to kill'. However, given that he was still under sixteen years of age at the time (which might have encouraged him to plead guilty:

if the case had gone to trial he would have turned seventeen by the time he appeared in court) he did not receive the death penalty, but was ordered to be detained 'At His Majesty's Pleasure', on 1 November 1921.

Given that he had committed two murders, and at a young age, Jones was regularly assessed in prison, and so we have a number of good sources in the National Archives – including all of his prison records – about what might have driven him to commit his crimes. Dr W. Norwood East, who joined the Prison Medical Service in 1899 and who would go on to co-write *The Psychological Treatment of Crime*, was convinced of Jones's sadism and dangerousness. In a 1923 report he said that he thought Jones fantasised about girls 'certainly during masturbation', and that 'all his desires seem to have been associated with girls considerably junior in age'. Dr Norwood East also thought that 'both murders were due to sadism', and that 'the sex impulse [in Jones] has developed in an irregular manner'. Specifically, that 'the manifestation of power over a woman, normal in the sexual act, has in him developed to an abnormal extent'. As a result 'the highest [sexual] gratification' comes when 'accompanied by cruelty'. Ten years later Norwood East commented that he had no reason to alter his opinion on Jones, and that if he was released this would involve a risk to the public – though he thought Jones might be less likely to re-offend after he had served twenty years. In 1936 Norwood East was more cautious, writing in the Prison Commissioners' file that he would view Jones's release with very grave anxiety and that he would not be surprised if he was convicted of another sex murder.

Jones served twenty years in prison and was released when

the country was at war. He never expressed remorse or regret for the murders that he committed. Nor did he ever live in Wales again. Jones married and the couple had a daughter, who I have interviewed at some length. He died of bone cancer in 1971, aged seventy-four, at his home in London, and suspicions remain as to other murders that he might have committed after his release from prison. In particular there is speculation about his connection to the 'Jack the Stripper' murders that took place between 1959 and 1963 in Hammersmith, around the area where Jones lived. It was when conducting research about those murders that I visited Abertillery to get a sense of Jones's childhood and found myself in the attic in Darran Road.

The attic where Jones hid Florence's body is small, cramped and impossible to stand up straight in without banging your head. I have no doubt that if he hadn't been arrested Jones would have moved Florence's body and found a better place to dispose of her remains – the attic was merely a temporary holding area to store and hide Florence's corpse before the smell of decaying flesh overwhelmed the house. In that sense Jones is different from the Wests, who used their cellar to prompt and then shape the murders that they committed as well as a place to store the bodies of their victims. However, what unites them is not only their sadism and the consistent belief that they might have committed many more murders, but the idea at the heart of this chapter: appearances can deceive.

We find this deception most clearly in Jones's willingness to address the crowd that had gathered in the restaurant after his acquittal. Standing on a table so that everyone could see him, he wanted them to know that he didn't bear a grudge against the people of his home town for his 'horrendous ordeal', and then happily played the returning hero. He was presenting himself as he would have preferred, almost as if he was the victim, and hiding the reality of his crime. Poor George Little, like the neighbour encountered by John Bennett in Cromwell Street, just couldn't believe that Jones had 'done it'. Seemingly very few people could. Perhaps, as time has moved on, we have all become more used to the fact that children can and do kill other children, but in 1921 that seems to have been inconceivable. Jones was not only a child who was a murderer, but also someone who was a neighbour and whose family was embedded in the life of Abertillery. It's always much easier for everyone to imagine that evil comes from outside a community. We want to believe that evil is perpetrated by a monstrous other, not one of our own. Did Jones also mislead the prison authorities so as to earn his release? Norwood East doesn't seem to have been deceived, but Britain was at war and so able-bodied men – even murderers – were at a premium, although it is difficult to be certain about what Jones did during the war. If Jones did offend again he was never arrested, let alone charged for any crimes, and suggestions as to other murders that he might have committed must remain as speculation as they can no longer be proven beyond reasonable doubt. However, like Norwood East we shouldn't be too surprised if Jones had indeed committed more 'sex murders'.

*

Stuart Hazell was a petty offender, with several convictions dating back to his youth, and had spent time in prison for drugs offences. By August 2012 he was in a relationship with Christine Bicknell, having previously dated Christine's daughter Natalie Sharp. He lived with Christine at her home 20 The Lindens, New Addington, about five miles from Croydon. Christine's granddaughter Tia Sharp, who was twelve years old, would often stay over and seemed to have formed a good relationship with Hazell, who had in effect become her step-grandfather. That's an important role within any family. What words do you associate with 'grandfather'? We will all have a unique way of answering that question based on describing our own grandfathers, but what about patience, generosity and empathy? Or perhaps, even better, unconditional love? In fact, in a press interview Hazell would say that he 'loved Tia to bits', although by the time he made that statement he had killed her.

The story of how Tia was murdered brings the various themes that have dominated this chapter to a conclusion, as well as allowing us to reconsider *descendre mal* – Hazell, at one stage after his arrest, claimed that he and Tia had been playing at the top of the stairs, and that she had accidentally fallen to the bottom and broken her neck. As a result he had panicked and hidden her body in the attic, although he later changed his plea and admitted to having murdered Tia. Presenting himself as fair rather than foul before his arrest, Hazell, like many murderers, even gave interviews to the news in which he spoke as if he was a concerned and increasingly anxious grandfather who had nothing whatsoever to do with Tia's disappearance, when the truth was that he had killed her. Also, he was using child pornography, had taken photographs of Tia before and after her death, and may well have tried to sexually assault her immediately prior to her murder.

In a bizarre sequence of events, the attic where Hazell had hidden Tia was searched by the police on three occasions, but it was only when the smell of decomposition became so over-powering that they eventually found her body, during their fourth search. Tia had been wrapped in a black bedsheet and her body had then been put in a number of bin liners which had been sealed with tape. The loft was described as 'extremely confined ... hot and quite chaotic' with 'a lot of boxes and bags' – in other words, like most attics. The day after Tia had been reported missing, a police constable had first gone up there and is reported to have said, 'From what I could see the loft seemed very clear. I thought "she's not hiding in here".' The following day a specialist team searched the loft for twenty-five minutes, and may well have moved the bin liners containing Tia's body, although the team believed that it was too light to have contained anything significant. On the third occasion, a search dog indicated that something might be in the loft, but the dog was too large to be taken into the loft and so nothing further was done. It was only on 10 August, a week after Tia was killed, that she was found. Scotland Yard would later apologise to Tia's family for these investigatory failures, and the advanced decomposition that happened during the delay meant that it was impossible to establish definitively the cause of her death.

Here I want to focus on the interview that Hazell gave to the criminologist Mark Williams-Thomas, which was broadcast just the day before her body was found. Tia's uncle had made an appeal for her to come home three days earlier, though the tragic truth was that she had never left. That appeal had resulted in fifty-five reports of sightings by members of the public, although clearly none of these were accurate. Let's look at Hazell's account of the last time Tia was seen:

MARK WILLIAMS-THOMAS: So Thursday night [2 August] Tia stays here with you and Christine is working?

STUART HAZELL: Yep, me and Tia are on the PlayStation, which is nothing unusual 'cos she's cheating all the time.

MWT: The CCTV footage released on Thursday with Tia, that actually has you on it as well?

SH: Yeah, yeah it did.

MWT: So talk me through Friday until the last moment you see her, tell me exactly what you did.

SH: Exactly what I did? Basically I woke up in the morning, I come downstairs, done my usual thing, let the dogs run around a bit as they're asleep in their beds, make myself a cup of coffee, had a cigarette, sat down, watched telly, just everyday things I guess, but [pauses] uhh, I can't remember ... sitting down here for about an hour, watching whatever rubbish is on, got up, went to the kitchen, started putting stuff away, then Tia comes downstairs, round about half ten, eleven. She'd been going on about going to Croydon and getting up early. She comes downstairs, sat down, watching telly, played the DS, she had toast, then wanted a sausage roll – she was always eating sausage rolls – then she doesn't take her washing-up so I take it out. I start doing a bit of washing-up. She was telling me what she was doing but I wasn't really logging it into my head. I cleaned the kitchen, then started sweeping up in here. Then hoovering – I hoovered the rug. Done all the hallway, had another cigarette, then gone upstairs, done the washing; made sure there was no washing. Went back upstairs and made the bed. Come downstairs. By then Tia is coming upstairs to get changed – she was mumbling – I can't remember about what. As I was hoovering she walked past me from the front room to go out the front door and that's all I knew and she left her phone on charge. I know because I told her to sit there and leave her phone on charge, 'cos I told her to not touch it [and] just leave it there charging, but she left it. She's responsible enough to go to Croydon by herself; she knows buses and trams. She's done it all on her own; it was just an everyday thing, but the one time you wanna listen to her and you don't.

MWT: So when she walked past you did she say anything?

SH: Uhh. She said 'goodbye' and I said, 'Well, make sure you're back at six.' She went, 'Yeah, yeah, yeah,' and that was it and the door closed and she walks out.

MWT: What about keys, things like that? Does she have a front door key?

SH: No, I would have been at home.

MWT: But does she have a front door key?

SH: No she doesn't. No, 'cos someone is always here. If no one's here then she goes to one of her friends, or neighbours, or someone like that.

MWT: Might be difficult for you to remember, but can you remember what she was wearing?

SH: I know exactly what she was wearing. She was
     wearing exactly what she had when she came up
     here because I washed her clothes that night ...
     It was yellow – one of them tight tube things;
     grey – like jeans – but they weren't jeans. Jeggings?
     Chinos? Something like that. I'm not up on women's
     clothes, but she had her trainers on because her Ugg
     boots were up there and she only had them. She was
     only going out to buy flip-flops; she was adamant
     about buying flip-flops.

MWT: Did she have a bag?

SH: She didn't have nothing – nothing at all. She
     didn't have an Oyster card because she lost that
     months ago.

MWT: So how was she going to buy the flip-flops?

SH: Well I'd given her a tenner. That was the agreement.
     When she's here for the weekend she helps me do
     things around the house – like do the back garden;
     do the front garden – oh it still ain't done! So I give
     her a tenner; she helped me do the washing-up like
     the night before. I gave her that then – it earns her
     responsibility and learn how to do things, plus it's a
     bit of pocket money.

MWT: Tell me about Tia. She stays here often?

SH: Yeah, she stays here loads of times. Well, she stays
     here when me and Christine are here, when I'm
     here, when Chris is.

MWT: And tell me more about her getting about.

SH: Yeah, sometimes she uses transport – if she wants
     to go to school and that. Or, if she wants to come

171

up here, she's come up here on the tram before –
straight from school, or whatever. She has done it
on her own.

MWT: And what's the most likely route if she's going
to Croydon?

SH: If she was going to Croydon, knowing Tia she'd walk
out of this house, take a right, go towards the bus
stop which is at the bottom of the road. She'd go
on there and I personally think that she would have
got the 231 because that's part of the tram system –
even though she didn't have her Oyster card. Then
[she] would have gone from there at the tram stop
to Croydon.

MWT: Tell me about Tia's life. Is she a happy girl? Has she
got any problems?

SH: No, she's got no problems at all. She's a happy-
go-lucky golden angel. She's perfect. There's no
arguments – nothing we can think of.

MWT: And tell me about the Thursday night.

SH: Did we have a meal? Yeah because when we went to
[the] Co-op we bought these things. Well, I bought
them, or Chris, but Tia ate them – three of these
lollies, Nobby Bobblys – she was going to eat the last
one but I told her to leave it for her nan. Yeah, we
had pizza and chips.

[FURTHER DISCUSSION ABOUT THURSDAY.]

MWT: I might be wrong here, but ten pounds to catch a
bus and buy flip-flops isn't enough.

SH: Nah, 'cos knowing Tia she might have had more
than a tenner. Her mum might have given her four

pounds and the day before I had given her a couple quid 'cos she'd bought some sweets which are still in the fridge now, 'cos in the Co-op you get three for a pound.

They've seen my dad and when they say something they just twist your words. They ask me stupid questions like did I do anything with Tia and no I didn't. I'd never think of that. I'd loved her to bits like my own daughter – we had that kind of relationship. She's got a loving home. She's never gone without anything. I can't work out what the hell is going on. They're talking to people round here that don't even know us and getting things off them but they don't know us!

[DISCUSSION ABOUT DIFFICULTIES FOR THE FAMILY.]

MWT: So do you feel under pressure – that people are looking at you?

SH: Well, if they believe what they read in the papers they can believe whatever they like, 'cos I know deep down in my heart that Tia walked out of my house – she walked out of there – I know damn well she was seen walking down the pathway. She made her own way down that track. What happened after that I don't know and I wasn't the last person to see her 'cos that was the one walking down the pathway.

[DISCUSSION ABOUT THE POLICE PRESS BRIEFING.]

MWT: Stuart, say Tia is watching this – talk to her ...

SH: Tia, come home babe, come and eat your dinner. I want my ten pound back for the garden. We love you. Come back babe, please.

MWT: Do you feel, Stuart, that people are pointing the
finger at you?

SH: I do feel that people are pointing the finger at me 'cos
till the other day it was known that I was the last
person to see her, but I wasn't. It's not about me, it's
about Tia and we've got to get her home, man. Just
don't know what more to do. If they laid off us a bit
I could actually be out there looking. I want to be
out there looking myself, but I'm stuck in here like a
prisoner. I feel helpless. I'm sitting here [and] I can't
do nothing. As soon as I go out there, they're all
over me. I want to find her in a McDonald's.

Despite being interviewed only feet beneath where Tia's
body had been hidden – and by then the smell of decomposition within the house must have been quite marked – Hazell
is trying to use this interview to suggest that he is a reliable,
trustworthy, responsible family man who has a wonderful
relationship with the 'happy-go-lucky golden angel' he treated
'like my own daughter'. I want to analyse the picture that
Hazell is trying to paint of himself: that he is fair rather than
foul, and how he attempts to convince us (perhaps even himself) of these lies.

It is interesting to look at the verbal clues Hazell offers as
to his guilt – clues that Mark was clearly aware of – and we
should note his almost complete avoidance of any substantive
discussion about what happened on the Thursday night, when
he was alone with Tia. He answers Mark's questions about the
night of 2 August with a non-sequitur about the PlayStation
on the first occasion, and about eating a meal on the second,

which would suggest to me that Tia was killed on Thursday night or in the very early hours of Friday. And, when he is having to invent details about what happened on Friday morning – which, I suspect, is why he is having to be so imprecise about the specific time – when Tia supposedly left the house, I was intrigued by his speech error in the phrase 'and the door closed and she walks out'. After all, it's impossible to walk out of a house after the front door has been closed.

Hazell's main defence technique within this interview is to offer almost endless detail about his domesticity. So he vacuums, washes up, cooks, makes the bed, watches TV, cleans the kitchen and lets the dogs out to run around – 'just everyday things I guess'. He makes Tia toast, then a sausage roll – 'she was always eating sausage rolls' – and gives her £10 as payment for helping out in the garden so that she can travel into Croydon and buy her flip-flops. Lying makes greater cognitive demands than telling the truth, and so I have no doubt that what Hazell is doing is stitching together events that had really happened in the past to create a narrative that sounds plausible in the present. At some stage he probably had made Tia toast and sausage rolls, but that was not what had happened on that Friday morning, and nor had Tia gone into Croydon. Indeed, he was caught out in this lie when he had to explain why Tia hadn't taken her mobile phone, her Oyster card or a bag, and Mark even questions whether £10 would have been enough money to undertake the trip and then make her purchase. Nor, as Hazell acknowledges, had any work been done in the garden. However, he clearly believes that the homely, domestic details he presents offer a form of reassurance that he could not be a murderer.

What Hazell is doing is using 'just everyday things' to create a sense of familiarity and presenting himself as just like us – that he is 'fair'. However, this merely takes us back to Freud, and the terrifying and unsettling of the everyday: the *unheimlich*. For Freud, the homely – those everyday things – were also the basis of what was terrifying and repulsive, as we encountered when discussing the sitting room where Edward Evans was murdered. The phrase 'I'd loved her to bits like my own daughter' hints at the foul (and we should remember that he had only recently moved into the house) as Hazell misunderstands who it is that is most likely to abuse a child: someone in their extended family; someone that they trust; someone in their own home. People who do harm to other people are rarely monstrous others but have often been in a relationship with their victims. However, more than anything else, it was Hazell's relentless *unheimlich* 'everyday things' that first made me suspicious of him.

On the opening day of his trial and before he changed his plea to guilty, the court heard how Hazell had repeatedly accessed paedophilic images of prepubescent girls on his mobile phone, and that the police had also found a memory card from one of his cameras hidden on top of a door frame in the house. This memory card included photographs of Tia when she was sleeping and lying naked on the bed at her grandmother's house – most likely after she had been murdered. There was blood visible on the bedding in the photograph and, in the corner, the hand of one her dolls could be seen. Might this have accounted for all the washing, vacuuming and making the bed that Hazell had been at pains to describe? Not so much the daily chores of domesticity but the requirements that come with the need to hide a crime scene. After his arrest and when he was on remand at HMP Belmarsh, Hazell had assured a prison officer: 'It wasn't sexual. I am not a nonce or pervert.' His murder of Tia was absolutely sexual in motivation and he was indeed, in prison argot, 'a nonce' – although he couldn't accept that that was what he had done and who he was. Like Macbeth, who was always searching for a secure identity, Hazell couldn't make sense of who he was and what he had become. In the same discussion with the prison officer at HMP Belmarsh, he concluded, 'I've got no money, no fags, no hope. It's the Hazell curse,' almost as if he too had met three witches on the heath.

*

These three case studies have been concerned with those spaces in our homes that we don't often use, and the means by which we access them – the stairs. These are liminal spaces which are attached to the house but not really part of it; they are the spaces where we hide, store and accumulate; spaces, moreover, that are usually hidden from public view. Their privacy – and what can be hidden there – plays a crucial part in allowing the public self to continue to perform as if nothing is untoward, and so lends weight to the sense that that public persona can be trusted. Not a murderer but a returning hero, a grandfather, a neighbour who would offer help to someone in the street or a lift to a hitch-hiker. However, even if the backdrop to *Macbeth* is the supernatural and kingship, the play asks us to question whether it is truly possible to trust our senses about who people really are, and what their intentions might be. Appearances deceive; things are not as they seem, and so it is always necessary to look more deeply to discover a person's true motivation.

So too with these case studies. Welcoming hosts could have evil intentions; the couple offering you a lift on a cold night were not good Samaritans; supposedly loving families, helpful neighbours or seemingly honest shop assistants were all simply convenient masks to disguise underlying sexual tensions and sadism; and the banality of completing everyday domestic routines could just as easily be used to cover up a murder. Neither Fred and Rose West, Harold Jones nor Stuart Hazell were trying to become king – their lives were firmly rooted in grinding reality, rather than royalty – but just like Macbeth, the vaulting ambitions of their intense desires drove them on and on and on until they eventually committed murder. And, in much the same way that Duncan was mistaken when he thought Macbeth's castle 'a pleasant seat', the houses in these case studies were also not as they seemed. This is most apparent in Cromwell Street, where the Wests' cellar was not only a place where children slept but also a torture chamber. In fact, the whole of 25 Cromwell Street seemed to have been harnessed to facilitate the dark, loathsome, fetishistic world of the Wests – including their back garden.

CHAPTER SIX

The Back Garden

'I believe that all good gardens are as much about
the people that make them as the plants growing
in them. You are an integral part of your garden.
It will not exist without you.'

Monty Don, *Down to Earth*

We have already encountered a number of domestic
gardens and how they were used within the commission or aftermath of a murder. I've described how Peter
Tobin used his back garden in Margate to bury the bodies of
Vicky Hamilton and Dinah McNicol, and how Reg Christie
employed the femur from one of his victims to keep a trellis
from falling down in his London garden. That particular
garden was described by Molly Lefebure in *Murder with a
Difference: The Cases of Haigh and Christie* as being filled with

dark, weedy earth in which proliferated flower-pot shards,
dry sticks and old mutton bones. There was a 'rockery',

which was little more than a collection of broken bricks, and a lawn, which comprised a very small mud patch on which struggled for existence several unkempt tufts of grass. Honeysuckle, jasmine, ramblers and forsythia each spring made further dejected efforts to clamber over the sooty garden walls.

Lefebure wrote this after visiting the garden, and in the full knowledge of what Christie had been doing in 10 Rillington Place. She was aware that the garden had been thoroughly searched by detectives and that the bodies of two young women had been buried there, as well as the gruesome discovery of three bodies in the kitchen alcove and Ethel Christie's body under the floorboards. This perhaps explains why she deliberately uses adjectives such as 'dark', 'unkempt', 'dejected' and 'weedy': she wants us to appreciate the gothic horror of what had been deliberately planted in that space, beyond the honeysuckle, jasmine and forsythia.

The gardens that we have encountered were not tranquil, and the gardeners who created them were not digging to get back to nature, soothe their senses in a busy world or improve their mental health – common reasons offered as to why people love gardening – but had more sinister motives in mind. They might be seen as being the exact opposite of who gardeners are, and what gardening as a hobby can achieve; they are deviant cultivators who give gardens and gardeners a bad name. There is of course a great deal of truth in this, but we should not simply consider gardening as being all about peace, beauty, fragrance, colour, form and verdant order. As a criminologist and an occasional gardener, I know only too well that gardens are really only superficially tranquil. In the spring and summer a Darwinian struggle takes place between those plants that will live and those which will be overcome by weeds; in the autumn and winter plants die; many of our most beautiful plants are poisonous and some, such as white lilies and chrysanthemums, are inextricably linked with death. The Alnwick Garden in Northumbria has a Poison Garden, which is 'filled with around 100 toxic, intoxicating and narcotic plants'. This garden – and there are others like it – is closely guarded and kept behind two black iron gates, and is only open to the public on guided tours, although visitors are 'strictly prohibited from smelling, touching, or tasting any plants'. Even so, some 'still occasionally faint from inhaling toxic fumes while walking in the garden'.

It is important not to overstate the abnormality of an association of gardens with death and even murder, although it is significant that the domestic gardens I have described were all back gardens. The back garden in Britain tends to be less cultivated and formal than a garden at the front of a house. Kate Fox, in *Watching the English*, noted that the back garden is where we are allowed to enjoy ourselves and therefore it is 'often relatively scruffy, or at least utterly bland'. On the other hand, front gardens, if you have one, are for show and display; they are part of the public, exterior face of the house. Back gardens tend to be secluded spaces hidden from the street, although we should also remember that Peter Tobin's back garden was actually overlooked by his neighbours – so perhaps they are not as secluded as we like to think, even if we presume that they are more private and personal and not on show. I suspect that Lefebure's description of Reg Christie's garden could have been applied to hundreds of other back gardens in the area – it was scruffy and private, and it is this privacy that can be exploited by murderers. Indeed John George Haigh – another serial killer who was active at the same time as Christie – wrote to his parents from prison as he awaited his execution, observing that 'leave your car outside in the street without lights and the police will be down on you in a flash, but if you're murdering someone at the bottom of your garden, they'll never discover that'.

What Haigh describes gets to heart of a puzzle inherent in how back gardens are managed by murderers: is their use of these spaces simply instrumental, or are they being harnessed for deeper, more psychological reasons? The instrumental is easy enough to explain. After a murder has been committed the killer needs to dispose of the body of his victim, or the risks of being apprehended increase. Add to this the sight, and especially the unpleasant smell, of a decomposing body, and the motivation for wanting to quickly get rid of it becomes all the more obvious. The killer can also control when he digs the hole to bury the body; so too he has all the tools that he needs at his disposal in the garden shed; and, of course, digging is accepted as being part and parcel of what happens in a garden – it is what you expect a gardener to do. As I've mentioned, Tobin told his neighbour the hole he was digging was for a sandpit for his son, when in truth it would eventually house Vicky and Dinah's bodies. There are greater risks for the killer if he was to wrap the body of his victim up, put it in the boot of his car and move it somewhere else. He could be stopped by the police, and most certainly he would now be caught on CCTV somewhere, which would offer opportunities to uncover his deposition site – as happened with Christopher Kerrell after the murder of his wife Hollie. The back garden is therefore convenient, private, and poses less of a risk than moving the body somewhere else.

Of course, Tobin did move Vicky's body down to Margate in the boot of his car, and his back garden on the south coast could be observed by his neighbours. However, he seems to have taken calculated risks in doing all of this, given that it is likely that he either hid Vicky's body in the attic of his house in Bathgate after he had killed her, or under a crude rockery in the garden and the new tenants would undoubtedly have found her remains if he had left her in one of these spaces. It also suggests the relative development in Tobin's abilities as a killer; like the Wests, he is an outlier, rather than the average murderer.

These all seem like compelling practical reasons to bury your victim in the back garden. But we should also note what Christie said about why he had put his wife's body under the floorboards of their front room: 'I think in my mind I did not want to lose her.' In other words, she was still physically close to him – even if she was now dead – and he also suggested that 'I thought that was the best way to lay her to rest'. We might simply see all of this as pseudo-romantic, self-serving nonsense, as Ethel was not in any formal sense being laid to rest, but the idea of wanting to stay close to your victims is not so illogical if you are motivated by the desire to have power and control over the person, or the people, that you have murdered. Burying their remains in the back garden means that the person is always there – still under the murderer's control – and their graves are a reminder of when the killer had taken their lives. Their bodies function as a form of 'evocative object', such as we encountered in the kitchen, and so become a source of memory, longing and nostalgia. Again we need not think of this as being so divorced from our own realities. I wonder how many people, for example, have buried the bodies of beloved pets in their back gardens.

There's one final psychological motivation for the killer to choose to bury the body of his victim in the garden: it serves to remind him how clever he is; how he has managed to outwit the police, and how he got away with murder. 'Catch me if you can' has been the motto of several killers I have worked with, which is exactly what the police failed to do for many years in Tobin's case. That's why I believe he didn't worry too much about being observed, or questioned by his neighbours about what he was doing. In fact, I get the sense that Tobin rather enjoyed all of that attention; he was fitting in with his neighbours, but standing out from them at the same time. He was cleverer than the lot of them, or so he believed, and each day that went by without his being arrested served as a testament to his ego, guile and cunning. And the longer that state of affairs continued, the greater his sense of invincibility – of being God-like – would have grown.

The case studies in this chapter allow us to see this tension at work, between the instrumental and the psychological in why a killer might choose to bury his victims in the back garden. There are two killer couples: Fred and Rose West, who we met in the previous chapter; and Christopher and Susan Edwards, who shot and murdered Susan's parents, Patricia and William Wycherley, in 1998, and then buried their bodies in the back garden of their semi-detached house at 2 Blenheim Close, Forest Town, Mansfield. The murders of Patricia and William would go undetected for fifteen years. The murders committed by the Wests are well known, and the case involving the Edwards featured in a 2021 TV series, *Landscapers*. My third case study has not had the same level of public attention and concerns Lee Sabine, who murdered her husband John Sabine in 1997 by hitting him over the head with an ornamental stone frog, and eventually buried his body in the communal garden at the retirement home where they lived. Lee was never arrested or charged with John's murder, and the circumstances surrounding his untimely death only came to light after she had died of cancer – John had never even been reported as missing. Given the lack of attention that he received during his lifetime, let's start with John.

*

John Sabine was an accountant who had been injured during the Korean War. He was nursed back to health by a young Welsh woman called Anne, who was training at St Mary's Hospital in Paddington, London. Even though John was married with two children and Anne was eleven years his junior, they started an affair, eventually marrying in 1960. John and Anne would go on to have four children in quick succession, and then they emigrated to Australia and later New Zealand, perhaps to give the children a fresh start. Another child was born after the family had emigrated, making five siblings in total: two boys, Steve and Martin, and three girls – Susan, Jane and Lee-Ann. Steve would later describe his father as a 'good man; a soft-hearted man', but he had nothing good to say about his mother, who in later life used the name Lee (which has sometimes been spelled 'Leigh') rather than Anne. Steve called her 'evil' and a 'conniving bitch – she controlled him [his father], but she loved him to pieces'. It would later emerge that John and Lee had abandoned their children in 1969, while they were living in New Zealand, and all five had been taken into care. Steve remembered that he and his siblings had simply been taken to a budget hotel in Auckland and left there; he described his childhood thereafter as 'miserable'. When the children were young adults they had a brief, tense reconciliation with their parents but that proved to be acrimonious, and very short-lived.

Lee and John invented different reasons to explain why they had abandoned their children. Sometimes it was suggested that John had run into financial difficulties; or, perhaps more honestly, that they got in the way of Lee's ambitions to have a career as a cabaret singer in Australia. However, others would also remember that the couple had been breeding springer spaniels in New Zealand and had been living not too far away from their children in care. It is difficult to be precise about their personal histories as the stories that they told could change depending on the audience. Later, Lee Sabine sometimes claimed to have been a supermodel, and that she had been married to a millionaire. None of this was true. We now also know that Lee herself had been abandoned by her parents when she was a toddler, and that she had been born in Gelli, a mining village just over ten miles away from Beddau, where she and John would eventually settle. In any event, Sabine was a Rhondda girl, rather than an Australian or Kiwi cabaret singer, and she had been brought up by her London-based aunt and uncle, which was how she came to be working at St Mary's Hospital, where her aunt was an assistant matron.

John and Lee returned to England, eventually moving in early 1997 to their retirement home in Beddau. No one seems to have noticed John – they were all too busy being dazzled by Lee – and although he registered with a GP in the town he never picked up his repeat prescription ordered for that April. In all likelihood he was already dead, although sadly he hardly seems to have been missed. If anyone did ask about her husband, Lee Sabine claimed that he had left her (sometimes suggesting that he had beaten her and that he was 'a bastard'), and gone back to Australia. She was described by her neighbours as 'theatrical' – she gave tarot readings, was strong willed and outgoing, and she called everyone that she met 'darling'. In other words, unlike her husband, people noticed Lee Sabine.

In 1998 she removed John's name from the tenancy agreement, but continued to receive his state benefits and army pension. In August 2005, when John would have turned seventy-five and been entitled to a free TV licence, Lee transferred the licence into his name. She was astute enough to continue to benefit financially from her marriage, and also adept at keeping John's murder a secret for nearly two decades, until she herself died of brain cancer in 2015. It was only then that those who had known and cared for her in the Beddau community began to unravel the mystery of the woman that one neighbour remembered as being 'as mad as a box of frogs', and 'a bit like Dame Edna Everage' – the outrageous alter ego of the Australian comedian Barry Humphries. In fact, just like something that Dame Edna might have said, it was a joke that Lee Sabine regularly told to her friends that would start the process of discovering what had actually happened to John, and some rare moments of honesty from her might help us to piece together why Lee killed her husband.

Lee loved gardening, and three years before her death she was interviewed by *RCT Homes* magazine, which promoted the work of the housing association where she lived, about her life and work, and her 'mission' to turn what had once been a small, neglected garden that she shared with three other residents into 'a little piece of paradise'. As she explained:

Coming from New Zealand I've grown up with dirt. I love being outside and I'd rather be mucking around in the garden than sat in front of the television. I do really love living in Beddau and feel part of the community – it's a special place. But when I first arrived sixteen years ago nobody was doing anything with the garden – it looked pathetic and neglected. The neighbours thought that I was mad when I started going out and working on the garden every day – especially as mine was the only flat with no views of the garden. I was doing a lot of digging and it was hard work but I knew I could do something beautiful. This is my property, my home – and I want to feel proud and I wanted my neighbours to feel proud too. The hard work paid off and my neighbours now love the garden. They can all see it from their flats and, because of the seating I have designed, we can sit outside together and catch up. Every summer I host a barbecue and all the neighbours come. It is a ball and it's brought us closer as neighbours. We all appreciate how special the space is and it's really coming together. I've chosen some plants that you would find in New Zealand to bring a little bit of the exotic to Beddau.

To accompany the article, Lee was photographed sitting in the garden. She fixed her gaze directly on the camera, and looked confident and stylish in a blue dress, with a large belt fastened around the waist; her frizzy bleached-blond hair framed her dark eyes. Behind her we can see the flowers that she had planted and also ornaments, as well as garden benches and tables that she had dotted about the space to allow people to sit and take in the beauty of the garden. It really did look like a little paradise, and I could also imagine from how she posed why she had been able to carry off the pretence of a life lived as a performer Down Under. However, even the very first thing she told the reporter from *RCT Homes* was a lie: she had not come from New Zealand and had not grown up with dirt.

Lee also provides other details which in retrospect seem to be important – we might even say that these amount to slips of the tongue in that they offer us a glimpse of the darker side of her personality. Let's think about this further by posing and then answering some questions. Why, for example, had she wanted to renovate the garden, especially when hers was the only flat that had no view of it? She had to do a great deal of work to get the garden into some semblance of order – she had to work on it every day and undertake a lot of digging, as well as buy the plants and ornaments – and so the effort involved in taking on the project seems like quite a liability. That burden of the cost and her labour was clearly something that Lee was prepared to shoulder because, I would suggest, not only did it offer an instrumental way of disposing of John's body, but it also meant that she was still physically close and therefore connected to her husband. Was that why she wanted to have a barbecue in the garden every summer, and invite all of her neighbours? John was at that barbecue too, and while he wasn't exactly participating, or having a 'ball', Lee could assuage her guilt just a little by imaging that at least she hadn't forgotten her husband and the relationship they had once shared. This is also an extreme form of dominance and control, and it seems to me that it was sadism which was the 'exotic' that Lee had brought to her 'little piece of paradise' in Beddau.

We now know that John's body was secreted in the garden, and in 2016 an inquest into the cause of his death concluded that he had been killed by blows to his head – most likely from the ornamental stone frog that Lee Sabine kept in her bedroom. His body had been wrapped in forty-one layers of shopping bags, bin bags and tin foil, and had been placed in a grey package buried under an old wooden frame, and then a baker's tray had been placed on top of the frame. John was still wearing his Marks & Spencer St Michael-branded pyjamas when he was found, which suggests that he had been murdered in his bed, although no forensic evidence was ever found to suggest that the body had been in the house. Something that has never been adequately explained is whether Lee initially stored John's body in the attic of the flat. If this was the case, she would have then needed to have transported his body to the garden – no simple task for one person. This raises the possibility that she may have been given assistance, although if this is the case, and there are rumours of her being in various romantic relationships locally, no verifiable information has ever been offered as to who might have helped her. As far as we can tell, Lee does not seem to have been part of a killer couple; there is no *folie à deux* – literally a madness shared by two – but rather she appears to have acted alone, killed and buried John by herself, and in that respect she is an outlier. Not only a female murderer, but also someone skilled in making her victim disappear.

The major mystery remains: why had she killed John? A neighbour called Valerie Chalkley, who had become friends with Lee when she and John were living in Reading, remembered telephoning and enquiring about John just after they had moved to Wales. 'I've killed him,' replied Lee matter-of-factly, and then described how she had 'battered him with a stone frog which was at the side of the bed. He was just driving me mad. Every night he would get into bed crying and weeping and saying "you don't fancy me".' Valery thought Lee was joking. This extraordinary outburst is in reality a pseudo-confession, as we now know that John was attacked with the stone frog, although we do not need to accept that Lee's motivation was that he had been driving her 'mad' because he was worried that she no longer found him attractive. In fact, this was not the only pseudo-confession that she would make. A hair salon owner in Beddau called Bernadette Adamiec remembered Lee telling her, 'People will talk about me long after I've gone to the extent I could be classed as famous.' When Bernadette asked why, Lee had replied, 'Because of the body in the bag.'

These pseudo-confessions are deliberate; Lee appears desperate to unburden herself and admit the truth, although she was also safe in the knowledge that people just wouldn't believe her because of her 'theatricality' and, ironically, her reputation for being as 'mad as a box of frogs'. In that sense she was hiding in plain sight, and comfortable enough in her disguise to host the annual barbecue. What seems to be less clear is why Lee sought to plant the seed of her post-mortem undoing within a joke that she told, and which was yet another form of confession.

Freud suggested that jokes bring to the surface repressed, unconscious ideas and feelings. They are able to do so only when our conscience – controlled by the 'superego', according to Freud – has been weakened, perhaps through using drugs, or drinking too much. And so it seems to have been the case here. When Lee realised that she had a terminal illness, and was taking some powerful medication, she told her friend and carer Michelle James that there was a medical skeleton hidden in the garden that she had acquired during her student nurse days. She joked that Michelle should retrieve the skeleton after her death and hide it in the attic to scare the next tenants of the flat. After Lee had died, Michelle remembered this, and thought that she would play a joke on her friend Gareth – she'd put the skeleton on her sofa and tell Gareth to come round and meet her new boyfriend. So Michelle and one of her friends dug up the package in the garden, but they quickly realised that this wasn't a medical skeleton at all. 'I saw the sludge inside,' explained Michelle, 'and there was a horrible smell. I just screamed – "There's a dead body; a dead body."' By December 2015 DNA tests revealed that the skeleton was John Sabine, and the following May the inquest concluded that John had been unlawfully killed.

*

It was another joke that would begin the process of uncovering the crimes committed by Fred and Rose West. Their eldest daughter, Heather, had disappeared on 19 June 1987, just a few months before her seventeenth birthday. She had done well at school and achieved eight GCSEs, although Heather had few friends, and had never had a boyfriend. She was also being sexually abused by her father, as she had been for most of her short life – according to one of the many biographers of the Wests, at least since the age of six or seven. Heather had found herself a job cleaning chalets at a holiday camp in Devon, and was determined to take up this opportunity, perhaps as a way of escaping Cromwell Street and the clutches of her father. That clearly frightened Fred and Rose, as they could easily control their children if they were still at home but would have less power over their lives once they had started to become independent. And nor should we forget that by the time Heather went missing, Fred and Rose had already killed at least eight young women, all of whom had been buried in their house and back garden. Letting Heather go to Devon was a risk that the Wests weren't prepared to take, and so Heather 'disappeared'.

The Wests explained Heather's disappearance to her sister and brother – Mae (sometimes her name is spelled May) and Stephen – that she had simply put a few of her things in a bag and then got into a red Mini that was waiting for her in the street. This was, according to West, driven by her lesbian lover, although there has never been any evidence for this suggestion about Heather's sexuality. Then, he explained, the pair had simply set off for Wales. When Stephen and Mae asked why Heather had never got in touch, Fred invented stories that she had become a drug dealer, was involved in credit card fraud, and later that she had become part of an organised crime network. He also sometimes claimed that Heather had been in touch with him, or that he had seen her on his travels. The children were not necessarily taken in by these stories, and Stephen and Mae even got in touch with the TV series *Surprise! Surprise!* in the hope of locating Heather. In fact, she had never left Cromwell Street.

Fred would sometimes joke to his children that Heather 'was buried under the patio', and even that he knew which slab she was buried under – 'three up and nine across'. This sort of joke was typical for a man such as West, who was totally dominated by his base, animalistic instincts and seemed to have no conscience. He behaved as he wanted, with little or no regard for anyone else's feelings – even those of his own children. He therefore told jokes not because he felt the need to repress his unconscious feelings, but because it would simply not have occurred to him that what he said was in poor taste. His humour was therefore different from Lee Sabine's, and his lack of inhibitions meant that the joke about Heather being under the patio was so regularly repeated that it eventually came to the attention of the police. By late February 1994 they had obtained a warrant to search the back garden of 25 Cromwell Street in relation to Heather's disappearance.

The Wests' back garden was long and thin, and mostly covered in concrete slabs. Fred had also, without planning permission, built an extension to the house, as well as a barbecue and a large Wendy house, which doubled as a play area for the younger children, and a tool shed. On 24 February the police went to Cromwell Street to give notice that they would start their excavations. At that stage only Stephen and Rose West were at home, as Fred was out at work. After the police served their search warrant, Stephen immediately contacted his father, but he would only return home around 6 p.m. that evening, even though he was working locally in Stroud, less than half an hour's drive away. Fred West clearly understood the gravity of what was about to happen, and so why did he not return home immediately? Had he gone somewhere else? What had he been doing in the time between Stephen's call and returning to Cromwell Street? I believe that Fred knew that the game was up, and spent that time strategising about how best to manage the coming days, and if it would be possible to limit his culpability.

On 25 February Fred admitted to the police that he had killed Heather, and was arrested. He explained that he had buried his daughter under the patio, near the back door of the house, and agreed to show the police exactly where they would find her remains. He said that he had 'just wanted to shake her, or to take that smile off her face'. He also offered the police an account of their last conversation: 'I said to 'er, now what's this about you leavin' 'ome? You know you're too young. You're a lesbian and there's AIDS and all that. I'm not going to let you go.' This is all self-serving nonsense, and typical of the sort of pseudo-sexual comments and allusions West would make during his police interviews. The question remains, given his lack of conscience, as to why he confessed at this time, and then made the offer to identify exactly where Heather's remains were buried. The obvious conclusion is that this was a way of preventing the police from discovering the remains of Alison Chambers and Shirley Robinson, both of whom had also been buried in the garden – Alison near the bathroom wall, and Shirley (and her unborn child) also close to the back door. West was trying to limit the body count. In fact, he was slightly off in his estimation of where Heather's remains might be found, but they were located the day after his confession, almost directly opposite the family barbecue area. The police, who continued their digging despite West's pleas not to, found the bodies of Alison and Shirley two days later. Some bones from all three bodies were missing, although West never explained what might have happened to them.

When Fred West was taken back to Cromwell Street he did not express remorse for what he had done, but merely complained about the damage that the police had made to his house and garden. He told the bemused detectives that they had better put everything 'back to normal' after they had finished their digging. That's a very revealing phrase: 'back to normal', implying 'as it had been before', and in the past. His house and garden were an extension of his personality, and so to dig up the garden and excavate the cellar was experienced by West as an invasive attack on who he was as an individual, and as a way of destroying him by disrupting history. Neither the house nor the garden would have existed without him; they were his creations – as, of course, were his children. He wanted to maintain power and control over what happened to these creations, and in that sense we can understand why he buried Heather opposite the barbecue area – everything, as he would have seen it, was 'back to normal'. Just as Tobin and Christie had kept their victims close after they had been murdered, and in the same way that Lee Sabine had held her annual barbecue celebrations near to where she had buried John, Heather too was also still under Fred's control, and present at the West family barbecues. She was never allowed to move away, and I wonder if Heather's missing bones were also kept by her father as 'trophies'.

*

The bodies of sixty-three-year-old Patricia Wycherley, known as Pat, and her eighty-five-year-old husband William Wycherley – Bill – were also never allowed to move away from their home. They were found in the back garden of their house in Mansfield on 9 October 2013, although we now know that they had been buried there fifteen years earlier, some time in May 1998. The couple had married in London in 1958, and at that time Pat was pregnant with their only child, a girl that they would call Susan. Number 2 Blenheim Close is an unremarkable, semi-detached house on the corner of a small cul-de-sac in Forest Town, an old mining village that has now been swallowed up by Mansfield's urban sprawl. Pat and Bill had moved there in 1987 and were described as 'reclusive' and as having led a 'quiet life'; they did not socialise and had little contact with their neighbours. It would later emerge that only one neighbour had ever been in their house, Brett Wilson, who had lived next door to the couple between 1990 and 1994. He remembered that they had moved in with an old Yamaha organ:

> It was very annoying because the house had thin walls. I could hear them singing most afternoons and evenings. They were fond of old music hall songs like 'Daisy, Daisy, Give Me Your Answer Do'. Mr Wycherley played the organ and his wife sat next to him. On one occasion I had to go round and politely ask them to turn the organ down. They invited me in and said they were sorry and promised to keep the noise down. They were fine after that.

Brett also remembered that the decor of the house had been 'shabby and yellowed' – perhaps the colour can be explained by the fact that both Pat and Bill smoked – and that the interior was covered in old ornaments, stacks of newspapers, books and bowls of sweets. They didn't drive, and so relied on buses. However, 'they would not stray beyond their own little world', Brett observed – and nor did they after they had died. When any of the neighbours went out into their back gardens, Brett recalled that Pat and Bill would either go back indoors if they too were outside or refuse to venture out. This lack of contact was perhaps why Brett referred to Bill as 'Mr Wycherley' and Pat as 'his wife'. 'They didn't mix; they didn't talk or communicate with anyone . . . you just used to see them moving around behind the net curtains like shadows.' Then, clearly thinking about the picture he had built up of them, Brett also commented, 'They never bothered anyone; they never did harm to anyone,' but added, 'You'd find it extremely difficult to bury two people and not be seen.' However, that's exactly what had happened and, as we've seen, happens more commonly than we like to think. Pat and Bill had been shadows during their lives and unseen after their murders; just like John Sabine, no one noticed they had gone.

Pat and Bill had been shot by their daughter and son-in-law, Susan and Christopher Edwards. At their trial, the judge, Mrs Justice Kathryn Thirwall, in her sentencing remarks described Susan Edwards as a 'liar and a fantasist', making it difficult to be precise about the circumstances in which Pat and Bill died, and the motivation for why the couple had turned to murder. Susan claimed that Bill had sexually abused her as a child, and at one stage maintained that she had visited her parents by herself over the bank holiday weekend in May 1998 and, after she had gone to bed, had been awoken by a loud bang. When she went to investigate, she found her father on the floor of his bedroom and her mother standing over his body holding a revolver. An argument had developed, and boiled over after Pat supposedly told Susan that she had had an affair with her husband Christopher in 1992, and it was this claim that had provoked Susan into shooting her mother. Susan had then left the house and called Christopher. She returned after speaking to her husband, wrapped the bodies of her parents in blankets and stored them under the bed, before returning home to London the next day. The following week, Susan claimed, she went back to Blenheim Close with Christopher and, after eating fish and chips and watching the Eurovision Song Contest, the pair buried the bodies in the garden.

This version of events was not accepted at court, and the judge proposed that Christopher Edwards – a gun club member – was in all likelihood with his wife when his in-laws had been shot, and it was probably him who had pulled the trigger. Four bullets from a .38 revolver had been fired – two each for Pat and Bill. Christopher is also believed to have been the one to have dug the hole where his in-laws were buried. After they had been shot, their bodies were wrapped in blankets and dragged down the stairs. Once outside, they were folded over and bundled into the hole, so that when Pat and Bill were found they were both in the foetal position, one on top of the other. The hole had then been filled with soil, and shrubs planted on top.

'On balance', Mrs Justice Thirwell accepted that Susan had been sexually abused by her father, but she did not conclude that this was what had motived the murders. After all, she reasoned, Susan had left the family home many years before, and had been married since 1983. Throughout most of her marriage to Christopher the couple had been in financial difficulties, and murdering her parents solved that problem. The prosecution made much of the fact that as soon as the bank holiday weekend ended Susan had gone to the Halifax Bank in Mansfield and withdrawn all of the money in her parents' joint bank accounts – nearly £40,000 – and opened another account in her own name and that of her dead mother. She also gave Blenheim Close as the address for any correspondence related to the account. The Edwardses profited from the murders of Pat and Bill by just under £300,000, claiming private and state pensions, industrial injuries benefits, Christmas bonuses and winter fuel payments. They obtained loans and credit cards in Pat and Bill's names, and they would eventually sell 2 Blenheim Close in 2005 for £66,938.

The judge suggested that this financial motivation for the murder of the Wycherleys had been brewing over a long period of time, as a result of a legacy of £10,000 that Susan had received from the second wife of her grandfather when she was twenty-one, in 1979. Susan had spent £5,000 from the inheritance on holidays, and the other half had been used to purchase a home for Pat and Bill in Edgware, London. Her name was on the deeds, but Susan claimed that her parents had then 'emotionally blackmailed' her into signing over her interest to them in 1983. Four years later her parents had sold that property and moved to Blenheim Close, having made a profit from the sale. They did not offer any of that profit to Susan and this, said Mrs Thirwall, had caused a great deal of resentment, and was more likely to have been the motivation for the murders than any historic sexual abuse.

Even so, despite their frauds over some fifteen years, when they were arrested Susan and Christopher Edwards had debts totalling £160,000, and only £17 in their bank account. They did not live a lavish lifestyle, and what they had spent all their money on allows us to glimpse their underlying personalities. It also offers us a way into thinking more about what might have happened to Pat and Bill, and how that differs from the gloomy back-garden fates of Heather West and John Sabine.

The Edwardses were described as 'a completely self-contained couple' and they had few, if any, friends. Apart from his gun club membership, Christopher was interested in military history and memorabilia, and then both he and Susan also become obsessed with collecting Hollywood souvenirs. The couple had signed photographs of Gary Cooper and other mementos of the actor, which had involved them spending just under £15,000; they had stamps featuring Frank Sinatra, and a signed photograph of the singer which had cost £20,000; and they also had other collectibles which at the time of their arrest were valued at £12,000. They were bingeing on Hollywood memorabilia, in much the same way that Ian Brady and Myra Hindley binged on tobacco and wine, and the Wests binged on pornography. Of course, over-spending in this way is a form of financial disorder, and while it is not necessary to understand why the couple had this psychological addiction, it is clear that this indicated that they lived in the 'here and now' – they spent, in other words, with no consideration of the future.

It was their need to live for the moment that explains why

they first killed Bill and Pat, and then buried their bodies in the garden, as opposed to moving them to another location. And to keep on bingeing on memorabilia, the Edwards had to maintain the idea that the Wycherleys were still alive. Susan in particular was adept at keeping up this fiction. She would write to relatives explaining that her parents were 'travelling abroad', or living in Blackpool, and would judiciously send Christmas cards to more intimate family members. Hilary Rose, a niece in Staffordshire, continued to receive Christmas cards until 2009, as did another family member called Vivien Steenson, who remembered correspondence from 'Uncle Bill' for several years after his death. One Christmas card sent by Susan read: 'I enclose a Christmas card for you – on behalf of myself and my parents. As for your note saying your card was returned from Blenheim Close – I am sorry about that, but not to worry. I should explain that – with my father getting elderly and my mother not always in the best of health – they have been travelling around Ireland, because of the good air, off and on for some years.' She also systematically forged signatures so as to keep the benefits of her parents being paid into the account that she had opened in her own and her mother's names, and wrote letters to doctors explaining why her parents didn't want to attend the GP's surgery for winter flu jabs.

The description of the Edwardses as being 'a completely self-contained couple' raises the issue of their living within a *folie à deux* – a description that can equally be applied to Fred and Rose West, and Ian Brady and Myra Hindley. This type of pathological relationship involves a shared psychosis characterised by delusional beliefs, which are then transmitted from one individual to another with whom they have formed a close relationship. Once the *folie à deux* becomes established, this delusional world view becomes fixed and immutable, and then characterises the couple's approach to their lives. Which member of the couple (and we do also see shared psychosis between larger numbers of people) is the dominant partner, and who is subservient? If one hadn't met the other, would they have developed this *folie à deux* at all? Was it Fred or Rose, Brady or Hindley who was dominant?

Sometimes it is difficult to tell, and so too in the case of the Edwardses. Susan might have forged the signatures and sent the Christmas cards, but it was Christopher who is likely to have pulled the trigger and then dug the hole where Pat and Bill were buried. Both seem to have been equally obsessed with spending the money that they had fraudulently acquired on Hollywood memorabilia. From what we now know, Christopher Edwards only seems to have disagreed with his wife on one occasion: the decision to sell the house in 2005, which must have been prompted by some new financial problem in their lives. Given that the sale went ahead, this perhaps confirms that Susan was dominant. Christopher is reported to have said that he was against the sale because it meant 'losing control of the burial site'. 'Control' is an interesting and illuminating word for him to have used, and the phrase 'burial site' is too elegant a description for what was in reality a deposition site. However, it was not the sale of the house that led to their downfall.

The fiction that the Wycherleys were alive only started to unravel when the Department of Work and Pensions made contact in 2013, in the belief that Bill was still alive and about to turn a hundred. This correspondence from the DWP spooked the Edwardses, who fled from their home in London to Lille in France, although their financial worries continued there too. As a consequence Christopher contacted his step-mother in the hope of raising some money, and admitted to her what had happened to Pat and Bill. Rather than lending him any money, Christopher's stepmother contacted the police, and so began the process of uncovering what had actually happened to the Wycherleys. Susan and Christopher Edwards would be found guilty of murder, and each was sen-tenced to a minimum of twenty-five years in prison. Both of their appeals against sentence have been turned down.

*

These three case studies help us to understand the tension at work between the instrumental and the psychological when a killer – or killer couple – decide to use the back garden to bury the bodies of their victim(s). Was it simply a convenient deposition site, or was there something more personal and significant in this choice of location? These case studies also underscore Lee Sabine's status as an outlier.

If, for the moment, we consider the murders of the Wycherleys, John Sabine and Heather West, and ignore the murders of Alison Chambers and Shirley Robinson, there are a number of commonalities about back-garden deposition sites. The first and most significant is control over the access to and use of this site. When Christopher Edwards talked about 'losing control of the burial site', he was identifying a reason why the back garden is important to the perpetrator. It is a private space that others can only enter with permission, and even then in a way that is managed by the killer. There are other advantages too, such as having the tools necessary to dig the hole close to hand, and in the immediate aftermath of the murder the back garden is obviously convenient, as it involves less effort than moving the bodies to another, more distant location. However, we should also remember that Fred West was a jobbing builder, owned a van and was regularly out and about in various parts of the Gloucestershire countryside, where he could easily have disposed of Heather's body. He chose not to, and while similar choices were more limited for Lee Sabine and the Edwardses, they all nonetheless had to move the bodies of their victims from where the murders had taken place – already wrapped in blankets, or bin liners – to the eventual garden deposition site, and then decided to leave them there.

Both Lee Sabine and the Wests regularly used their gardens to socialise, especially at their barbecues. Their back gardens – even remembering that Sabine's was a shared garden, though one over which she exerted proprietary rights – were not off-limits after the burial of their victims, but continued to be used by family and friends. This too seems to be significant. Their murder victims were still under their control, and even if some killers such as Reg Christie might have characterised this deadly presence of a corpse almost in romantic terms, it was a demonstration of power rather than of love. Neither Heather nor John were ever allowed to leave home or escape that control, but were always under the thumb – or at least the foot – of their killer. Nor was there ever any remorse expressed by either Sabine or the Wests. They were not ashamed of what they had done, and their pseudo-confessions and jokes were not prompted by regret or penitence, but by their weakened or non-existent superegos. In fact, both the Wests and Lee

Sabine were happy to offer self-serving justifications for why they had taken the lives of their victims.

This is all slightly different for Susan and Christopher Edwards. Most obviously, they lost control of their back garden by selling the house. This was not what prompted the discovery of the bodies, but after the sale of the house they were clearly at the mercy – or at least the gardening interests – of the new owners. How were they to know whether the new owner might want to completely change the garden, and dig up all the existing plants and shrubs? The decision to sell Pat and Bill's house was in that sense an error, and in all likelihood dictated by the fact that, more than the other killers I have described, the Edwardses lived in the present, rather than thinking about the future. They seem to have been the killers who used the back garden in the most instrumental way, and were prepared to allow their control of that space to pass to other people when the need arose. Nor did they ever socialise in the back garden; there were no barbecues being held near the bodies of Pat and Bill, which might have hinted at more psychological motivations for burying their victims there. To the Edwardses, Pat and Bill were just like a piece of furniture that you leave behind for the new owners of your house, as it won't suit where you are now going to live. However, just like Lee Sabine and Fred West, they were also happy to offer a self-serving justification for why they had committed murder, and obfuscate when the need arose, as opposed to expressing remorse for what they had done.

*

Perhaps what unites these case studies is the status of the victims. No one missed John Sabine after he was killed – he was hardly noticed even when he was alive – and Pat and Bill were 'shadows' behind the net curtains. This latter editorial does not seem to have been made as a *post hoc* justification by their former neighbours to explain away any lack of interest in what had happened to the couple, but an honest assessment of the fact that the Wycherleys liked to keep themselves to themselves. Heather was missed – at least by her siblings – but neither Alison Chambers nor Shirley Robinson was reported as missing. In fact, none of the victims that I have described was ever reported missing, and Fred West, and especially Susan and Christopher Edwards, were adept at first explaining and then maintaining a fiction that their victims were still alive. Brothers and sisters, nieces, cousins, aunts and uncles, GPs, the police, and the various civil servants who administered state and army pensions, winter fuel payments, and the TV licence scheme all had to be kept accepting of a narrative that had been devised to conceal murder. This was yet another means by which Pat and Bill, John and Heather were never allowed to 'leave' the control that was exercised over them by their killers. Even after they were dead and buried, they were still useful and therefore had to be managed.

As I have argued, the Edwardses used the back garden in the most instrumental way, while the Wests and Lee Sabine had other, more psychological motivations. Their gardens – their little paradises – really were extensions of their self and being; they were an integral part of who they were, and so for Fred West an attack on his garden was experienced as a visceral attack on him personally. Our next chapter considers that phenomenon more broadly – when the whole house is viewed as an extension of the identity of the killer, and under his total control.

CHAPTER SEVEN

Whole-House Murders

'Watch out, you might get what you're after
Cool babies, strange but not a stranger
I'm an ordinary guy
Burning down the house.'

Talking Heads, 'Burning Down the House'

When I was a student, I spent a considerable amount of my time living in New York. I loved being in the 'Big Apple', especially as I was able to visit some amazing galleries, theatres and especially CBGB, a club in the East Village where American punk bands performed. It was there that I first saw Talking Heads in 1978, the year after they had released the song 'Psycho Killer'. The band's lead singer, David Byrne, who was born in Scotland, has consistently denied that the lyrics are about David Berkowitz, the New York serial killer better known as 'Son of Sam' who was arrested in August 1977, instead claiming it was inspired by Hitchcock's fictional Norman Bates. However, the timing of Berkowitz's arrest, and the single's release a few months later in December 1977, were enough to persuade me that they were somehow connected. And they have remained so ever since in my imagination – *Qu'est-ce que c'est.*

This wasn't the last time Talking Heads touched on criminal themes. In 2020, Byrne told the *Wall Street Journal* that their 1983 hit 'Burning Down the House' was not about arson. He explained that 'when I wrote the lyrics in 1982, the title phrase was a metaphor for destroying something safe that entrapped you. I envisioned the song as an expression of liberation, to break free from whatever was holding you back.' He went on to say that there were no hidden meanings in the rest of the lyrics – they were not telling a story or signifying anything in particular. Rather, 'I simply combined aphorisms and non-sequiturs that had an emotional connection.'

Given Byrne's comments, it might seem a little unfair to use the chorus from 'Burning Down the House' to peg this chapter. However, if we accept that the song's lyrics were inspired by words, aphorisms and non-sequiturs – in other words, conclusions that do not logically follow from previous statements – there are many reasons why the song is emblematic of what I want to describe. I love that it is about 'an ordinary guy', and even Byrne's clarification that the song was about breaking free and destroying something which was safe is useful in thinking about the case studies I am going to present. Above all, whether intentionally about arson or not, the song perfectly captures what some men do to the houses where they have lived. These are often men who had previously been seen by family, friends and neighbours as ordinary guys, but, for different reasons, they then went on to kill their partner and their children before attempting to take, or succeeding in taking, their own lives. In doing so they destroyed everything that they had helped to create – actions which were non-sequiturs. This annihilation is usually not just about a murder in a specific room, but murders that took place throughout the house. And then, as a final demonstration of their power and control, even the house itself is symbolically murdered too. We have a criminological label for the men (and a few women) who behave in this way: we call them 'family annihilators'.

I first started to study this phenomenon with my colleague Professor Elizabeth Yardley – Liz – at what was then called the Centre for Applied Criminology at Birmingham City University. We were prompted to do so because there had at that time been some high-profile cases of men killing their families and then destroying the house where they had once lived, and we wanted to know how unusual this form of murder might be, and whether or not it was becoming more common. We also wanted to see if the overwhelmingly American criminological and psychological theorising about this type of crime could be applied to what had been happening in the UK. That theorising viewed family annihilation as a subset of mass murder – the killing of four or more victims in a single location during one event – and the family annihilator himself was seen as someone who had had a life that had been characterised by a long history of failure and unhappiness. One American academic further suggested that the men who behaved in this way could be divided into two groups: either 'altruistic' or 'revenge killers'. This first type of family annihilator, the altruistic, believed that the breakdown of the family unit – most commonly as a result of divorce or separation, though sometimes bankruptcy or redundancy – was the 'end of the world', and that killing everyone within the family unit was a way of sparing them future pain and suffering. The second type, the revenge killer, murdered his children because he viewed it as the ultimate way to hurt his partner, or former partner, as they would then have to live with that loss for the rest of their lives.

This binary theorising did not seem to us to capture the diversity of the phenomenon at all, and we found the tacit acceptance that taking the lives of other family members could be in any way altruistic ludicrous. This judgement failed to acknowledge the agency of those who had been killed, and gave priority to the killer's warped and deadly view of the world. Blithely accepting the view of the killer – who would sometimes leave a note, or telephone someone prior to the annihilation – was, we reasoned, a way of silencing his victims after their deaths. We wondered what these victims might have said about what had happened if they had lived, or what surviving members within the extended family made of the annihilator. Was he really just an ordinary guy? Had his life always been patterned by failure and disappointment? Above all, weren't there broader cultural issues about masculinity, the family and the economy that needed to be considered when explaining this phenomenon, beyond speculation about the individual motivation of the annihilator?

We started our research in 2012, and to begin Liz and I used a newspaper search engine to identify cases of family annihilation in Britain since 1980. From then until 2012 we identified seventy-one cases that matched our search criteria, and fifty-nine of those involved male family annihilators. This showed a smaller subset of women who commit family annihilation, although they were not the focus of our attention at this stage – we wanted to concentrate on the majority of men who committed family annihilation. It became clear that this phenomenon was becoming more common, and there have been many other cases since we completed our research. We found only six cases of family annihilation in the 1980s, and reasoned that this couldn't simply have been the result of changes in media reporting over our time frame – after all, this type of murder was newsworthy whether in the 1980s or the present day. We also found that the first decade of the twenty-first century produced nearly half of the cases we uncovered.

We made some surprising findings: family annihilation is most likely to occur on a Sunday in August, during the school holidays; most took place in the home; stabbing, carbon monoxide poisoning, strangulation and arson were the most common ways that the annihilation took place; the majority of the annihilators – more than 70 per cent of our sample – were in their thirties and employed. The range of occupations of the killers was striking: surgeon; doctor; accountant; librarian; marketing executive; postman; soldiers; law enforcement; several lorry and taxi drivers; builders; painters and decorators; and businessmen.

We were also able to suggest primary motivations for most of the annihilations, based on suicide notes that were discussed at the coroner's inquiry, and as Liz and I got closer to more recent cases, newspapers would often report what surviving family members, neighbours, friends and work colleagues said about the killer's motivation. Family break-up was the most commonly reported primary motivation, although this hid a number of different domestic situations, such as the annihilator's anger after the family had already broken up, or alternatively when there was a threat that the family would break up. There were other primary motivations related to financial difficulties which might involve bankruptcy, the threat of bankruptcy or being made redundant, as well as so-called 'honour killings'.

All in all, what we discovered differed markedly from the binary picture of the motivations of family annihilations presented in the North American literature. Most notably, far from the family annihilator being an unhappy and frustrated man whose life had been characterised by a long history of failure, many of the men who killed in this way in Britain had been highly successful and accomplished professionals. We also felt that we could identify a taxonomy – a system of classification – of family annihilators that went beyond the 'revenge' and 'altruistic' categories that had previously been suggested, although we were at pains to point out that what linked all of these killers was their need to exert power and control in situations where they felt that their masculinity was threatened in some way. For them, the role of father, 'bread winner' or 'head of the household' was central to their masculine identity but, in the time leading up to the murders, the family had ceased to perform its masculinity-affirming function.

The taxonomy we devised for male British family annihilators had four categories: self-righteous; disappointed; anomic; and paranoid. The *self-righteous* annihilator sought to blame his partner, or ex-partner, for the annihilation. He had likely been controlling and possessive in their relationship and had a narcissistic personality. That narcissism would play out in the annihilation itself, which was often dramatic – both in relation to the method and what the annihilator would say prior to the murders to family or friends, or in notes or mobile phone messages left behind. We also reasoned that the self-righteous annihilator would take his own life as a way of avoiding being judged by the criminal justice system. The *disappointed* annihilator believed that his family had let him down; that they had failed either actively or passively in fulfilling his vision of what a family should be. As such, he saw the family as an extension of his own needs, desires, hopes and aspirations. The *anomic* annihilator had lost the source of his income, either because he had been sacked, made redundant or declared bankrupt, or was facing the threat of bankruptcy. We suggested that this type of killer has been over-socialised into a belief that consumption determined the quality of our lives and that life itself could be reduced to possessions. Like the self-righteous annihilator, the anomic family annihilator was likely to be narcissistic and his consumption often conspicuous. Finally, the *paranoid* annihilator believed that an external threat – whether real or imagined – such as from social services, who might take his children into care, would destroy his family. In his own mind he saw killing his family as a way of managing that threat and protecting his family.

We found that over half of our sample fell into the self-righteous category – which might be seen as our version of the 'revenge killer'. People like Brian Philcox, a security guard and chairman of the Federation of English Karate Organisations, who picked up his two children – Amy, aged seven, and Owen, who was three – on an agreed access day in June 2008 and drove them to an isolated spot in North Wales. Philcox had been divorced from his wife in May because of his 'violent and controlling personality', and the legal proceedings had been bitter and acrimonious. Philcox claimed that 'she's trying to take me to the cleaners and leave me with nothing – well, I'm not going to let her'. He drugged Amy and Owen with chloroform, and filled the car with carbon monoxide from the exhaust of his Land Rover, texting his wife as this was happening. He also encouraged her to go to his house, where he had left her a note in which he described her as a 'bitch', and had also secreted a booby-trapped bomb. He hoped, in other words, to kill his former partner, although thankfully she did not visit the house.

This precis of the research that I undertook with Liz should provide context for the rest of this chapter. I'll be looking at: the murders of Caneze Riaz and her daughters Sayrah, Sophia, Alisha and Hannah by Mohammed Riaz at their home 61 Tremellen Street, Accrington in November 2006; and the murders of Jill Forster and her daughter Kirstie at their home, Osbaston House, in the village of Maesbrook, Shropshire by Christopher Foster in August 2008.

I am also going to use our findings to see if it can help us to make sense of a third and more controversial case of family annihilation – the 'Clydach murders', which took place at 9 Kelvin Road, Clydach, near Swansea on 27 June 1999. David Morris was convicted for these killings and died in prison in August 2021. However, Morris had always maintained his innocence of the murders of Mandy Power, her two daughters Katie and Emily, and her eighty-year-old mother Doris

Dawson. After these murders the killer set a number of fires in the semi-detached house in what must have been an attempt to destroy evidence. Can our research help to explain the Clydach murders, and did the criminal justice system get this right – no matter Morris's continued pleas of innocence until his death?

*

In 2016, on the tenth anniversary of the murders of Caneze Riaz and her four daughters – Sayrah, Sophia, Alisha and Hannah, all between the ages of three and sixteen – June Khanan, Caneze's mother and the girls' grandmother, told the *Accrington Observer* that she would never be able to forgive her son-in-law, Mohammed Riaz, for their deaths. June's husband, Abdul Khanan, who died in 2003, was Mohammed's uncle and the extended Riaz family lived in north-west Pakistan, close to the Afghanistan border. Mohammed and Caneze had first married in a Muslim ceremony held in Pakistan in 1987, and then married under English law in Accrington in 1992. By that stage the couple had two children, Adam and Sayrah. Video taken at their English wedding ceremony shows Mohammed wearing a Western suit, with a flower in his buttonhole, and he seems to be relaxed and comfortable with the marriage traditions of his adopted homeland. However, this was not to last: he would later be described as 'a strict Muslim' and, according to June Khanan, his refusal to integrate and learn English became more pronounced after the death of his uncle, showing Riaz's desire to become head of the family.

Riaz seems to have been especially angered by Caneze's success as a social worker, and was regarded by her family and friends as being 'jealous of his wife'. Caneze was described as a 'popular community leader', and 'a pillar of the local community' – she was a school governor, and had also helped to set up a support group for Asian women and girls. Riaz, perhaps because of his refusal to learn English, was not well integrated in the community, worked in a plastics factory and earned significantly less than his wife. Prior to her murder, Caneze was openly discussing leaving her husband with her family. Caneze had also made it clear that she would not allow her daughters to have an arranged marriage, and Sayrah had spoken of her ambition to become a fashion designer. Riaz, on the other hand, would have preferred for all of his daughters to wear traditional Asian clothes, and would often dump their jeans in the dustbin. All of this contributed to growing tensions within the family, which had been made worse as a result of their eldest child and only son being diagnosed with terminal cancer in 2006. Adam was being treated in the Christie Hospital in Manchester, but Riaz rarely went to see him as he said that his lack of English made it difficult for him to speak to the doctors, and so Adam's visitors were usually his mother and uncle.

On the night of Wednesday 1 November 2006, Riaz waited until his wife and children had gone to bed, and then sprinkled petrol throughout the house. Lancashire Fire and Rescue later identified three specific 'seats' of the fire – in other words, where it had been started: at the top of the stairs; outside Sayrah's bedroom; and outside Caneze's bedroom, where she was sleeping with three-year-old Hannah. He also seems to have poured petrol onto his wife's bed. Riaz then set the house alight and went downstairs, only to go back upstairs as this was where the fire was burning most strongly – presumably in the hope of committing suicide. Perhaps because the fire had been very carefully planned, a spokesperson for Lancashire Fire and Rescue stated that this was the 'worst fire they had ever seen', and 'I don't know of anything on that scale before or after. It was an inferno in seconds.' Riaz was pulled alive from the blaze, but he had 60 per cent burns to his body and died two days later, without ever regaining consciousness. Caneze and her daughters died of smoke inhalation at the scene and, six weeks later, after the funerals of his mother and his four sisters had taken place, Adam died of cancer.

In trying to work out what might have prompted Riaz to kill his family, a complicated intra-familial picture emerges, with a number of different layers involving culture, illness and jealousy. This was not a 'spur of the moment' crime, but something that had been carefully planned. It is significant that two of the three seats of the fire were outside his wife's and his eldest daughter's bedrooms, as he seems to have harboured his greatest anger for them. More generally, it seems inescapable that Riaz felt disappointed that he had lost control and influence over his family, and that they were no longer prepared to accept the values that he felt were important. He viewed their rejection of these values as reflecting badly on him and who he was as a husband and father, as a man, and as a Muslim. Killing his wife and their children allowed him to regain control of a situation in which he felt that he had become increasingly powerless and shamed. As he would have seen it, his family had let him down – they had disappointed him. Ironically, at his post-mortem, it was discovered that Riaz was suffering from cirrhosis of the liver and was a secret alcoholic. He was a hypocrite, in other words, rather than a 'strict

Muslim', and his public anxiety about his family becoming too Western was merely a cover to hide his own, all-too-common Western vice.

*

Almost exactly two years later, on a bank holiday Monday – 25 August 2008 – Christopher Foster, his wife Jill and their fifteen-year-old daughter Kirstie were attending a friend's barbecue and shooting party in Shropshire. A photograph taken of them at this event shows them happy, relaxed and smiling at the camera. Kirstie, a talented rider who had recently celebrated her birthday and was about to start her GCSEs, turns in her chair to look at the photographer, who is behind her, but her father and mother are facing the camera. They look prosperous, confident and well-groomed; they seem to fit in; they belonged. The Fosters left the party at 8.30 p.m. and drove the fifteen minutes back to their home, Osbaston House in Maesbrook, a village much favoured by what one journalist described as 'self-made millionaires from Wolverhampton and Birmingham'.

The Fosters had bought Osbaston House in 2004 for £1 million, and had then spent more than £200,000 refurbishing the sixteenth-century farmhouse. Foster said to friends that he had bought the property for Kirstie, as she would be safe there – but just to be certain he installed CCTV cameras around the walls of their new home, which was set in several acres of land, with stables for Kirstie's five horses, kennels for their dogs and a garage for two Porches, an Aston Martin and Jill's 4x4.

On their return from the party, Kirstie went upstairs to her bedroom and sent various messages to a friend, before her father switched off the internet at around 11.30 p.m. The house's CCTV captures Foster moving about the grounds at 3.10 a.m. on Tuesday. By that stage, both Jill and Kirstie had been shot dead by Foster – he kept several custom-made guns and rifles in the house – as had the family's four dogs, three of the horses and all of their chickens and the ducks. Foster moved their horsebox into the driveway and shot out the tyres, making it very difficult to move, and almost impossible for any emergency vehicle to get into the house. He then flooded the property with two hundred litres of oil from the tank in the basement, and set the whole house alight. It would take several days and twelve fire crews to put the inferno out, and when they did, they discovered Foster lying beside Jill; he had died of smoke inhalation rather than gunshot wounds.

Foster did not leave a suicide note, but it was quickly established that he was several millions of pounds in debt; had remortgaged Osbaston House on three different occasions; had over twenty different bank accounts – one of which was overdrawn by £300,000; that he didn't have a job or any visible means of support. That Tuesday morning had been the day that the house was going to be repossessed. One of the forensics officers who was among the first to enter the smoking ruins noted that '[Foster] shot the dogs in the head, shot the horses in the head, shot his wife in the head. No distinction is there? It indicates he classes them as all the same.' Kirstie died in exactly the same way too. Foster is almost the perfect paradigm of the anomic family annihilator: his family, like his house, was an indicator of his financial success, and so with his economic failure his wife and daughter became obsolete; they no longer served a function. This may be an accurate conclusion, but it hardly captures everything that needs to be described about this astonishing and appalling case, or explains why people like Foster become family annihilators.

Foster was born in July 1958 and so had celebrated his fiftieth birthday in the month prior to the annihilation. His family came from Lancashire, where his father sold mattresses door-to-door in Blackpool before they moved to Wolverhampton. His roots, in other words, were very different to the world of Osbaston House, and one journalist described him as 'an ordinary bloke from Wolverhampton'. Foster did not excel at school and was often in trouble for fighting; on one occasion he had his nose broken, and his behaviour was troubling enough to result in his appearing in juvenile court. His younger brother Andrew described Foster as 'a bully', and recounted an incident in their childhood when Foster accidentally set him on fire. Then, in 2011, Andrew also revealed to *The Times* that he had been groomed and then sexually abused by his brother:

When I was eleven and Chris was fifteen or sixteen, he told me about the facts of life. This continued on and off and eventually he showed me pornographic magazines with pictures of naked women. After a while he started to sexually abuse me. This would happen at least once a week until I was sexually mature and I told him I wouldn't do what he wanted any more. The abuse was about control and I had to break away from him. He always denied it but there was a pattern in Chris's life and it revolved around controlling other people.

We can now see this pattern of grooming and coercive controlling behaviour that Andrew describes in how Foster treated his family, and these historic teenage behaviours of fire-starting and sexual assault are in themselves important indicators of how Foster would go on to kill. I don't think that we should simply accept that setting his brother alight was an accident, and instead we should see this as further deliberate and calculated behaviour. Foster's parents were aware of their son's attraction to fire to the extent that his father nicknamed him Little Nero. Ironically, it was Foster's invention to put fires out that was to create his fortune.

His first job had been as an apprentice electrician, but he later followed in his father's footsteps and became a salesman. In 1988, while watching news coverage of the Piper Alpha oil platform fire, Foster realised that he could devise a product for fire-proofing oil rig valves, which he then patented as ULVAShield, and set up Ulva Ltd, a Telford-based company through which his product would be sold. His business boomed. It was a busy time – the previous year he married Jill, whom he had met through her sister Anne. Anne didn't like Foster – 'he had a huge ego and was a Mr Know All. I couldn't stand the sight of him and was stunned when Jill fell for him. He was false and flash – and the only person he cared about was himself.' She was not invited to her sister's wedding, at which Andrew was best man, although he has since stated that he never understood why, given what had happened in the past during his childhood. In fact, Andrew was never invited to Osbaston House, and only visited the site in the wake of the annihilation.

With the success of Ulva Ltd the Fosters bought a

five-bedroomed house with an indoor swimming pool in the village of Allscott in Shropshire in 1993. The money also allowed Foster to indulge in his love of cars, motorbikes and shooting, although in Thatcher's Britain it was the house that had become the ultimate symbol of success and prestige. The couple would move to Maesbrook and Osbaston House in 2004, by which stage Ulva Ltd was estimated to be worth more than £10 million. However, the roots of Foster's financial problems were already well established, and by late 2005 he was deeply in debt.

In 2003 Foster had signed a contract with a company called DRC Construction to exclusively manufacture ULVAShield. Perhaps because his spending was already out of control – in the year before the annihilation Foster, for example, spent just under £100,000 on shooting – he found a cheaper manufacturer in the USA. DRC Construction took Foster to court for breach of contract and won their case, though by that time Foster had set up another company and so began to asset-strip Ulva Ltd. In short, he was behaving above the law so as to secure his own financial success, regardless of anyone else. In February 2008 Lord Justice Rimer, at the Royal Courts of Justice, described Foster as 'bereft of the basic instincts of commercial morality – he was not to be trusted', and the bailiffs were hovering. Belinda Feathers, the Fosters' housekeeper, remembered coming to work a few months later, on Friday 22 August, and finding an envelope pinned to the gate of Osbaston House. On it was written 'To be opened only by Christopher Foster', and so she handed the envelope over to her employer. It was a letter from the bailiffs, informing Foster that they would be repossessing the house on Tuesday

26 August – but by then, of course, everything had been destroyed.

In business Foster acted improperly – he couldn't be trusted, and was bereft of the basic instincts of commercial morality – and the same was true of his behaviour towards his family. We can even view his purchase of Osbaston House as not 'for Kirstie', but for himself; his conspicuous consumption and his family were mere proxies for his success, and the stage on which he performed his achievements. Jill and Kirstie, in other words, were props in Foster's performance; he seems to have loved them, but more as possessions that he owned, in the same way that he owned his cars and guns. As a result, Osbaston House appears more like a prison than a home that was safe and secure, as the walls, fences and CCTV cameras could keep the occupants inside just as easily as they might deter others – like his brother Andrew – from entering. The home was a place where Foster felt in control and where he could dominate, and that domination would ultimately be expressed through annihilation. Of course, by taking his own life Foster also ensured that he would never be judged by the criminal justice system, and nor would he ever again be just 'an ordinary bloke from Wolverhampton'.

Despite being different types of family annihilator, there are nonetheless a number of issues that connect Riaz and Foster. In particular the murders they committed did not take place on the spur of the moment; neither of them had simply 'snapped'. These murders were well planned and carefully controlled, and were motivated not just as a result of the individual pathology of the perpetrator but also by the cultures and environments in which they took place. Arson was also central to each of these murders – as a way both to kill and to destroy the houses in which the annihilations had taken place. Both murders were dramatic, perhaps even theatrical; they seemed to make a point, which is of course how they came to public attention. Foster committed suicide and Riaz attempted to. Taking their own lives, or planning to do so, must be seen as a deliberate form of behaviour that served their purpose. Most obviously, suicide (or intended suicide) prevented them from being judged and held accountable by the formal processes of the criminal justice system, and it also prevented information coming into the public domain via a trial. This is yet another form of the coercive and controlling behaviour which they had demonstrated in other aspects of their lives. Foster did have control over his family, whereas Riaz wanted to exert it within a situation in which he felt increasingly out of control and powerless. In addition, the house was the symbolic site that held meaning for both of these annihilators, which was why it had to be murdered too. Might all of this allow us to make sense of another set of dramatic murders, where arson in an attempt to destroy the house was also central to how events unfolded, and which saw four people from the same family lose their lives?

*

The murders of Mandy Power, her daughters Katie (ten) and Emily (eight), and her eighty-year-old disabled mother Doris Dawson, who all lived together at 9 Kelvin Road, Clydach, near Swansea, on Saturday 26 and Sunday 27 June 1999 are notorious, largely because of the conviction of David Morris for these deaths – crimes for which he always maintained his innocence. The Clydach murders, as they became known, have been the subject of a book, *The Clydach Murders: A Miscarriage of Justice* by former solicitor John Morris; a much more sober BBC Wales documentary, *The Clydach Murders: Beyond Reasonable Doubt*, which uncovered two new potential witnesses; a Sky documentary series in 2022 called *Murder in the Valleys: The Case for and against David Morris's Conviction*, which interviewed some of the key participants; and various online websites and petitions. The conviction of Morris and a belief that there had been a miscarriage of justice also became the focus of a determined campaign by the University of Winchester's Crime and Justice Research Centre. As recently as January 2021, South Wales Police announced an independent review of some aspects of the case, although that is now too late for Morris, who died at HMP Long Lartin in August 2021, still maintaining his innocence. At the time of the murders there was no usable DNA or fingerprint evidence to connect him to the crime scene, and no witnesses to place him in Kelvin Road, although he had been in a sexual relationship with Mandy. Morris was convicted twice for the murders, in 2002 and 2006, although the need for two trials is yet another feature of the notoriety of the case.

These murders remain notorious because in many ways they are outliers, and thankfully it is still rare for four people to be murdered in the same location during the same event in this country. However, even characterising the Clydach murders in this way is fraught with difficulties: should we label what happened as mass murder, or more specifically as a family annihilation? These difficulties are not eased by the fact that one of the first suspects – long before David Morris became the focus of the investigation – was a woman called

Alison Lewis, a former South Wales Police officer, who had left the force because of PTSD, had previously attempted suicide and, in the aftermath of the murders and while under intense public scrutiny, had to spend ten days in a psychiatric unit. She had been in a lesbian relationship with Mandy for several months prior to the murders, and gave evidence at Morris's 2002 trial of the 'intense' relationship that had developed between her and Mandy after they had first met in November 1998. She also had to face questions from Morris's defence barrister accusing her of the murders.

At the time of the murders Alison was still married to Stephen Lewis, a serving officer in the South Wales Police, who had a twin brother called Stuart, who was an acting inspector on the force. Indeed, Stuart was on duty the night the murders took place and attended Kelvin Road on his own after the murders had been reported, but left after only ten minutes without preserving the crime scene, and his log book for that night went missing. All three were arrested in July 2000 – Alison and Stephen on suspicion of murder, and Stuart on suspicion of perverting the course of justice. However, no charges were ever brought, and all three were ruled out as suspects in January 2001. In response to the BBC Wales documentary, which was first broadcast in October 2020, Alison, Stephen and Stuart all vigorously maintained their innocence, and reiterated their belief that Morris was guilty. Alison and Stuart would later appear in the Sky documentary series – again maintaining their innocence, and describing the impact of the murders on their lives. They were clearly aware that many of the questions hanging over Morris's conviction had still not gone away.

Within the murders themselves there were a number of bizarre pieces of post-mortem staging behaviour by the killer: Mandy's body was washed, a watch was placed on her wrist and her killer inserted a vibrator into her vagina; Doris had had her hands wrapped in newspapers and magazines, and these were then placed at either side of her body and set alight; Mandy's denim skirt was found downstairs, although all of her other clothing was upstairs; pictures of Katie and Emily were found on a table downstairs, and it is clear that the killer had tried to burn these photographs and the table on which they lay, but they had failed to ignite properly; and, finally, the killer set a number of different fires in the house at different times, although all four victims died of blunt force trauma from blows to their heads by a metal pole – which may have been a martial arts weapon that was kept in the house for protection.

There is evidence of escalation as Doris, who is believed to be the first of the four to have died, had been murdered by receiving five or six blows to the head, while there were twenty-two blows on Mandy's body, and she may also have been strangled. This is a clear indication of 'overkill' – the technical term that is used to describe violence which is beyond that needed to achieve the killer's objective – and which therefore suggests that it was Mandy who was the main target. From evidence collected by the police, how the killer got into the house, and the fact that they fixed a fuse, suggests they were familiar with the layout of the house. After the murders, the killer remained in the house for a number of hours. Taken as a whole, the motive would appear to have been about sadistic pleasure – a motivation which is a common theme in family annihilation.

I want to focus here on the previously mentioned post-mortem staging behaviours – and specifically the presentation of Mandy's body and the killer's behaviour towards Doris. Above all, what interests me in relation to this chapter is how the perpetrator set a number of fires, which appear to have been an attempt to burn the whole house down. The house seems to have held symbolic importance for the killer – it was not just the site of the murders, but a place in itself that acted as a constant reminder of what their relationship had once been, or which he still wanted it to be and therefore it needed to be destroyed.

This latter feature is a crucial difference between the Clydach murders and, for example, the murders at White House Farm in August 1985, when five people were killed in one incident within the same location and so offers a good comparison. The White House Farm murders also involved a number of staging behaviours and the convicted killer, Jeremy Bamber, has consistently maintained that he did not commit the crimes. However, in that family annihilation there was no attempt to symbolically murder the house too – White House Farm clearly retained value for the killer; it was in his interests to ensure that the house 'survived'.

I want to start by looking at why Morris really was – and remains – a credible perpetrator, before going on to analyse whether the evidence is consistent with Morris as a perpetrator. However, I should make it clear that I have not been privy to all the information that I would need to establish definitively Morris's guilt or innocence, nor have I been able to discuss these murders with any of the detectives who worked the case. These are important qualifications in relation to my criminological analysis, and I would also reiterate that Morris was found guilty of these murders on two separate occasions.

David Morris was a petty offender who had also been convicted of violent offences, and on the night that the murders took place he was high on a cocktail of drugs and alcohol. He knew Mandy Power, had been to her home in Kelvin Road on a number of occasions, and knew where he could find a key to enter the house. In fact, Morris had been in an on-off sexual relationship with Mandy behind his girlfriend's back, and the jury accepted that the motivation for the murder was that he had turned up at Kelvin Road wanting to have sex, but Mandy had refused. When he was first interviewed by the police Morris denied that he was in a sexual relationship with Mandy, and he also told a lie that would come back to haunt him: he stated that a broken, bloodstained gold chain found at the property did not belong to him. He said to the police that 'on the lives of my children' the chain wasn't his, only admitting the truth just days before his original trial. Morris explained the chain's presence by claiming that he and Mandy had had sex on the day before the murders, and that he had left it in the kitchen. After the murders he had gone to great lengths to buy an identical chain in an effort to deflect attention away from the one that had been found at Kelvin Road.

In summary: Morris knew the house and was in a clandestine relationship with Mandy – a fact that he wanted to hide from his then girlfriend. He lied about the gold chain before admitting that it was his, and on the night of the murders was intoxicated by drink and drugs, which might explain some of the unusual features at the crime scene. Morris had a history of petty offending, and had in the past also used violence. All of these factors make him someone that the police would have wanted to investigate, if only to rule him out of their enquiries. However, no DNA or any other form of forensic evidence connecting him to the murders was recovered from the house that was usable at that time, although in the weeks after he died the police released a statement that a bloodstained sock found at the murder scene did belong to Morris – a claim that was in turn dismissed by his family as 'nonsense'. However, Morris does not seem to have changed his behaviour in the days after the murders. There are no reports of his acting strangely, or in a disinhibited fashion, which would be the sort of behaviour that we would expect from someone who had committed this type of crime – even someone who might have killed whilst high on drink or drugs. In fact, he only seems to have come to the police's attention two years after the killings, when an off-duty police officer overheard a conversation about Morris having been in a relationship with Mandy. With all of this in mind, might it be possible to connect Morris to the murders through an analysis of the killer's post-mortem staging behaviours?

Murderers normally attempt to leave the scene of their crime(s) as quickly as possible, as this not only reduces their chances of being caught but also because people tend not to want to be near dead bodies. Staying in Kelvin Road for several hours after four murders had taken place is unusual behaviour, and offers an insight into the thinking of the perpetrator. I suggest that we can see the decision to remain in the house as a form of psychological reversal – the killer has achieved his original objective in that Mandy was dead, but he was now going through a process of self-sabotage to undermine what he had done. We can see the staging behaviours as creating a narrative – of telling a story – about what had taken place, and why the killer had wanted to take Mandy's life. So, we might read the washing of her body as an attempt to destroy any forensic evidence that would connect the murder to Morris and, if the motivation was to have had sex, we should remember that no semen was ever found at the crime scene, although it is possible that he had used a condom and took that with him when he left the house. The insertion of the vibrator into Mandy's vagina could be read as an angry man's revenge on her lesbian lover, and in this scenario placing the watch, which had been Alison Lewis's gift to Mandy on Valentine's Day, on her wrist can be interpreted as a way of implicating her for the crimes, deflecting attention away from Morris.

All of this seems logical enough, although I am not convinced that this is the only, or the best, way to analyse what happened post mortem. There are a number of different ways to understand all of this, and the criminological analysis that I have offered above does not account for the staging behaviours connected to the other murders in Kelvin Road. Why would Morris murder Doris, and why attempt to set her body alight? Why would he have wanted to have killed the two children? Of course this might be explained instrumentally. Given that the children could identify the culprit, they could have been killed to ensure their silence. However, why then attempt to set fire to their photographs? This is a very unusual behaviour in an already confused crime scene, especially as the pictures weren't kept on the table on which they were found, but instead moved there by the perpetrator. The photographs were not torn or defaced, and the frames were intact. The attempt to set the table on fire – which would have destroyed the photographs – was unsuccessful, which, unlike with Christopher Foster and Mohammed Riaz, perhaps suggests the killer's lack of understanding about how to set fires. It seems logical to conclude that burning the photographs of the children transcends the instrumental and can instead be seen as part of the killer's underlying need to destroy not just Mandy but the whole family and the house itself, making it a symbolic manifestation of what he was trying to achieve. His goal was to destroy everything and everyone, and so burning down the house and killing Doris, Katie and Emily was not a form of 'collateral damage' in the murder of Mandy, but something deliberate and planned.

It is difficult to see how all of this fits with what we know about Morris on the night of the murders, and the circumstances surrounding his relationship with Mandy and the rest of her family. He may well have been angry, drunk and high – or a combination of them all – and he can plausibly be described as being out of control and not thinking through his actions. However, that would not explain why, after committing the murders, he would then spend several hours posing his victims and staging the crime scene. He can't be both out of control *and* carefully deflecting the police's attention onto another suspect. It would make more sense to see these behaviours as those of someone intent on committing family annihilation, and if that is the case we would also expect the perpetrator – if he survived – to be in a hyper-emotional state after having committed the crimes.

At his trial the prosecution alleged that Morris's motivation for murdering Mandy was that he had wanted to have sex with her and that he had become enraged when she refused. However this does not really explain why he also felt the need to murder Doris and the two children. We might accept that the primary target had been Mandy, but if the killer had always intended to commit family annihilation then everyone in the household had to die. There is also a potential clue to the killer's state of mind hidden among the magazines that Doris's hands were wrapped in; a headline on one read 'Deborah looked at the bloody body; was a mother dead because of a fleeting affair?' (It has not been possible to establish who this 'Deborah' actually was and what the headline might have been referring to.) Might we interpret this as being more than coincidental? It is possible to read this and conclude that those words perfectly capture a potential motivation for murdering Mandy: it is a punishment for an affair and it was known that she had in the past taken several lovers in the town.

And, as I am suggesting, if this was a family annihilation, where would it fit on the taxonomy that I identified with my colleague Liz Yardley? It seems to me that the evidence at the scene of the crime suggests that the Clydach murders are about disappointment, although of a different kind from that at the heart of the Riaz case. In Accrington, the disappointment was about the Western values that had come to characterise the family, and the corresponding feeling of powerlessness that Mohammed Riaz felt in trying to impose his will on his wife and children. Taking their lives and then his own was a way of regaining his power over them. In Clydach and taking into account only what the crime scene tells us, the disappointment might better be characterised as the feeling of powerlessness that comes when someone who believes they are, or were, in a relationship discovers that their hopes and aspirations for the relationship are no longer, or perhaps never were, reciprocated. The way to resolve that emotional conflict, and to regain control is for the family annihilator to take everyone's life, and then their own.

Here it is important to re-emphasise that I have not been privy to all the information that I would need to access in order to 'prove' David Morris's guilt or innocence. I should also re-state that Morris was found guilty on two different occasions and, even though his barrister twice sought to per-suade a jury that there was a reasonable doubt as to his guilt by trying to build a case against Alison Lewis, she was never charged with these murders, and has consistently denied any part in what happened. Indeed, as part of the Sky documen-tary series about the murders, Alison spoke of how she was not a murderer and that 'all I wanted to do was love Mandy' and that 'there hasn't been a day when I haven't missed her. I loved being with her and everything about her made me happy.' So all that I am attempting here is to offer a reading of the stag-ing behaviours that we see within the Clydach murders and how, for me, they relate to the phenomenon of family annihi-lation – something that does not seem to be consistent with the behaviour of David Morris on the night of the murders, and his subsequent behaviour in the community. He may well have been a liar and a petty offender who had in the past used violence, but he does not seem to me to be the person who committed the Clydach murders, despite his two convictions.

*

I've been concerned in this chapter with murders that take place in different rooms of the same house, during one killing incident – even if this event might last for several hours. The house itself is then symbolically murdered, and in the case studies I chose all of the perpetrators used arson to achieve that end. However, other family annihilators have employed explosives, bulldozers and even a crane. The post-annihilation behaviour of the killer is important: the family annihilator will always commit suicide or attempt to do so, and it is that behaviour which creates a difference between this criminological phenomenon and mass murder. Whether *anomic*, *disappointed*, *paranoid* or *self-righteous*, none of these annihilators simply 'snapped'. What happened was the result of planning, their personal history within the family, how they gave meaning to the idea of family, the significance to them of the home in which they lived, and more broadly the culture and community in which the annihilation took place.

I now want to use these ideas about family annihilators and 'whole-house' murders to think further about the room-specific murders I have described, as a way of bringing some conclusion as to why the home should be the primary site of murder in this country. However, I can only draw some of the contours of such a conclusion because murder as a more general phenomenon is always built up of unique cases, which makes it impossible to show the fine detail in every example. So my conclusion has to be partial rather than definitive, but it is offered in the spirit of a builder digging the foundations of a house, rather than an expensive architect showing you the grand plans for a structure that might or might not get planning permission, and so may never actually see the light of day. To begin, let's revisit the family annihilators, as they really do exhibit some of the more extreme examples of several common trends that are possible to discern in the room-specific cases I have presented.

It is very obvious that the family annihilator viewed his house as an extension of his being. It was a visible manifestation of his self, his values and tastes, and therefore also the primary site where he could perform who he was, or would prefer to be. The symbolic function of the house for this type of murderer carries a number of different, often competing, meanings. It could be a sanctuary, a place that was safe and cut off from the external world – which is what Christopher Foster claimed was the motivation for buying Osbaston House – but it could just as easily be a prison that shaped the behaviour of those who lived there. It might also be a site of punishment, a place from which people would want to escape, rather than want to return to. For some family annihilators, the house became a constant reminder that they had failed or had been disappointed in what they had once wanted from life – and from their family. The meanings therefore that they attached to these houses are significant, for those meanings could facilitate an atmosphere of tolerance, nurturing and loving, or instead create the conditions which, in extreme circumstances, would produce violence and sometimes lead to murder.

These meanings are not just fixed to whole houses but can also become attached to specific rooms. Kitchens, bedrooms, dining rooms, the places where we sit and socialise, and even the humble door, doorstep and back garden are also all invested with a historic, cultural and personal significance. In short, these spaces are filled with a history of what happens there – not just in the lives of the individual, couple or family who live there at that moment in time, but more broadly and stretching back over the centuries. It might be a new show home, as opposed to a Victorian villa, or shared, rented accommodation, but these spaces have been constructed (or reconstructed) to reflect how people live their lives, within rooms that come to constitute what it is that is called a home. Our lives are then performed within these rooms for good or for ill, with all the messy, complicated inconsistency, tension, hope, love and despair that goes hand in glove with what it means to be human. If 'I' exist inside my body – in my brain and heart, and shaped by a genetic inheritance that goes back to my parents and grandparents – that 'I' then lives in a home, which also has a history of adaptation, change, evolution, secrecy and tension. It is a place where 'I' can be born, live, love and, in some circumstances, die.

These meanings might be acknowledged, underappreciated or even ignored, but they are nonetheless what gives shape to how we live, and whether that life will be happy or troubled. Sometimes these spaces, and what they might mean to the people who occupy them, will first facilitate and can even go on to characterise the violence that takes place there and, occasionally, as I have suggested, that violence will turn to murder. This takes us back to the old criminological chestnut of 'nature versus nurture'. Does someone commit a crime because the roots of violence are already in their genes, or is their criminality more to do with how they've been brought up, the relationships that they have with their parents and the people that they've been socialised with? Is it the house, a room in the house or the people who are living there that 'cause' the crime? Throughout my career I've always answered the 'nature v nurture' question by saying it is neither one nor the other, but a messy combination of the two, and that any combination would be unique to the individual. To me, that answer seems to work just as well here too, thinking about the houses and rooms that we encountered where a murder had taken place. These houses and rooms only become spoiled and guilty spaces when they were used by an individual who was motivated to do harm. However, this conclusion should offer to us only a limited consolation. The significance and power – including the guilt – of these spaces is already there, lying dormant beneath the floorboards, having seeped into the walls and beams, and stained the ceiling and the carpets. It might lie dormant, perhaps masked by the new sofa or a kitchen table, but it is always ready to bubble to the surface and make a nuisance of itself when the occasion is demanded by someone with murder on their mind. In doing so, the red-olent history of these spaces re-emerges and helps to create a 'house of horror', or a 'monster mansion'.

This might seem like too bleak and totalising a conclusion about the place which we have come to call our home, but it is one that I think can be sustained not only by the evidence that emerges from the stories of family annihilators but also from the room-specific murderers I have described. After all, as I have drawn attention to, it is not the street, an unlit park, a pub or a nightclub that is the primary site of murder in this country, but the home. This stubborn reality needs to be explained rather than brushed under the carpet, and the case studies I have presented offer a way of beginning to understand how and why this should be the case. These examples of murders, and the guilty domestic spaces where they occurred, allow us to really see inside the home and actually view how people live and die in those spaces – spaces that have already been saturated in the accumulated cultures of living rooms, kitchens and bedrooms. Of course, 'real life' within these rooms seems a million miles away from the sanitised, pristine photographs we see of house interiors, which purport to tell us all about houses, interiors, decor, and how we exist as individuals, as a couple or as a family. Indeed, what interests me about those images, in magazines or online, is their inauthenticity. Look for yourself at the remarkable absence of scuffs on the paintwork or stains on the wallpaper. Nor is there ever mess on the sofas and chairs – no discarded bags and coats, or stubborn dog hair that refuses to be sucked up by the vacuum – or abandoned shoes on the rugs and carpets. I have yet to encounter a photograph in these magazines where the bathroom includes a shaving kit, or where there are dirty plates mounting relentlessly one on top of the other in the kitchen sink. Ironically, it is murder that would therefore seem to expose how and where we really live when the front door is closed, and the curtains are drawn.

Social media also presents us with idealised images of the home and the people who live there, and, with some honourable exceptions, the same holds true for TV and cinema, where a domestic setting is rarely the site for the action if the drama is about a murder. It's far more common for stories about violence and murder to be set out on the streets, in a pub or in some other shared space far away from the routines of domesticity and life at home. It's now almost a cliché to have these dramas begin with a lone woman walking down an unlit alley – it's out there, in that sort of space, that the woman is in real danger, and as the audience we long for her to make it home, where she will be 'safe'.

Perhaps it is these idealised images that have blinded us to the more depressing, criminological reality of the home. Magazines, social media, cinema and TV sell us a romanticised, faultless, but ultimately unrealistic picture of where and how we live. But let's be honest with each other: we already knew that. What emerges from these murder stories is that we collectively choose not to acknowledge that reality – we know, but we pretend not to, and soon we come to convince ourselves that we actually don't know after all. It's a game that we play with ourselves, with our friends and family, over and over again in all kinds of different interpersonal situations, and in more cultural ways too – including our knowledge about murder. Playing that game allows us to be shocked, when in fact we knew all along what the outcome would be, and so we had no right to be surprised at all.

I think that's why Freud's *unheimlich* – the unhomely, the uncanny – still has relevance. We are not really scared of the alien 'other', but have always been fearful of those ordinary things in the everyday spaces that surround us, and the danger that we have conveniently chosen to 'forget' by storing that knowledge in our subconscious. Yet those unhomely things have played just as important a role in making us who we are, as much as everything else that we choose to acknowledge about ourselves and the culture in which we live – including the place we call home. They also help to explain the violence in our lives much more clearly than thinking about an evil, fantastic 'other' that exists out there, somewhere else, and not within the home where we have dinner, socialise with our friends, sleep with our partners and live with our family. Yet as W. H. Auden says, evil is always unspectacular because it shares our bed and eats at our table, and surely that's the message that emerges from thinking about murder in the way that I have outlined. Evil doesn't need to be invited to come into our home, because it's already there.

I've used a few age-old phrases that we associate with our homes – there's no place like it, for example, or that it's 'where the heart is', that home is 'sweet home', but I could equally have suggested that the best journey that we can make is always 'to come home'. So too we might want to grumble about the jingoism associated with the common-law proverb that 'an Englishman's home is his castle', but even so it does still highlight the centrality of the domestic in British life, what it is that makes us this way and the basis of the stories that we like to tell each other about ourselves. It was this very idea that Orwell employed in 'Decline of the English Murder'. And, of course, the phrase is also sexist – there's a gender in that Englishman. Perhaps it is no surprise that most of the murders that I have described were committed by men, although that gets us only so far. I've also mentioned some women who committed murder, and many men who were the victims of other men in the home that they shared. Thankfully, most men do not kill. That having been said, this should not deflect us from calling out the toxic nature of how some men perform masculinity – a performance that can sometimes lead to murder in the very space where we are all supposed to be safe.

So home is often not 'sweet', but troubled and problematic. And here's my take-home message. We will never deal with that reality culturally, legally or criminologically until we give up our pleasant domestic fantasies and begin to address why it is that where we live is the most likely place where we will be killed, and therefore start the process of having a long, hard conversation with ourselves. And what should that conversation be about and where should we begin? Let's start with domesticity, misogyny, masculinity – toxic and otherwise – and with the centuries of accumulated routines, responsibilities and cultures that have come to be attached to the rooms in the place that we call our home, and which all too often can lead to death.

The answer really has always been staring us in the face.

And Afterwards?

'I once had a barbecue at Dennis Nilsen's house.'

Rhiannon Evans, 'How Much Does a Gruesome
Murder Affect the Price of a House?', *Vice UK*,
28 April 2015

April Jones was a five-year-old girl who disappeared from outside of her home on the Bryn-Y-Gog estate in Machynlleth, Powys on 1 October 2012, after having been seen by her friend getting into a Land Rover driven by a man. There did not appear to have been a struggle; April seemed to be willing to get into the vehicle. The following day, Mark Bridger, a local man with a string of offences, was arrested in connection with April's disappearance, and three days later he was charged with her abduction and murder; it would later emerge that he was known to the Jones family. On 30 May 2013 Bridger was found guilty and sentenced to life imprisonment, with the trial judge ordering that he should never be released from prison. During the trial Bridger, who was found to have downloaded indecent images of children, claimed that he had run April over with his car, but he couldn't remember what had then happened to her – such was his panic, and the fact that he had been drinking so much alcohol. However, forensic evidence found April's blood in Bridger's rented cottage, which was called Mount Pleasant, in the nearby village of Ceinws, and fragments of human bone consistent with a 'younger individual' – believed to be pieces of April's skull – in the cottage's fireplace. It is likely that Bridger sexually assaulted and then murdered April in the cottage, dismembered her and disposed of the bulk of her remains in the surrounding countryside.

Bridger's conviction – and his whole-life tariff – might be seen to offer closure to the case. However, that was only the formal, criminal-justice ending to this awful story, and there are a number of other issues to consider. April's body was never recovered, for example, and what should be done about the cottage where she had been killed? Should that have been left standing, or destroyed like the Wests' house in Cromwell Street? With no body, the Jones family could not have a proper burial for their daughter, and Bridger's rented cottage was, according to April's father Paul, 'a constant reminder of the tragic events'. Coral Jones, April's mother, commented that 'even driving on the main road near the village is difficult. You go past and your head ultimately turns to that house. It brings back horrible memories of what happened. It was a dreadful thing that happened there.' Both Paul and Coral appealed to the Welsh government to buy the cottage, which was worth about £150,000, and then have it destroyed. The

Senedd agreed to their request and in November 2014 the process of demolition began. Paul and Coral, accompanied by April's older siblings, watched on as a digger smashed Mount Pleasant to pieces, and April's father described his thoughts to a local newspaper:

Having this house demolished is symbolic. It's a sort of closure; the end of a chapter. All the time it has been here, its existence plays in the back of your mind. Even when you are not thinking about it, it's there in the back of your mind.

However, even after the cottage had been razed Coral concluded 'it will not be a final closure', and that coming back to witness Mount Pleasant being destroyed had 'really opened a wound'. Her comments suggest that there can never really be closure after a murder, only different ways of coming to terms with the grief that will be unique to each family.

How the Jones family reacted to the house where their daughter had been murdered raises a number of more general questions about what should happen to the properties where murders have taken place. Should they be demolished, or is that too impractical, as it was with the mid-terraced house in Margate where Peter Tobin buried two young women in the back garden? What if the murder takes place in a flat in a block of flats, such as where Gulistan Subasi was murdered? In April's case the Welsh government were willing to buy the cottage and Gloucester City Council also compulsory purchased 25 Cromwell Street so that they could obliterate every last trace of where so many young women lost their lives. However, is that really a viable option for every house or flat where there has been a single murder, or even in houses where there has been a spate of murders? Is there some empirical formula that might be established, which could be used to determine what should happen to a house where there has been a murder?

Of the forty-some houses and flats that appear in this book, the vast majority have been left intact and, even if we were to exclude those murders which took place on the doorstep – and so the interior of the house was never tainted by the murder – the majority are not only still standing, but are also occupied. Only four houses are no longer in existence, with those in London disappearing as a consequence of more general urban development. In any event, is erasure really enough to establish closure about a property where a murder has taken place? It would seem not, if we accept what Coral Jones describes.

Osbaston House in Maesbrook was destroyed as part of the family annihilation committed by Christopher Foster. In that sense, he seemed to have created his own form of closure. But what about the land on which the house had been built? Kevin Gorski bought the site in 2014 but in 2020 claimed that the 'murder mansion plot' was a 'death trap', and 'it's like there's a curse on the land'. The property that he is trying to build on the ashes of Osbaston House has been beset with problems, and Kevin feared the structure that had been erected would fall down at any moment. The two other properties that I have described that were part of a family annihilation – 61 Tremellon Road in Accrington and 9 Kelvin Road in Clydach – are both still standing and, as far as I am aware, have now been re-inhabited.

There's an interesting clue in what happened to Osbaston

House's plot that helps us to understand why many people might be prepared to live in a house where a murder has taken place. They are cheap to buy or rent. Most, especially in the immediate aftermath of a murder, can be bought for a 'knock-down price' – Kevin Gorski only paid £400,000 for the sixteen-acre site – although they do still retain a commercial value. Despite various property surveys suggesting that as many as 40 per cent of people wouldn't buy a house where someone has died, and a staggering 67 per cent of homebuyers in one survey claiming that they couldn't imagine living in a house which had a history of violent death, there remains a resilient market for these flats and houses to either rent or buy.

A student called Azarias Fontaine had no qualms about moving into a flat on the outskirts of Bradford where the 'Crossbow Cannibal' – Stephen Griffiths – had murdered and dismembered three women in 2009 and 2010. He said at the time, 'I can see it would freak out a lot of people but not me. Just because some crazy murders took place here, does not make it a bad place.' By the time Azarias moved in, in 2017, the flat had been redecorated, and the carpets in the kitchen and bathroom – including the bath itself (where some of the bodies had been dismembered) – had been replaced by the landlord. It was cheap to rent – just £360 per month, which was lower than the then going rate. So too there have been several tenants who have occupied the flat at 4 Hartland House, overlooking the Royal Veterinary College in London, where Anthony Hardy – the 'Camden Ripper' – killed at least three people before his arrest in 2002. Camden Council took the view that 'because the flat is part of a block, it's not viable to demolish it. [However] because of the circumstances, the council has taken the decision to completely gut the flat – including the removal of all fixtures and fittings, and decorations and woodwork – and replace as new.' This refurbishment cost the council £20,000, and when the flat came up for rent in April 2004 more than thirty prospective tenants expressed an interest in renting the property.

The house in a cul-de-sac in the village of Helmshore, Rossendale, where sixty-year-old Sadie Hartley was murdered by Sarah Williams, was sold after the asking price was reduced by £50,000. The house was listed on Rightmove as 'a substantial five-bedroom detached family home set in a highly regarded woodland setting. Originally built by Hurstwood these sought-after family homes are ideal for the modern professional family being close to local amenities and countryside and a short drive to the motorway network.' Williams, who had been in a relationship with Sadie's partner and wanted him back, used a high-voltage stun gun to paralyse Sadie when she answered the door, and then attacked her with a knife. Williams was convicted of murder. It is also interesting to note that the two-bedroom house on Somerset Road, Drolysden, belonging to the notorious police killer Dale Cregan – who murdered PCs Fiona Bone and Nicola Hughes in 2012 – was sold at auction for £71,000, double the guide price. This sale shows that not every house where a murder has taken place has to reduce its asking price, although the proceeds from the auction of Cregan's former home went to support police charities, and this probably influenced the final amount paid by the new owner.

The serial killer Dennis Nilsen's attic flat, 23D Cranley Gardens in Muswell Hill, north London, has had several owners since Nilsen was convicted in 1983. It sold at auction for £240,000 in 2013, then was renovated and put back on the market the following year at an asking price of £350,000. There were no takers, although a cash buyer was eventually found in June 2015 – at £300,000. The flat was back on the market in under two years, this time with a price tag £30,000 above the average for flats in the area. It was sold again in 2016 'for the relatively cheap price' of £493,000, although the owners were not troubled by what had happened in the flat in the past. They are quoted at the time of their purchase as saying, 'We've looked it up and read all about the history. But it was all thirty-five, forty years ago. For us it was never an issue.'

Estate agents will often note in their listings of these properties that 'a crime was committed at the premises'. In the case of Cregan's former home, for example, Barnard Marcus advised potential buyers that 'the registered proprietor of the property is a convicted criminal and the buyer purchases the property in the full knowledge of this fact and shall raise no further questions in this regard'. Indeed, under Consumer Protection from Unfair Trading Regulations (CPRs), an estate agent is duty bound to disclose any information that might affect a consumer's decision about purchasing a property, which would include disclosing information that might decrease the value of the property or cause distress by living there. The CPRs include incidences of criminal activity that took place in that property, as well as murder or suicide.

In the United States these homes are referred to as 'stigmatized properties', and three states – Alaska, California and South Dakota – have specific laws requiring vendors to disclose if an occupant has died in the house in the previous three years. This does not mean that such properties do not sell, but they will usually take longer to do so, and often at a reduced price. One Californian realtor called Randall Bell reportedly makes $375 an hour as a self-styled 'Master of Disaster', having consulted on the sale of properties belonging to Nicole Brown Simpson, JonBenet Ramsey's home and the mansion of Charles Manson's victim Sharon Tate. His top tip when selling such a home is to rent the property first, so as to allow time 'to take the stigma away'. Other advice for owners of these 'tainted properties' includes 'extensive remodelling', changing the name or address of the property and, in extreme cases, demolishing and rebuilding.

One issue which is rarely discussed is the active desire that some people have to live in a house where a murder has taken place. The journalist Rhiannon Evans, quoted at the start of this chapter, might indeed have been interested in how a murder could affect the price a house would be sold for, but she also seems to have been incredibly keen to visit Cranley Gardens. As she says in her article, 'I'd be lying if I said icy chills ran down my spine' when she was invited to attend a barbecue at the basement flat, and was instead intrigued by the fact that a serial killer had once lived at the property. There's an echo here too of Sandy McNab's sales pitch for visiting Dr Crippen's house in Hilldrop Crescent.

Others go further and actively choose to live in a house where a murder has taken place. One new homeowner, who preferred to remain anonymous when he spoke to the press, said he was 'curious' about 'the aggressive murder' that had taken place in the house, and didn't object to the fact that 'the blood is stained in the wood beams, the ceilings and even on the curtains. You can see blood splatters [*sic*] everywhere.' The glee with which this was said left me with the impression that his curiosity masked more than simply his desire to buy the property to learn and understand – qualities which are the essence of being curious.

Indeed, this seems to me to be another example of murder-abilia, where buyers seek articles which were used or owned by murderers, or created by them, and which has become a booming industry. Dark Crime Collectables – 'Europe's largest murderabilia website' – was created in 2020 by Rory Everett, a software engineer from London, and specialises in 'gangland, global crime and serial killers', although the last category seems to dominate what's for sale. Everett sells paintings, drawings and letters by various American serial killers, alongside Dennis Nilsen's keyboard (£5,000), his typewriter (£2,500) and his CD player (£200); although he had sold out of Nilsen's reading glasses, and his 'one and only hairbrush with strands of hair found in his cell'. It's really only a short jump (and a large mortgage) from buying artefacts such as these to purchasing the flat where Nilsen murdered his victims.

We can perhaps also see this as a form of dark tourism, a loose label that gets applied to people wanting to visit sites that owe their notoriety to death and disaster. This is some-times also called thanatourism – from the Greek *thanatos*, which means 'death'. I witnessed this phenomenon myself in Ipswich, when, out of the gloom of a dark, cloud-filled morn-ing in 2006, headlights lit up the crime scene where the body of a young woman had been found. A minibus pulled up in a layby and disgorged its eager passengers. Believing that they might be the family and friends of the dead woman, I went over to introduce myself, but as I put out my hand by way of greeting the first passenger waved me away, saying, 'Oh, don't worry about us – we saw what was happening on the TV and just wanted to come down and look for ourselves.'

More recently, in the wake of the fire at Grenfell Tower in west London in June 2017, when seventy-two people lost their lives and a further seventy were injured, dark tourists started to arrive, wandering around the site of the charred building and taking selfies. In response, hastily drawn posters by survivors started to appear on lamp posts and fences surrounding the site. One read 'Grenfell: A Tragedy Not a Tourist Attraction'. A resident told a BBC interviewer, 'It's not the Eiffel Tower,' and a few weeks later there was criticism when a coachload of tourists visited to take photographs on what seemed to be an officially organised tour. We might see these criticisms as legitimate, especially as some people who escaped the blaze were still recovering in hospital, other survivors were homeless and almost everyone was still in shock.

However, we have to consider how much of this kind of dark tourism is engrained in the human psyche. Just look to Pompeii and its inhabitants, who were covered in lava and volcanic ash from Mount Vesuvius in AD 79. We are separated from that admittedly natural tragedy by a millennium or two, whereas what happened at Grenfell Tower, and the ongoing enquiries into the fire, are still very present and in living memory and are much more concerned with negligence and a basic disregard for some of the very people we should be protecting in our society. Of course, the passage of time creates a distance between the disaster of the event and how it might thereafter be processed, consumed and understood. Pompeii, for example, is now presented as a way of understanding the culture of the Roman Empire, and how people lived at that time. We get to see into their accidentally preserved houses, with the furniture and kitchenware that they used; we can visit Pompeii's shops, where some of the walls are covered in electoral propaganda and jokes; and we also discover taverns and brothels on the less respectable side of the town. However, we can also see more than a hundred preserved bodies of the two thousand people who are estimated to have perished – some of whom were captured clenching their hands and feet at the very moment that they died in their houses as a result of the heat and the volcanic debris that poured down on the town. That's dark by any stretch of the imagination.

This is all presented as an educational experience – one that involves buying a ticket to gain entry, and where you can purchase a guidebook at the gift shop, or you can hire an official tour guide. Later, the same gift shop will sell you postcards to send to your family and friends back home. As the official website makes clear, visitors are requested to observe customary rules of decorum to preserve the site, and promptly report any breaches and problems to the security staff. There are also rules governing dropping litter, reminding visitors not to touch any objects and banning the use of 'commercial photography'. In other words, this is a controlled and regulated experience of dark tourism, which can therefore be consumed without any feelings of guilt that you are actually entering the houses where people died – and that some of those people are still frozen in the very moment when they perished.

The educational dimension of visiting Pompeii is also at the heart of a trip to Auschwitz. Cheap air travel has now meant that more than two million people visit the infamous Nazi concentration camp each year – that's an average of almost 5,500 visitors a day – and the majority travel to the site from Krakow's international airport. It is now a UNESCO World Heritage Site. Having visited Auschwitz myself, I know that it is a profoundly moving experience and one that seems to perform a consciousness-raising function, as well as keeping the 'man-made' Holocaust, as opposed to the natural disaster of Pompeii, in our collective memory. Does this happen as a result of the numbers who died there – more than a million, as opposed to the two thousand at Pompeii – or because what happened at Auschwitz took place in the last century, rather than AD 79? Even closer to the present day we now have the National September 11 Memorial and Museum in New York, which I also found profoundly moving.

However, how might we accommodate a Jack the Ripper walking trip into these official and educational tours? Is the objective of such an experience to raise consciousness about the plight of working-class women in the East End of London in the 1880s, or is it more of a parlour game about trying to identify the person whom we have come to call Jack the Ripper? One tour operated by Secret Chamber Tours Ltd advertises that it will use 'state-of-the-art RIPPER-VISION' – hand-held projectors to help recreate the atmosphere of Victorian London, 'using spooky images, film clips and moving images' to bring Whitechapel to life. The experience is described as a 'spine-chilling' night tour, which will show the locations of the murders 'and the lives of the unfortunate victims'. We might want to grumble that how this tour is being presented does seem to err on the side of entertainment rather than consciousness-raising, but has it actually blurred our moral guidelines about how we should interact with the reality of murder and death, or merely found another way of getting us to engage with a subject we too often choose to avoid?

Thinking about the issues that surround the ethics of dark tourism perhaps also offers us an opportunity to put the questions about what we should do with the properties where a murder has taken place in a much broader cultural context, and a way to think more critically about what is appropriate, or improper, in our response to these properties. At a general and more cultural level, we should acknowledge that dark tourism seems to hold a mirror up to our own mortality, and is therefore an emotionally challenging, existential experience, as well as one that might be viewed as voyeuristic. It gets us to discuss the inevitability of our own ultimate demise – something which we tend to ignore until it is too late – and that has to be a good thing. There do also seem to be some general rules that might help us to think about what is appropriate, and what it less so. For example I've drawn attention to the passage of time as a way of processing and understanding death and disaster, and I have also described how dark tourism can be regulated and controlled. All of the sites and the walking tour that I have mentioned require a ticket – a simple mechanism that formalises what happens, as opposed to 'just seeing for yourself'. These tours were not DIY experiences where you could choose what you wanted to do at a site, but ones which constrained your behaviour – put the rubbish in the bins, don't touch the objects, and which prohibited commercial photography – as well as trying to increase our understanding about what had happened.

So the lessons that we might want to take from dark tourism have nothing to do with 'body count', or if the murderer was a serial killer. Neither are they to do with the mechanics of the murder itself, and whether these might have been especially gruesome or attracted media attention. Nor does it seem necessary to destroy every property where a murder has occurred, or we would already have bulldozed Auschwitz, and never have excavated Pompeii. Rather, these lessons suggest that there will always have to be an appropriate time gap between what has happened and then being able to process the murder in another way, and that time gap might be relatively quick, or could be much longer. However, there must be a dignified moratorium between the event and moving on. Who it is that will determine all of this should be someone who might still live in that property, the survivors of an attack, or anyone else who might be associated in other ways with the person who has died. They of course might choose to remodel the flat or house, or even have it destroyed, but that is their choice. If no one still lives in the property, then the American advice for 'stigmatized properties' seems like good, practical actions, and ones that would appear to have already been employed in this country. I can see no fixed rules in all of this; there's no empirical formula that I can devise that will guide people in every circumstance, and frankly nor should we want there to be. People should react to what has happened to them – including when a loved one or a friend has been murdered – in ways that make the best sense to them, and so just as there are no empirical rules about grief and how long, or in what form, the grieving process might take, nor can there be definitive rules about when and what should happen at a property where a murder has occurred.

I know, it's getting late.

At times, the stories that I have told in this book were particularly distressing, and one or two brought back some difficult personal and professional memories. As I have discovered over the course of my career, talking about death, let alone a murder, is never easy, and is more often than not painful and problematic, even when that murder might have happened many years ago. My goal is never to cause distress, but to find ways to bring comfort by illuminating the gloom; by shining a light into those places where we fear to tread, and which seem dark and frightening. Death in all of its forms is one of those places; hidden away in our culture and all too often silenced. My aim throughout has therefore been to attempt to bring a taboo subject into view, and to start a discussion for good, or for ill.

That's been my goal, but I need to stop now: it's time to go home.

A Guide to Further Reading and Study

Introduction

I used Harry Mount, *A Lust for Window Sills: A Lover's Guide to British Buildings from Portcullis to Pebble Dash* (London: Abacus, 2011) – and, for the curious, a crocket is a small, sharp, medieval ornament on the inclined edges of spires and gables. I also quote from Judith Flanders, *The Making of Home: The 500-Year Story of How our Houses became Homes* (London: Atlantic Books, 2014). Also of interest is Lucy Worsley, *If Walls Could Talk: An Intimate History of the Home* (London: Faber & Faber, 2011). For the idea that the house is an extension of the self, see Russell W. Belk, 'Possessions and the Extended Self', *Journal of Consumer Research*, 15:2 (September 1988), 139–68; Russell W. Belk, *Collecting in a Consumer Society* (New York: Routledge, 1995); and Jeremy Paxman, *The English: A Portrait of a People* (London: Penguin, 1998). It was Paxman who drew my attention to the very British habit of naming houses, despite there being 'a perfectly adequate numbering system', because 'names express individuality. A number implies communality, or anonymity.' For how this might work in practice, see Kitty Go, 'Home is an Extension of Yourself', *Financial Times*, 10 November 2007, about the homes that she created in New York and Hong Kong; and, more recently Ros Byam Shaw, 'The Storeys of My Life: Every Home Reflects its Owner's Personality, and the Interiors of these Three Characterful Townhouses Speak Volumes about Theirs', *Mail Online*, 18 March 2018. A more scholarly introduction to the subject is Shelley Mallett, 'Understanding Home: A Critical Review of the Literature', *The Sociological Review*, 52:1 (2004), 62–89.

I built the story of Dr Crippen and the murder of his wife Cora from Roger Dalrymple, *Crippen: A Crime Sensation in Memory and Modernity* (Woodbridge: The Boydell Press, 2020). This rather wonderful book has photographs of Crippen being arrested, and of Sandy McNab standing outside his new purchase of 39 Hilldrop Crescent wearing a top hat. Orwell's 'Decline of the English Murder' has been reprinted in various places and can be found on the internet. I used George Orwell, *Shooting an Elephant and Other Essays* (London: Penguin, 2009). The 'decline' in the title of Orwell's essay was a reference to the murder committed in October 1944 by Karl Hulten, an American GI deserting from the army, and his eighteen-year-old Welsh girlfriend Betty (Maud) Jones, which became known in the press as the 'Cleft Chin Murder'. Their victim was a taxi driver with a cleft chin called George Edward Heath, from whom they also stole £8, and it is very doubtful if this murder would ever have become as infamous had not Orwell decided to write about it. Hulten was the first and only American soldier to be tried and condemned to death in an English court – under special dispensation from President Roosevelt – and was later executed at HMP Pentonville in March 1945. Jones was also sentenced to death, but was later reprieved, and would eventually be released from prison in May 1954. Hulten had told Jones that he was a paratrooper called Ricky Allen, a Chicago gangster sent to England by Al Capone, and Jones claimed she was a showgirl called Georgina Grayson awaiting a screen test, but that her secret dream was to be a 'gangster's moll'. See Marjorie Bilbow, 'Love, Lies and Murder in 1944', *New York Times*, 2 September 1989. The stories of Hulten and Jones were turned into a 1990 movie directed by Bernard Rose, called *Chicago Joe and the Showgirl*, starring Kiefer Sutherland as Hulten and Emily Lloyd as Jones.

Sigmund Freud wrote about the uncanny in his 1919 essay 'Das Unheimliche', which is widely available in his collected works and can also be downloaded from the internet, and in it he draws on the work of both Friedrich Nietzsche and especially Ernst Jentsch. The basics of Freud's argument can be found in Stephen Frosh, *A Brief Introduction to Psychoanalytic Theory* (London: Palgrave Macmillan, 2012) and an excellent secondary text remains Nicholas Royle, *The Uncanny* (Manchester: Manchester University Press, 2003), which was the first book-length treatment of the subject. I wrote about Peter Tobin, and the crimes that he committed, with the former Sky News journalist Paul Harrison in *The Lost British Serial Killer: Closing the Case on Peter Tobin and Bible John* (London: Sphere, 2010), which includes chapters on both Tobin in Margate and his murder of Angelika Kluk. As a side note, I remain convinced that Tobin is the notorious Glasgow serial killer who has been dubbed 'Bible John' by the press. Abigail Dengate explained her decision to move into Tobin's house in Margate to *KentOnline* – see Marijke Hall, 'Living in Serial Killer Peter Tobin's House in Irvine Drive, Margate, 13 Years after Tragic Discovery of Vicky Hamilton and Dinah McNicol', 10 October 2020, and I use quotations from this article. The crimes committed by H. H. Holmes have been memorably described by Erik Larson in *The Devil in the White City: Murder, Magic and Madness at the Fair that Changed America* (New York: Vintage, 2003).

The various statistics that I quote in relation to the numbers and places where people are murdered in England and Wales can be found at www.ons.gov.uk, and for Scotland at www.gov.scot. A more general introduction to murder is Fiona Brookman, *Understanding Homicide* (London: Sage, 2005) and, more recently, Adam Lynes, Elizabeth Yardley and Lucas Danos, *Making Sense of Homicide* (Winchester: Waterside Press, 2021). I have also written about murder in *My Life with Murderers: Behind Bars with the World's Most Violent Men* (London: Sphere, 2019) and *Death at the Hands of the State* (London: The Howard League, 2005). This latter book drew attention to the fact that the murder rate in prison is often higher than the rate of murder in the community – something that still shocks me. How do we control the murder rate in the community when we can't even control it within a setting that should be monitored by staff and highly controlled?

Chapter One

The basis of this chapter is my academic work with a variety of colleagues and former PhD students at Birmingham City

University. See, in particular: Donal McIntyre, David Wilson, Elizabeth Yardley and Liam Brolan, 'The British Hitman: 1974–2013', *The Howard Journal of Criminal Justice*, 53:4 (September 2014), 325–40; David Wilson and Mohammed Rahman, 'Becoming a Hitman', *The Howard Journal of Criminal Justice*, 54:3 (July 2015), 250–64; and Liam Brolan, David Wilson and Elizabeth Yardley, 'Hitmen and the Spaces of Contract Killing: The Doorstep Hitman', *Journal of Investigative Psychology and Offender Profiling*, 13:3 (2016), 220–38. The various hitmen who appear in this chapter, including Santre Sanchez Gayle, are mentioned within these articles, and also the case of Frank McPhie. In relation to the murder of Frank McPhie, I discuss in the chapter how he had been given an Osman Warning by the police. This is named after the 1998 legal case of Osman vs The United Kingdom, which was heard before the European Court of Human Rights (ECHR). The applicants were the widow of Ali Osman – who was shot and killed by Paul Paget-Lewis – and her son Ahmet. The Osmans complained that the police had been given information that Paget-Lewis, a teacher who had become infatuated by Ahmet Osman, posed a serious threat to the family, but had not acted on that information. The Osman Warnings were developed in response to the judgment of the ECHR. I have not previously discussed in my academic work the cases of Jill Dando or Alistair Wilson, although I have written about the Nairn hit in a number of newspapers and discussed it on a podcast called *The Doorstep Murder* (see below).

An account of a journalist delivering the 'death knock' is offered by Samira Ahmed, 'A Moment that Changed Me: How a "Death Knock" Taught me about Grief, Respect and Truth',

Guardian, 3 November 2021; and for a police officer, Zoe Zaczek, 'Behind the Dreaded "Death Knock": Senior Constable Shares a Heartbreaking Christmas Message Describing what it's like to Stand at a Family's Door and tell them a Loved One has Died', *Daily Mail*, 8 December 2020.

For the background to the murder of Jill Dando I used a number of journalistic pieces including: Adam Lusher, 'Who Killed Jill Dando? The Main Theories Behind the Murder of British TV's Golden Girl', *Independent*, 26 April 2019; Press Association, 'Jill Dando Murder Will Never Be Solved Says Lead Detective', *Guardian*, 29 March 2019; and Suzi Feay, 'Jill Dando: The 20 Year Mystery – The Whodunnit Continues', *Financial Times*, 19 April 2019, which is a review of an ITV documentary on the twentieth anniversary of the murder. There was a variety of true crime documentaries about the case at this time, the best being BBC 1's *The Murder of Jill Dando*, directed by Marcus Plowright, which was broadcast on 2 April 2019. Dando's former *Crimewatch* co-host Nick Ross, who appeared in that documentary, also used his website to discuss the case: see 'Who Killed Jill Dando', www.nickross.com, April 2019. In this blog post he is scathing about the idea that she might have been murdered by a Serbian hitman – a theory he describes as 'risible', although I beg to differ. There are a number of books about this particular murder, but I would only recommend David Smith *All About Jill: The Life and Death of Jill Dando* (London: Sphere, 2002) and Brian Cathcart, *Jill Dando: Her Life and Death* (London: Penguin, 2001). For the assassination attempt on Nikola Štedul in Kirkcaldy see 'Who is Nikola Štedul?', *Fife Today*, 18 October 2018, and Steven Taylor, 'Margaret Thatcher Warned

Not to Mention Yugoslav Dissident Shooting on Fife Street', *Daily Record*, 11 January 2021.

The former Metropolitan Police officer Peter Bleksley writes about the Alistair Wilson case in *To Catch a Killer: My Hunt for the Truth Behind the Doorstep Murder* (London: John Blake, 2018). I was interviewed for this book, and subsequently wrote about the case in the *Herald*, 18 November 2017. There is an excellent podcast, presented by Fiona Walker, on BBC Sounds called *The Doorstep Murder*, which expertly discusses the various theories about what happened to Alistair Wilson. I have also contributed to this podcast, and have been interviewed several times on BBC Radio Scotland about the case in general and in relation to the package sent to me at my office at Birmingham City University entitled 'Alistair Wilson: A Cold Case Thesis'. This thesis was signed Nate. For the record, I do not know and have never met Nate, but I do get the impression from what he writes that he is a former or serving police officer – he certainly seems to understand police procedure, and often gives the impression of having an axe to grind about the case. Nate re-emerged in January 2022 when he issued a press release about a book he had written about the Glasgow serial killed Bible John. In that press release he described himself as a 'community detective' (which I take to mean armchair detective) and gave a surname: Campbell. He also provided an email address and I have contacted him. As yet I have not been able to meet up with him, as Nate says that he would prefer all communication to be done via email.

Arnold van Gennep was a Dutch-French ethnographer who died in 1957. He writes about rites of passage and introduces the concept of liminality in his most famous work, *Les Rites de Passage* (1906). This book would influence Victor Turner's work, and in particular *The Ritual Process: Structure and Anti-Structure* (Chicago: University of Chicago Press, 1969).

Chapter Two

Walter Benjamin was a German Jewish philosopher and cultural critic associated with the Frankfurt School, a broad philosophical and sociological movement preoccupied with a critique of modernity, mass culture, capitalism and commodification. Benjamin's best-known works are two essays, 'The Work of Art in the Age of Mechanical Reproduction' (1935) and 'Theses on the Philosophy of History' (1940), completed just before he committed suicide, while fleeing from the Nazis in September 1940. Both are widely available in print and can be downloaded from the internet. I know from teaching undergraduates that Benjamin's theoretical work can sometimes be a little intimidating, and so perhaps as a way into understanding his arguments it's best to look first at one of his biographies: Howard Eiland and Michael Jennings, *Walter Benjamin: A Critical Life* (Cambridge, MA: Harvard University Press, 2014). The journalist Stuart Jeffries also offers a good review of this biography in the *Guardian*, 7 August 2014, and would later write an excellent article about the Frankfurt School more generally: 'Why a Forgotten 1930s Critique of Capitalism is Back in Fashion', *Guardian*, 9 September 2016. Howard Eiland (mentioned above) and Kevin McLaughlin translated and then published for the first time Benjamin's enormous collection of writings about city life in nineteenth-century Paris – these writings are without doubt one of the greatest ever contributions to cultural theory. See Walter Benjamin, *The Arcades Project* (Cambridge, MA: Harvard University Press, 1999).

I mention Kate Fox's *Watching the English: The Hidden Rules of English Behaviour* (London: Hodder, 2004) in the chapter, and also discuss Edgar Allan Poe's 'The Murders in the Rue Morgue' (1841). This can be downloaded from the internet, but is widely available in collections of Poe's work – for example, *The Portable Edgar Allan Poe* (London: Penguin, 2006). For an excellent introduction to his life and works see Peter Ackroyd, *Poe: A Life Cut Short* (London: Chatto & Windus, 2008), which has a very useful discussion about the importance of 'The Murders in the Rue Morgue' to detective fiction. The idea that Poe had a 'life cut short' is a reference to the fact that he died in 1849 at the age of forty, in very mysterious circumstances. Poe had actually been en route to Philadelphia, but was found by an acquaintance in a Baltimore public house called Gunner's Hall on election day, semi-conscious, wearing soiled clothes that did not belong to him and repeatedly calling out 'Reynolds'. He would die a few days later without ever regaining consciousness, or offering an explanation as to what had happened to him, and clarifying who Reynolds might have been.

I have written about the murders committed by Ian Brady and Myra Hindley in my own *A History of British Serial Killing* (London: Sphere, 2008). This book can also be used to prompt further reading about Dennis Nilsen, Peter Sutcliffe, the Wests and other serial killers. I specifically refer to here, and quote from: Alan Keightley, *Ian Brady: The Untold*

Story of the Moors Murders (London: Robson Books, 2017) and David Smith with Carol Ann Lee, *Witness: The Story of David Smith, Chief Prosecution Witness in the Moors Murders Case* (Edinburgh: Mainstream Publishing, 2011). In passing I mention Brady's own *The Gates of Janus: Serial Killing and its Analysis* (Los Angeles: Feral House, 2001). This is a rather self-serving account of the history of serial murder. The first part of the book is taken up with Brady's personal philosophy, and the second half with his ideas related to offender profiling, based on his own analysis of eleven serial killers. However, of perhaps greater interest is the fact that Brady does not mention the murders that he and Hindley committed. About those crimes he is, as I have observed in my own writing, like many other serial killers, 'silent and uncommunicative'.

There have been no book-length accounts of the murders of Connie and Janice Sheridan, or the murder of Julia Rawson. However, the murders of the Sheridans were the subject of an episode of ITV's *Real Crime* strand on 24 April 2007, called 'A Killer Came Calling', in which a number of the investigating officers were interviewed. See also Cahal Milmo, 'Salesman Gets Life for Killing Dog Breeders', *Independent*, 17 August 2013; 'Salesman Jailed for Double Murder', *BBC News*, 3 April 2000; and 'Fenland Murders Featured on TV', *Wisbech Standard*, 27 April 2007 – which also carries interviews with the investigating officers. West Midlands Police produced and released their own twelve-minute documentary about Julia Rawson's murder (it can still be found on YouTube), which featured exclusive drone footage showing the extensive area that the police had searched looking for Julia's body. A number of the investigating officers were also interviewed, and the release of the documentary was widely covered in the press. See, for example, Charlotte Regen, 'Police Documentary reveals Inside Story of Julia Rawson Murder Investigation', *Birmingham Mail*, 10 November 2020; Jordan Coussins and Oprah Flash, 'Watch Dramatic Bodycam as "Flat of Horrors" Killers Confronted by Cops in the Street', *Birmingham Mail*, 9 November 2020; and Charlotte Paxton, 'The Seven Key Moments that Snared Julia Rawson's Killers', *Birmingham Mail*, 14 November 2020.

I mention staging in this chapter, which is when an offender will deliberately attempt to alter the crime scene prior to the arrival of the police – most often something done to direct attention away from the most logical suspect. Research suggests that this is a relatively unusual crime scene behaviour as far as murder is concerned, and estimates of its occurrence have varied from less than 1 per cent to 8 per cent. We can see this type of staging as being either ad hoc or pre-planned, and there is also a form of staging – sometimes known as secondary staging – which manipulates the crime scene without any intention to misdirect the investigation, but rather to shock or create a narrative. What results from the first type of staging is a misleading appearance about the true nature of the crime that has taken place, which is presented as a legitimate death instead of murder. The academic literature on this area can be found at: Robert R. Hazelwood and Michael R. Napier, 'Crime Scene staging and Its Detection', *International Journal of Offender Therapy and Comparative Criminology*, 48:6 (2004), 744–59; John E. Douglas and Lauren K. Douglas, 'The Detection of Staging, Undoing and Personation at the Crime Scene' in John E. Douglas, Ann W. Burgess, Allen G. Burgess and Robert K. Ressler (eds), *Crime Classification Manual: A Standard System for Investigating and Classifying Violent Crimes* (Hoboken: Jossey-Bass, 2006); and Laura G. Pettler *Crime Scene Staging Dynamics in Homicide Cases* (Boca Raton: CRC Press, 2016).

My observations about CCTV are taken from James Treadwell and Adam Lynes, *50 Facts Everyone Should Know About Crime & Punishment in Britain* (Bristol: Policy Press, 2019); the statistics related to the National DNA Database can be found at www.gov.uk; I use the idea of 'wound culture' from Mark Seltzer, *Serial Killers: Death and Life in America's Wound Culture* (London: Routledge, 1998); and the work of Sir Alec Jeffreys and the development of DNA fingerprinting, which would lead to the arrest of Colin Pitchfork, was featured in a 2015 two-part ITV crime docudrama called *Code of A Killer*, directed by James Strong, with John Simm playing Jeffreys. Pitchfork, who raped and murdered Lynda Mann and Dawn Ashworth, was released from prison in September 2021 but has since been recalled.

Chapter Three

Much of my initial thinking about kitchens was prompted by reading Judith Flanders and Lucy Worsley, op. cit., and then amplified by listening to an episode of Radio 4's *Thinking Allowed*, 'The Making of the Modern Kitchen', which was first broadcast on 1 September 2004. This edition of the programme, presented by the sociologist Laurie Taylor, inspired me to read June Freeman, *The Making of the Modern Kitchen:*

A Cultural History (Oxford: Berg, 2004) and I followed up on a number of the issues raised in this book. For the importance of evocative objects in shaping how we think, and as things which will act as companions to our emotional lives, see Sherry Turkle (ed.), *Evocative Objects: Things We Think With* (Cambridge, MA: The MIT Press, 2011).

For the statistics related to knife crime see www.gov. uk and www.benkinsella.org.uk, and, of course, there are a number of easily accessible reports about the prevalence of knife crime. See, for example, Danny Shaw, 'Ten Charts on the Rise of Knife Crime in England and Wales', *BBC News*, 18 July 2019; 'Knife Crime in England and Wales at Record High, Figures Show', *BBC News*, 17 July 2020; and Nadeem Badshah, 'Knife Crime Hits Record High in England and Wales', *Guardian*, 17 October 2019. I built the stories of the women who were stabbed in their kitchens from various local newspapers, amplified by other reporting about their murders in the national press. Charlotte Huggins: Catherine Wylie and Richard Duggan, 'Mum of One Stabbed to Death by Jealous and Controlling Boyfriend', *MyLondon*, 4 July 2019. Mary Annie Sowerby: Emily Parsons, 'Life for Workington Man who Admitted Killing Annie Sowerby in Dearham', *Times & Star*, 24 July 2019. Alison Hunt: Ashlie Blakey, 'Stabbed 18 Times on her Doorstep – the Grotesque Murder of a Mum Whose Ex was Furious She had a new Boyfriend', *Manchester Evening News*, 19 July 2019. Eliza Stevens: Katy Clifton, 'Man who Stabbed Partner 86 Times out of Rage and Resentment in Hendon Flat Jailed for Life', *Evening Standard*, 20 August 2019.

There are a number of books about the murders committed at 10 Rillington Place and the controversy surrounding Reg

Christie – specifically whether he was also responsible for the murders of Beryl and Jeraldine Evans (crimes for which Timothy Evans was hanged). See, for example, F. Tennyson Jesse, *Trials of Timothy Evans and John Reginald Christie* (London: William Hodge, 1957) and Ludovic Kennedy, *Ten Rillington Place* (London: Victor Gollancz, 1961). These two books have become the 'standard version' of the Evans case, while John Eddowes, *The Two Killers of Rillington Place* (London: Little, Brown, 1994) refutes much of what they argue. In any event, wherever you might stand in relation to this controversy, these books build an excellent picture of the crimes that Christie committed. I also mention Molly Lefebure, the former journalist who became the Home Office pathologist Professor Keith Simpson's secretary during the Second World War. She wrote about these experiences in *Evidence for the Crown: Experiences of a Pathologist's Secretary* (London: Heinemann, 1955) and followed this up with *Murder with a Difference – Studies of Haigh and Christie* (1958). It is in this book that she describes Christie's garden. I also mention *Policeman, Pilot and a Guardian Angel* (London: Four O'clock Press, 2008) by Len Trevallion, whom I had the pleasure to meet before his death in 2017 at the age of 102. In his book Trevallion describes interviewing Christie in his cell, and of being told of the abortions that the Christies performed on sex workers at 10 Rillington Place.

There are no book-length accounts of the murders of Hollie Kerrell or Ellie Gould, and I relied on newspaper reporting and TV documentaries about these cases. See in particular: Cathy Owen, 'Murdered by Her Husband: How Hollie Kerrell was Killed and Buried in a Child's Duvet', *WalesOnline*, 26

November 2019; and 'Hollie Kerrell: Man Killed Wife While Kids Were in House', *BBC News*, 2 November 2018. The Crime + Investigation channel covered this case in a documentary called *Murdered by My Husband*, which was aired on 25 November 2019. For Ellie Gould's murder see: 'Ellie Gould Murder: Thomas Griffiths Jailed for Fatal Stabbing', *BBC News*, 8 November 2019; Tom Seward, 'How Wiltshire Police Caught Ellie Gould's Killer Thomas Griffiths', *Swindon Advertiser*, 8 November 2019; Alison Maloney, 'My Teenage Daughter was Stabbed 13 Times in Our Kitchen by Her Ex – We Must Toughen Up Sentences for Domestic Killers', *Sun*, 1 November 2020; and Tomas Mallow, 'Ellie Gould Murder: Victim's Mum Can't Bear Thomas Griffith Leaving Prison Before He's 30', *SomersetLive*, 16 September 2020. Ellie's murder was featured in two TV documentaries: Quest Red devoted an episode of *Britain's Deadliest Kids* on 31 October 2020 to this case, and the Crime + Investigation channel aired *Murder at My Door* on 2 November 2020. I should acknowledge that I contributed to the first of these documentaries, and subsequently spoke with Carole Gould, Ellie's mother.

Chapter Four

You can view the Great Bed of Ware for yourself without having to travel to London, as the Victoria and Albert Museum uploaded a short video about it onto their YouTube channel in 2021: see 'The Most Famous Bed in the World?' Charles Dickens mentions the bed in 'The Boots at the Holly Tree Inn', published in 1855. This is a short story about a snowbound traveller who has been disappointed in love and who finds himself stuck for a week at the Holly Tree Inn prior to travelling to the United States. He entertains himself by recording the stories of other lodgers, and especially the tale of two eight-year-olds who have fallen in love, and turn up at the inn on their way to Gretna Green. In Shakespeare's *Twelfth Night* (1601) the character Sir Toby Belch describes a sheet of paper as 'big enough for the Bed of Ware!' I also read: Elizabeth Collins Cromley, 'Sleeping Around: A History of American Beds and Bedrooms', *Journal of Design History*, 3:1 (1990), 1–17; Annie Carlano, *Sleeping Around: The Bed from Antiquity to Now* (Seattle: University of Washington Press, 2006); Brian Fagan, 'The Bizarre Social History of Beds', *The Conversation*, 13 September 2019; and enjoyably followed the various news stories about the archaeologist Lyn Wadley of the University of Witwatersrand, South Africa, and her discovery at Sibudu Cave of the oldest known bedding.

I have written extensively about Mary Ann Cotton and drew on my existing writing and research – see, in particular, *Mary Ann Cotton: Britain's First Female Serial Killer* (Winchester: Waterside Press, 2013). Quotes are taken from this book and my more academic work about the case – see Elizabeth Yardley and David Wilson, *Female Serial Killers in Social Context: Criminological Institutionalism and the Case of Mary Ann Cotton* (Bristol: Policy Press, 2015). This book also considers female serial killers more generally. Anyone interested in the original sources related to Cotton should consult the National Archives in Kew, Home Office Box 140/141. I am always surprised that there is a small but persistent belief, especially in the north-east of England, that

Cotton was innocent of the charges against her. I doubt that I will ever be able to convince these local historians, but I would make a special plea that they should read the sources, specifically those contained within the Brotherton Library Special Collections at Leeds University Library. This houses Dr Thomas Scattergood's (he could have been named by Dickens himself!) medical case histories and notebooks. These are important but underused sources as Scattergood was the toxicologist who examined the remains of several of Cotton's victims and discovered the arsenic poisoning. There can be no doubt about what happened to many of the people that she encountered – including members of her own family. My book about Cotton became the basis for a 2016 ITV drama, starring Joanne Froggatt as Mary Ann, called *Dark Angel*. There really is only one other book about Cotton which is worth reading: Arthur Appleton *Mary Ann Cotton* (London: Michael Joseph, 1973).

For the murder of Alida Goode and the crimes committed by Lee Baker see: 'Youth Faces Death Charges', *The Times*, 30 July 1986; 'Life for "Sick" Man who Decapitated his Girlfriend's Mother', *The Times*, 11 June 1987; and 'How Award-Winning Cop Tony Nott Helped Solve Some of Dorset's Most Shocking Crimes', *Bournemouth Daily Echo*, 3 July 2010. An episode of CBS Reality's series *Murder by the Sea* featured this case in January 2020, and a number of detectives who worked on the investigation were interviewed on the documentary. I also discuss whether Baker's offending might be explained as a catathymic crisis. The best starting point to understand this concept is Louis B. Schlesinger, 'The Catathymic Crisis, 1912–Present: A Review and Clinical Study', *Aggression and*

Violent Behaviour, 1:4 (1996), 307–16, and F. Wertham, 'The Catathymic Crisis: A Clinical Entity', *Archives of Neurology and Psychiatry*, 37 (1937), 974–7.

For the murder of Alice Rye I used: Ian Herbert, 'Suspect Told Detectives Horrific Murder Details', *Independent*, 5 July 1999; 'Informer Blamed Friend for Murder', *Guardian*, 5 July 1999; 'Mutilated in Her Own Home', *Warrington Guardian*, 8 July 1999; 'Police Informant Jailed for Life', *BBC News*, 16 July 1999; 'Cruel Lunatic Tracked Victim Using Electoral Roll', *Wirral Globe*, 22 July 1999; 'Wirral Pensioner Alice Rye's Killer Fails in High Court parole Bid', *Liverpool Echo*, 17 May 2011; and 'Killer who Tried to Blame Ellesmere Port Man for Murder of Pensioner Alice Rye in 1996 is Refused Parole', *Cheshire Live*, 18 May 2011. There was obviously an element of post-mortem staging within this murder – see my notes above. I spoke with detectives who worked on this case, and was shown a number of the crime scene photographs. I later discovered a rather strangely satisfying book discussing crime scene photographs by Henry Bond, *Lacan at the Scene* (Cambridge, MA: The MIT Press, 2012), which has a foreword by Slavoj Žižek called 'The Camera's Posthuman Eye'. Bond imagines the French psychoanalyst Jacques Lacan coming to England and working as a police detective, and wonders how 'Lacan's tripartite model of human mental functioning [could be] put to use in the service of crime investigation – particularly through a consideration of visual evidence present at scenes of murders'. Bond uses the crime scene photographs of murders committed in England between 1955 and 1970, which have been collected at the National Archives, to make this seemingly fanciful idea come to life. There are various books about Lacan, but perhaps the best place to get started is Slavoj Žižek, *How to Read Lacan* (London: Granta, 2006).

Chapter Five

My thinking about *Macbeth* (as opposed to having to learn large chunks of it at school for exams) was prompted by listening to an episode of the BBC Radio 4 series *In Our Time*, presented by Melvyn Bragg. The episode on *Macbeth*, in which Professors Emma Smith, Kiernan Ryan and David Schalkwyk appear, was first broadcast on 1 October 2020 and is still available to download as a podcast. As a result, I also consulted Emma Smith, *This is Shakespeare: How to Read the World's Greatest Playwright* (London: Pelican, 2020); Jonathan Bate, *The Genius of Shakespeare* (London: Picador, 1997); and Peter Ackroyd, *Shakespeare: The Biography* (London: Vintage, 2006). I also benefited from reading Terry Eagleton, *On Evil* (New Haven: Yale University Press, 2010), which has an excellent discussion of evil within *Macbeth*, and in which he cheekily argues that the three witches are in fact the heroines of the play.

I have written a number of academic articles about Harold Jones's offending behaviour with my colleague Professor Michael Brookes – see, in particular, 'Making Sense of the Sexual Sadist Between the Wars: The Case of Harold Jones', *The Journal of Forensic Psychiatry & Psychology*, 22:4 (2011), 535–55. A useful local historical account of the case is Neil Milkins, *Every Mother's Nightmare: Abertillery in Mourning* (Abertillery: Old Bakehouse Publications, 2008), which contains numerous photographs of Jones, his victims and the town. Milkins himself still lives in Abertillery. The various issues surrounding the case, and the question as to whether Jones is also the 1960s serial killer known as 'Jack the Stripper', were featured in a BBC Wales documentary called *Dark Son*, which was first shown on 12 January 2019, and was later broadcast on BBC 4. I contributed to this documentary, which involved me visiting Abertillery on a number of occasions to view the sites of the murders, including entering the attic where Jones stored Florence Little's body. I also walked the various locations connected to the murder of Freda Burnell and spoke at length with Neil Milkins. The best book about Jack the Stripper is Robin Jarossi, *The Hunt for the 60s Ripper* (London: Mirror Books, 2017).

There are numerous press reports about the murder of Tia Sharp, and also a number of TV documentaries. I used in particular: the ITV News broadcast of the interview between the criminologist Mark Williams-Thomas and Stuart Hazell which aired on 9 August 2012, and the longer transcript of the interview that was published in *The Times* the following day. Other newspapers also covered this interview in some depth. Mark presented a documentary about the case, *Tonight: Living with a Killer*, on ITV on 16 May 2013, and there have been several other documentaries – such was the interest in the case. Those that I used were: an episode of *Britain's Darkest Taboos – The Murder of Tia Sharp*, on the Crime + Investigation channel, which was broadcast on 14 March 2014; and *The Murder of Tia Sharp: My Daughter*, Channel 5, 4 September 2017. Mark Williams-Thomas also very kindly discussed the interview that he conducted with Hazell when

I started to research this case. Finally, there is a book about the murder: Nigel Cawthorne, *Tia Sharp – A Family Betrayal: The True Story of how a Step-Grandfather Murdered the Young Girl Who Trusted Him* (London: Pennant Books, 2013).

There are many books and several documentaries (including, most recently, one about the murder of Mary Bastholm – *Fred and Rose West: Reopened*, broadcast on ITV in September 2021) about the crimes committed by the Wests. Of particular interest for this chapter are: John Bennett and Graham Gardner, *The Cromwell Street Murders: The Detective's Story* (Thrupp: Sutton Publishing, 2005); Howard Sounes, *Fred & Rose: The Full Story of Fred and Rose West and the Gloucester House of Horrors* (London: Time Warner Books, 1995); Gordon Burn, *Happy Like Murderers: The True Story of Fred and Rosemary West* (London: Faber & Faber, 1998); and Stephen and Mae West, *Inside 25 Cromwell Street: The Terrifying True Story of Life with Fred and Rose West* (Monmouth: Peter Grose, 1995). Also of interest is Martin Amis, *Experience* (London: Vintage, 2001). Amis was Lucy Partington's cousin, and he writes movingly about her in this memoir. He allows us to see the human being behind the headlines, and before she got caught in 'the troglodytic squalor', as he describes it, of 25 Cromwell Street. Bernard Knight, the Home Office pathologist who excavated 25 Cromwell Street, does not mention any of this in his semi-autobiographical *Murder, Suicide or Accident: The Forensic Pathologist at Work* (London: Endeavour Press, 2016) but he very kindly discussed the case with me. There are a growing number of documentaries about the Wests, but I found most helpful for this chapter the two-part series called *Lost Girls*, which was broadcast on Channel 4 in April 2002.

For the stories of *descendre mal* I used the following sources. Linda Rainey: 'Great Yarmouth Murder Trial: Rosalind Gray Killed Linda Rainey by Pushing Her Down the Stairs', *BBC News*, 5 August, 2020; 'Rosalind Gray Jailed for Killing Linda Rainey in Row over £200 Debt', *BBC News*, 10 September 2020; and Jemma Carr, 'She Tried to Get Away with the Perfect Murder', *Daily Mail*, 7 August 2020. Michelle Morris: Danielle Hoe, 'Tragic Mum Michelle Morris Died after Falling Down the Stairs as Three Friends Accused of Murdering Her', *Yorkshire Live*, 27 April 2021; 'Doncaster Fatal Assault Victim Named as Michelle Morris', *BBC News*, 3 June 2020; and Danielle Hoe, 'Police Issue Major Update in Michelle Morris Murder Investigation in Doncaster', *Yorkshire Live*, 20 January 2020. David Thomson: 'David Thomson Death: Man Not Gulty of Manslaughter', *BBC News*, 18 December 2020; 'Two Men Charged with Murder of David Thomson in Weymouth', *Dorset Eye*, 6 April 2020; Diarmuid MacDonagh, 'Two Charged with Murder as Victim is Named', *Dorset Echo*, 6 April 2020. Nicholas Tame: Ruth Halkon, 'Two Men Fought to Death Outside Bedroom of Woman They Both Loved', *Mirror*, 8 July 2015; Sion Morgan, 'Nicholas Tame Murder Trial Set to Start in Swansea Crown Court Today', *Wales Online*, 8 July 2015; Robin Turner, 'Kevin Syms Jailed for Life after Pushing Love Rival Nicholas Tame Down a Flight of Stairs', *Wales Online*, 16 July 2015. Frederic Pallade: Sandra Hembery, 'Suspected Murder Victim Frederic Pallade Found Fatally Injured at Bottom of Flight of Stairs', *Wales Online*, 21 May 2019; 'Frederic Pallade Death – Clydach Man Charged with Murder', *BBC News*, 20 April 2019; 'Man Sentenced to Four Years in Prison for Manslaughter of Partner Frederic Pallade', *ITV News*, 16 October 2019. Louise Evans: Steven Morris, 'Cheating Husband Jailed for 17 Years for Wife's Murder', *Guardian*, 6 November 2013; Christine Challand, 'A Lovely Family has Been Destroyed ... And It's My Fault', *Mail on Sunday*, 9 November 2013; and 'Alan Evans Jailed for Life for Wife's Kidderminster Murder', *BBC News*, 6 November 2013.

The Staircase, which first aired in Britain in 2018, can still be viewed on Netflix. There is an official website about the series at www.netflix.com which takes viewers through various theories related to what happened. Also of use is Rose Minutaglio, 'The True Story Behind the Staircase, the Netflix Series About Michael Peterson's Bizarre Murder Case', *Esquire*, 1 June 2018; and Mahita Gajanan, 'Here's the Story Behind Netflix's Latest True Crime Docuseries The Staircase', *Time*, 11 June 2018. For the Alford plea – which stems from the case North Carolina v Alford in 1970 – see Megan Rose and ProPublica, 'The Deal Prosecutors Offer When they Have no Cards Left to Play', *The Atlantic*, 7 September 2017. Henry Alford, a black man indicted for first-degree murder in North Carolina in 1963, and who pleaded guilty to second-degree murder – even though he continued to protest his innocence and declared so to the court – died in prison in 1975. There is no British equivalent of an Alford plea. Peterson's lawyer has recently written an excellent book about the US criminal justice system – David S. Rudolf, *American Injustice: Inside the Underbelly of the Criminal Justice System* (London: HarperCollins, 2022) – although he does not discuss the

Peterson case. I interviewed Rudolph for my BBC Scotland series *David Wilson's Crime Files* in 2020.

For guidance related to the difference between murder and manslaughter see 'Homicide: Murder and Manslaughter', www.cps.gov.uk.

Chapter Six

I have previously mentioned Molly Lefebure's book on the murders committed by the serial killers Reg Christie and John Haigh, and the quotes that I use about Christie's garden are taken from there. The eighty letters Haigh sent to his parents while he awaited execution can be found at the Institute of Criminology, Cambridge University. I have also written about these letters in 'A Very English Serial Killer', *Guardian*, 19 November 2007. Of note, like Ian Brady in *The Gates of Janus* (see above), he makes no mention of the murders for which he had just been convicted. Most of his correspondence is taken up with discussing the weather, gardening and the Royal Family. In this sense he is yet another example of the 'silent and uncommunicative' serial killer that I have met and had to work with. I have also already referenced the books and documentaries (see above) that I have used and found useful about the crimes committed by Fred and Rose West. Indeed, Fred West might also be seen as a 'silent and uncommunicative' serial killer, as nothing that he ever told the police could be relied upon. The forensic psychologist Professor David Canter, for example, notes that the 111-page autobiography left by West contained no mention of his crimes, and was instead a rambling 'Mills & Boon' account of his life as a hardworking, loving father, who was regularly put upon by others. The notable exception to the 'silent and uncommunicative' rule in my working life has been Dennis Nilsen, who talked endlessly – although not necessarily with any insight – about the murders that he committed.

For the different role played by the back garden in English homes see Fox (mentioned above) who notes, 'The back garden, the one we are all allowed to enjoy, is often relatively scruffy, or at least utterly bland, and only very rarely the pretty, colourful, cottagey profusion of roses, hollyhocks, pansies, trellises, little gates and whatnot that everyone thinks of as a typical English garden.' On the other hand, the historian Dominic Sandbrook, in *Seasons in the Sun: The Battle for Britain, 1974–1979* (London: Penguin, 2012), notes that front gardens are 'severely controlled'.

For the murder of John Sabine see: Barbara Davies and Tom Kelly, 'Haunting Truth About the Evil Wife Accused of Committing the Perfect Murder of her Husband and First Glimpse Inside the Flat His Body Was Kept for 18 Years', *Daily Mail*, 18 December 2015; Katie Sands, 'Wife of Man Whose Body Lay Undiscovered for 18 Years Confessed to a Friend She Murdered Him with a Stone Frog', *Wales Online*, 7 March 2016; Sam Tonkin, 'The 2lb Stone Frog Used to Commit the Perfect Murder by Wife Who Smashed in Her Husband's Skull then Mummified his Body and Kept it Secret Until She Died 18 Years Later', *Daily Mail*, 20 May 2016; Karen McVeigh, 'When Lee Sabine Died a Year Ago her Friends Found her Husband's Skeleton on the Patio – the First in a Series of Discoveries that Stunned their Welsh Mining Village',

Guardian, 8 October 2016; and Philip Dewey, 'Murdered With a Stone Frog: The Grisly Story of the Man Whose Mummified Remains Were Hidden in his Wife's Garden', *Wales Online*, 18 July 2021. The story also attracted a great deal of broadcast media attention – see, for example, *BBC News*, 19 May 2016. For information about the Sabine children in New Zealand see Bridget Jones, 'Dumped at a Nursery, and Abandoned into a Life of Misery – Jane Sabine's Story' on *I Am* Season Two, TVNZ on demand, 29 October 2019.

For the murders of Pat and Bill Wycherley see: Paul Bracchi, 'The Great Whodunnit of No. 2 Blenheim Close: 15 Years Ago Bill and Pat Vanished but Relatives Still Received Christmas Cards', *Daily Mail*, 19 October 2013; 'Patricia and William Wycherley's Daughter Lost It and Shot Mother', *BBC News*, 13 June 2014; 'How the Wycherley Murder Went Unnoticed for 15 Years', *Press Association*, 20 June 2014; 'Mansfield Couple Found Guilty of Murdering Parents', *ITV News*, 20 June 2014; Jenny Kleeman, 'The Murderers Next Door', *Guardian*, 25 October 2014; and Rachel Gorman, 'Wycherley Murders Detective Explains Why He Has Mixed Emotions Ahead of Bodies in the Garden TV Show', *Nottingham Post*, 12 January 2020. Before *Landscapers*, starring Olivia Colman and David Thewlis, was released there were a number of discussions about the four-part series – see, for example, Naomi Gordon, 'See Olivia Colman in True Crime Drama Landscapers: Here's Everything you Need to Know', *Good Housekeeping*, 11 September 2021. The series was first broadcast in December 2021 on Sky Atlantic, and while critics praised the acting of Thewlis and Colman there was a more mixed reaction to the blurring of genres within the series – true crime and black comedy, and also disquiet about scenes where the actors broke the 'fourth wall' and spoke directly to camera and therefore the audience. For the sentencing remarks of Mrs Justice Thirwall, see: In the Crown Court Nottingham R v Christopher Edwards and Susan Edwards, www.judiciary.uk.

Chapter Seven

David Byrne describes writing 'Burning Down the House' in Mark Myers, 'David Byrne and Talking Heads on Burning Down the House', *Wall Street Journal*, 6 July 2020. The history of 'Psycho Killer' is told most recently in Tyler Golsen, 'The Story Behind the Song: Talking Heads Murderous Bop Psycho Killer', *Far Out*, 10 August 2021. For my academic research about family annihilators see Elizabeth Yardley, David Wilson and Adam Lynes, 'A Taxonomy of Male British Family Annihilators, 1980–2012', *The Howard Journal of Criminal Justice*, 53:2 (May 2014), 117–40.

For the murders of the Riaz family see: Danielle Roper, 'Ten Years On – Family Say Riaz Blaze Victims Must Never Be Forgotten', *Manchester Evening News*, 29 October 2017; Charlotte Bradshaw, 'Tormented Husband Killed Riaz Family', *Lancashire Telegraph*, 21 February 2007; 'Man Killed Family in House Arson', *BBC News*, 20 February 2007; 'Father Dies in Arson Attack', *Guardian*, 3 November 2006; and Ian Herbert, 'Father of Family Killed in House Fire Dies from Burns', *Independent*, 4 November 2006. This family annihilation has featured in a number of TV documentaries – see, for example, *Honour Kills*, BBC 3, 23 October 2007; and it was an episode of the *Killer in the Family* series, called 'The Firestarter', first shown in 2009, and which can still be viewed on YouTube; this documentary opens with the video footage of the couple's Western wedding ceremony.

For the murders of the Foster family see: Jon Ronson, 'I've Thought About Doing Myself In Loads of Times', *Guardian*, 22 November 2008; Sally Ramage, 'Case Study of Christopher Foster's Ulva Ltd', criminal-lawyer.org.uk, September 2008; Penny Wark, 'Christopher Foster's Brother Speaks Out: Why Did No One Stop Chris from Killing His Family?', *Telegraph*, 27 November 2011; Martin Robinson, 'Aftermath of a Murder Spree', *Mail Online*, 20 April 2016; Scarlet Howes, 'Sister of Mum Killed by "Mansion Monster" Refuses to Visit Her Grave Because He is Buried Next to Her', *Mirror*, 27 October 2018; Elizabeth Yardley, 'The Snapping Myth: Men Who Kill Women are Exerting Control, Not Losing It', elizabethyardley.com, 2 January 2020; and John Siddle, 'Owner of Murder Mansion Plot Where Tycoon Killed Wife and Daughter Fears Land is Cursed as New Build is Falling Down', *Sun*, 7 November 2020. This family annihilation was the subject of a 2012 TV documentary called *Murder Mansion*, which is still available to view on YouTube and I would particularly recommend the work of my colleague Professor Elizabeth Yardley on this case.

For the Clydach Murders see: 'Detective Denies Planting Evidence', *South Wales Guardian*, 7 June 2002; David Rose, 'Who Killed Mandy and Her Family?', *Observer*, 23 November 2003; Julia Stuart, 'The Clydach Murder Mystery', *Independent*, 16 August 2013; Paul Turner, 'Clydach Murders Killer David Morris's Family Refused Appeal Against

Conviction', *WalesOnline*, 5 July 2018; 'Clydach Murders: Forensic Review Agreed for Evidence', *BBC News*, 19 January 2021; Katrina Rowe, 'South Wales Police Statement – Clydach Murders', *West Wales Chronicle*, 19 January 2021; Adam Aspinall, 'My Dad Didn't Kill Four People and I'm Fighting to Clear His Name', *Mirror*, 10 February 2021; 'Clydach Murders: Killer David Morris Dies in Prison', *BBC News*, 20 August 2021. See also John Morris, *The Clydach Murders: A Miscarriage of Justice* (Bridgend: Seren Books, 2017). For the University of Winchester's work in relation to this case see Brian Thornton, 'Clydach Murders: Five Years Working on a Hopeless Case', *The Justice Gap*, 25 November 2014. The murders were featured in a BBC Wales Investigates documentary called *The Clydach Murders: Beyond Reasonable Doubt*, which was first broadcast on 22 October 2020, and can still be viewed on iPlayer. My former colleague, the forensic psychologist Professor Mike Berry, was interviewed for this documentary, and I benefited enormously from my discussions with Mike about the case. I discuss staging, and the various references and further reading that are helpful in the guide to Chapter Two.

I briefly mention the murders committed at White House Farm in August 1985, when Nevill and June Bamber, their daughter Sheila and her two sons, Nicholas and Daniel, were murdered – crimes for which Jeremy Bamber was convicted. The best book about the case is Carol Ann Lee, *The Murders at White House Farm: The Shocking True Story of Jeremy Bamber and the Killing of His Family* (London: Sidgwick & Jackson, 2015).

And Afterwards?

There are a number of good pieces of journalism about the April Jones case, and I found Steven Morris, 'April Jones Murder: How Detectives Pieced Together Her Final Hours', *Guardian*, 30 May 2013, and 'Mount Pleasant Cottage in Ceinws, Wales – The Former Home of Mark Bridger Demolished', *Press Association*, 17 November 2014, particularly useful. Quotes from April's parents are taken from these articles. Rhiannon Evans wrote about her friend's barbecue at Dennis Nilsen's old property in 'How Much Does a Gruesome Murder Affect the Price of a House?', *Vice UK*, 28 April 2015. Evans also writes about Randall Bell, the American realtor who describes himself as the 'Master of Disaster', in this same article. The various stories about what happened to properties after a murder had been committed are usefully summarised in Helen Carter, 'The Houses Linked to Notorious Murders – and the Bargain Hunters who Don't Mind', *Manchester Evening News*, 17 May 2020, which even quotes my research about the house occupied by Mary Ann Cotton in West Auckland. For the statistics related to the house-buying preferences of British people see the blog post by Tamir Davies, '36% of Brits Wouldn't Buy a Property where Someone has Died', www.sellhousefast.uk, 2016.

There are now a number of specialist academic books about thanatourism, thanatology and dark tourism. See, for example, Richard Sharpley and Philip Stone, *The Darker Side of Travel: The Theory and Practice of Dark Tourism* (Bristol: Channel View Publications, 2009) and Philip Stone, Rudi Hartman, Tony Seaton, Richard Sharpley and Leanne

White (eds), *The Palgrave Handbook of Dark Tourism Studies* (London: Palgrave Macmillan, 2018). Thanatology is the scientific study of death, and a thanatologist would be someone who had developed expertise on the subject of dying, death, grief and loss. Stone, mentioned above, is the director of the Institute for Dark Tourism Research at the University of Central Lancashire, and their website contains a number of useful resources, interviews and guides. The term 'dark tourism' was coined by Professors Malcolm Foley and John Lennon, two Scottish academics working at Glasgow Caledonian University, in relation to their work about people fascinated with the assassination of President John F. Kennedy. A useful introduction to the subject can be found in Simon Usborne, 'Dark Tourism: When Tragedy Meets Tourism', *National Geographic*, 9 April 2019. I used the official webpages of Pompeii, which can be accessed at www.pompeiisites.org, and Auschwitz (at www.auschwitz.org), and an internet search of the various Jack the Ripper tours that are currently being offered. I should also acknowledge that in 2018 I co-presented with Emilia Fox a BBC 1 documentary called *Jack the Ripper: The Case Reopened*. I would also recommend Hallie Rubenhold, *The Five: The Untold Lives of the Women Killed by Jack the Ripper* (London: Penguin Books, 2019). For the story of tourists at Grenfell Tower see Eleanor Rose, 'Pictured: Moment Coachload of Chinese Visitors Stops to Gawp at Remains of Grenfell Tower, Despite Warnings Site is Not a Tourist Attraction', *Evening Standard*, 29 September 2017.

For the various pieces of 'murderabilia' that I mention are for sale, or have been sold out, see www.darkcrimecollectables.co.uk. A little background about Rory Everett, who set up the website, can be found in Dan Warburton, 'Yorkshire Ripper's Letters and OJ signed Memorabilia for Sale on Grim New Website', *Sunday Mirror*, 16 May 2020, and Dan Warburton, 'Fury Over Murder Tour to Pub Where Scots Serial Killer Dennis Nilsen Hunted for Victims', *Daily Record*, 1 August 2021.

Acknowledgements

I would like to thank the many people who have helped in the research and then the writing of this book. At Curtis Brown my thanks as ever to Gordon Wise, my stalwart literary agent, and to Jacquie Drewe, Emma Power and Bella Smallwood; and at Little, Brown Kirsteen Astor, Zoe Gullen, Aimee Kitson and of course the wonderful Rhiannon Smith, who is a friend as much as she is my very resourceful and redoubtable editor. Thank you also Meryl Evans who I always trust to 'legal' my books with sympathy and diligence. I benefited enormously from discussing ideas in the book with: Professor Mike Berry; Andrew Roberts – who talked me through Churchill's use of his bed (although this does not appear in the text); Mark Williams-Thomas; Donal MacIntyre; Melissa Mayne – one of the most respected makers of true crime documentaries in the country, and Paul Sommers of Alaska TV; and Harry Bell, Diane Dunbar, Emma Fentiman and Ruth Mulcahy of Tern TV in Scotland. My thanks too to a number of former colleagues within HM Prison Service who did not want to be publicly identified, but who were prepared to discuss a number of the cases that appear in the book – those discussions helped to shape my thinking. I would also like to thank my colleagues at Birmingham City University (BCU), where I continue to teach, and especially Professor Elizabeth Yardley, Professor Michael Brookes, Dr Liam Brolan and Dr Dan Rusu. Many of the ideas, especially those related to my work about British hitmen, were developed with colleagues at BCU, and I continue to discuss most things psychological and criminological with Michael every Saturday when we conduct our Twitter #SaturdaySeminars.

I would like to thank the vast number of my friends who have over the years invited me into their homes. Chief among this motley crew would be Neil and Sue Foster, with whom we have shared Friday nights around a kitchen table for over two decades to discuss all the things that life can throw at us; Peter and Linda Lee-Wright; the Bucknills – Sarah and Mark; Simon and Camilla Theobald; Antony and Verity Woodward; and Emma and Simon Winlow, whose joyous wedding I attended during the writing of the book – and I am ashamed to admit I have still not given them their wedding present. It would be wrong not to acknowledge Jane Hamilton at the *Daily Record* and Emilia Fox and Dr Graham Hill, whose company I have enjoyed when discussing all things criminological during the filming of *In the Footsteps of Killers* for Channel 4, and with Mils on our podcast *If It Bleeds, It Leads*.

Of course, as we get older, my wife Anne and I find ourselves increasingly being invited to the home of our son and daughter-in-law, and I would like to thank Hugo and Suzi for welcoming Cillian's grandparents into their midst on such a